GAMBLING
WHAT'S AT STAKE?

ISSN 1543-4915

GAMBLING
WHAT'S AT STAKE?

John W. Weier

INFORMATION PLUS® REFERENCE SERIES
Formerly Published by Information Plus, Wylie, Texas

Detroit • New York • San Francisco • New Haven, Conn. • Waterville, Maine • London

Gambling: What's at Stake?

John W. Weier

Paula Kepos, Series Editor

Project Editor
John McCoy

Permissions
Lisa Kincade, Robert McCord, Lista Person

Composition and Electronic Prepress
Evi Seoud

Manufacturing
Cynde Bishop

ISBN-13: 978-0-7876-5103-9 (set)
ISBN-10: 0-7876-5103-6 (set)
ISBN-13: 978-1-4144-0754-8
ISBN-10: 1-4144-0754-8
ISSN: 1543-4915

This title is also available as an e-book.
ISBN-13: 978-1-4144-2868-0 (set), ISBN-10: 1-4144-2868-5 (set)
Contact your Thomson Gale sales representative for ordering information.

Printed in the United States of America
10 9 8 7 6 5 4 3 2 1

TABLE OF CONTENTS

PREFACE vii

CHAPTER 1

Gambling in America: An Overview 1

This chapter traces the history of gambling from ancient and medieval times through nineteenth-century Europe and America to the modern era, including several twenty-first-century developments. It concludes with a look at social and practical issues surrounding the subject and a report of public opinion on the moral acceptability of gambling.

CHAPTER 2

Supply and Demand: Who Offers Gambling? Who Gambles? 13

Corporations, small businesses, criminals, charities, and governments profit from offering gambling opportunities. Profiles of each appear in this chapter, which also describes the participation rates, favorite wagering activities, and demographics of American gamblers. A discussion of gambling addiction concludes the chapter.

CHAPTER 3

An Introduction to Casinos 27

They may be as small as a single room or as large as a megaresort, but casinos all offer games of chance and skill played at tables or machines. The historical and current status of casinos, their social acceptability, the wide variety of games they offer, and the types of gamblers they attract are examined in this chapter. It also takes a look at the growing popularity of poker.

CHAPTER 4

Commercial Casinos 37

Casinos owned and operated by large and small companies are the focus of this chapter, which describes the history and current status of casinos in the eleven states where they are legal: Nevada, New Jersey, Mississippi, Louisiana, Indiana, Illinois, Missouri, Michigan, Iowa, Colorado, and South Dakota. Legislation authorizing and regulating these establishments, plus the economic impact casinos have had on these states, are described in detail.

CHAPTER 5

Native American Tribal Casinos 53

Gaming establishments operated by Native American tribes have spread throughout the country since Congress passed the Indian Gaming Regulatory Act in 1988. As explained in this chapter, these casinos can be legally operated only by officially recognized tribes, and they are subject to regulation by federal, state, and tribal governments. Chapter 5 also offers information on tribal gaming revenues and their uses and focuses on Native American casinos in Connecticut and California, two of the states where they are most profitable.

CHAPTER 6

The Economic and Social Effects of Casinos 63

Though impartial data on the positive and negative effects of casinos are not widely available, this chapter provides a general assessment. It provides the pros and cons of Native American tribal casinos and considers how casinos affect economics, crime, suicide rates, personal bankruptcy, compulsive gambling, underage gambling, and politics.

CHAPTER 7

Lotteries. 77

U.S. lotteries are operated by state governments to raise public funds. This chapter considers the types of games offered (such as lotto, instant, scratch, and second-chance); multistate games (such as Powerball); the role of retailers in selling tickets; lottery players; and the economic and social effects of lotteries.

CHAPTER 8

Sports Gambling 93

Three types of sports gambling exist in the United States: parimutuel betting on horse and dog races as well as the ball game jai alai; betting through a bookmaker (legal only in Nevada); and illegal wagering. Each is described in detail and assessed in terms of positive and negative effects.

CHAPTER 9

Internet Gambling 113

In existence only since the mid 1990s, Internet gambling appeals to younger people but poses problems for regulators, largely because the Internet transcends political boundaries. This chapter details the Internet and how it generated an international gaming industry; examines the applicable federal and state laws that prohibit Internet gambling; and assesses the economic and social effects of online casinos.

IMPORTANT NAMES AND ADDRESSES 125

RESOURCES 131

INDEX 133

PREFACE

Gambling: What's at Stake? is part of the *Information Plus Reference Series*. The purpose of each volume of the series is to present the latest facts on a topic of pressing concern in modern American life. These topics include today's most controversial and most studied social issues: abortion, capital punishment, care for the elderly, crime, gambling, health care, the environment, immigration, minorities, social welfare, women, youth, and many more. Although written especially for the high school and undergraduate student, this series is an excellent resource for anyone in need of factual information on current affairs.

By presenting the facts, it is Thomson Gale's intention to provide its readers with everything they need to reach an informed opinion on current issues. To that end, there is a particular emphasis in this series on the presentation of scientific studies, surveys, and statistics. These data are generally presented in the form of tables, charts, and other graphics placed within the text of each book. Every graphic is directly referred to and carefully explained in the text. The source of each graphic is presented within the graphic itself. The data used in these graphics are drawn from the most reputable and reliable sources, in particular from the various branches of the U.S. government and from major independent polling organizations. Every effort has been made to secure the most recent information available. The reader should bear in mind that many major studies take years to conduct and that additional years often pass before the data from these studies are made available to the public. Therefore, in many cases the most recent information available in 2007 dated from 2004 or 2005. Older statistics are sometimes presented as well, if they are of particular interest and no more-recent information exists.

Although statistics are a major focus of the *Information Plus Reference Series*, they are by no means its only content. Each book also presents the widely held positions and important ideas that shape how the book's subject is discussed in the United States. These positions are explained in detail and, where possible, in the words of their proponents. Some of the other material to be found in these books includes: historical background; descriptions of major events related to the subject; relevant laws and court cases; and examples of how these issues play out in American life. Some books also feature primary documents, or have pro and con debate sections giving the words and opinions of prominent Americans on both sides of a controversial topic. All material is presented in an even-handed and unbiased manner; the reader will never be encouraged to accept one view of an issue over another.

HOW TO USE THIS BOOK

Gambling has long been a favorite pastime worldwide, and its history in the United States dates back to the founding of the nation. It has been estimated that Americans spend more than $1 trillion per year on charitable gambling, betting on horse and greyhound races, lottery purchases, casino wagering, and other legal and illegal gambling activities. Much controversy surrounds the gambling industry. While gambling proponents argue that the economic benefits of gambling far outweigh any potential risks, some individuals oppose gambling on moral grounds or argue that it can cause an increase in various types of social problems. This book presents in-depth information on how casino gambling, sports gambling, lotteries, and Internet gambling work, provides up-to-date financial data for each, and discusses the effects of these and other gambling activities on the communities in which they take place. Also discussed are American attitudes toward gambling.

Gambling: What's at Stake? consists of nine chapters and three appendixes. Each of the chapters is devoted to a particular aspect of gambling in the United States. For a summary of the information covered in each chapter, please see the synopses provided in the Table of Contents at the front of the book. Chapters generally begin with an overview of the basic facts and background information on the chapter's topic, then proceed to examine subtopics of particular interest. For example, Chapter 8: Sports Gambling begins with a historical survey of wagering on sporting events and a summary of American attitudes about sports gambling. A substantial section on pari-mutuel gambling defines and explains the term and then goes on to discuss horse racing, greyhound racing, jai alai, and the future of pari-mutuel gambling in general. Next, legal gambling on college and professional sports (which mainly takes place in Nevada) is covered. Finally, sections illuminate the prevalence and effects of illegal sports gambling in the United States. Throughout the chapter the emphasis is on controversial aspects of these topics, such as the treatment of racing animals and the impact of gambling on sports. Readers can find their way through a chapter by looking for the section and subsection headings, which are clearly set off from the text. Or, they can refer to the book's extensive Index, if they already know what they are looking for.

Statistical Information

The tables and figures featured throughout *Gambling: What's at Stake?* will be of particular use to the reader in learning about this topic. These tables and figures represent an extensive collection of the most recent and important statistics on gambling, as well as related issues—for example, graphics in the book cover how much consumers spend on casino gambling as compared with other recreational pursuits; public opinion on the economic benefits of casinos; types of modern lottery games; horse-racing purses paid out by state; and participation in gambling by college student-athletes. Thomson Gale believes that making this information available to the reader is the most important way in which we fulfill the goal of this book: to help readers understand the issues and controversies surrounding gambling in the United States and reach their own conclusions.

Each table or figure has a unique identifier appearing above it for ease of identification and reference. Titles for the tables and figures explain their purpose. At the end of each table or figure, the original source of the data is provided.

In order to help readers understand these often complicated statistics, all tables and figures are explained in the text. References in the text direct the reader to the relevant statistics. Furthermore, the contents of all tables and figures are fully indexed. Please see the opening section of the Index at the back of this volume for a description of how to find tables and figures within it.

Appendixes

In addition to the main body text and images, *Gambling: What's at Stake?* has three appendixes. The first is the Important Names and Addresses directory. Here the reader will find contact information for a number of government and private organizations that can provide further information on aspects of gambling. The second appendix is the Resources section, which can also assist the reader in conducting his or her own research. In this section the author and editors of *Gambling: What's at Stake?* describe some of the sources that were most useful during the compilation of this book. The final appendix is the Index. It has been greatly expanded from previous editions and should make it even easier to find specific topics in this book.

ADVISORY BOARD CONTRIBUTIONS

The staff of Information Plus would like to extend its heartfelt appreciation to the Information Plus Advisory Board. This dedicated group of media professionals provides feedback on the series on an ongoing basis. Their comments allow the editorial staff who work on the project to continually make the series better and more user-friendly. Our top priorities are to produce the highest-quality and most useful books possible, and the Advisory Board's contributions to this process are invaluable.

The members of the Information Plus Advisory Board are:

- Kathleen R. Bonn, Librarian, Newbury Park High School, Newbury Park, California
- Madelyn Garner, Librarian, San Jacinto College—North Campus, Houston, Texas
- Anne Oxenrider, Media Specialist, Dundee High School, Dundee, Michigan
- Charles R. Rodgers, Director of Libraries, Pasco-Hernando Community College, Dade City, Florida
- James N. Zitzelsberger, Library Media Department Chairman, Oshkosh West High School, Oshkosh, Wisconsin

COMMENTS AND SUGGESTIONS

The editors of the *Information Plus Reference Series* welcome your feedback on *Gambling: What's at Stake?* Please direct all correspondence to:

Editors
Information Plus Reference Series
27500 Drake Rd.
Farmington Hills, MI 48331-3535

CHAPTER 1
GAMBLING IN AMERICA: AN OVERVIEW

What is gambling? *Merriam-Webster's Dictionary* gives half a dozen definitions, such as playing a game of chance for money and making a bet on an uncertain outcome. One definition says that gambling is staking something on a contingency. Another says that gambling is taking an action with an element of risk. Combining various terms together provides the following overall definition: gambling is an activity in which something of value is risked on the chance that something of greater value might be obtained, based on the uncertain outcome of a particular event.

Organized gambling has become an industry because so many people are willing and even eager to risk their money in exchange for a chance at something bigger and better. The elements of risk and uncertainty actually add to gambling's appeal—and to its danger. Throughout history, various cultures have considered gambling harmless, sinful, respectable, corrupt, legal, illegal, and tolerable. Some people love it, some people hate it, and some people just ignore it. Societal attitudes are dependent on customs, traditions, religion, morals, and the context in which gambling occurs.

Lawmakers have struggled to define gambling and determine which activities should be legal and which should not. For example, betting activities with an element of skill involved (such as picking a horse in a race or playing a card game) might be more acceptable than those based entirely on chance (such as spinning a roulette wheel or playing slot machines). Acceptability also depends on who profits from the gambling. Bingo games held for charity and lotteries that fund state programs are more commonly legal than casinos run for corporate profit.

In the article "In Defense of Gambling" (*Forbes*, June 23, 2003), Dan Seligman estimated that Americans legally gamble $900 billion per year. But why do people gamble at all? Common sense suggests that risking some-

thing of value on an event with an uncertain outcome is irrational. Scientists have found a variety of reasons for gambling, including the lure of money, the excitement and fun of the activity, and influence from peers. At its deepest level, gambling may represent a human desire to control the randomness that seems to permeate life. Whatever the drive may be, it must be strong. An entire gambling culture has developed in the United States in which entrepreneurs (legal and otherwise) offer people opportunities to gamble, and business is booming.

HISTORY OF GAMBLING

Ancient Times

Archaeologists have discovered evidence that people in Egypt, China, Japan, and Greece played games of chance with dice and other devices as far back as 2000 BCE. According to *Encyclopedia Britannica*, loaded dice—which are weighted to make a particular number come up more often than others—have been found in ancient tombs in Egypt, the Far East, and even North and South America.

Dice are probably the oldest gambling implements known. They were often carved from sheep bones and known as knucklebones. They are mentioned in several historical documents, including the *Mahabharata*, the epic poem and philosophy text written in India some 2,500 years ago. A story in the New Testament of the Bible describes Roman soldiers throwing dice to determine who would get the robe of Jesus. Roman bone dice have been found dating from the first to third centuries CE. The Romans also gambled on chariot races, animal fights, and contests between gladiators.

The Medieval Period

During medieval times (approximately 500–1500 CE) gambling was legalized by some governments, particularly in areas that are now Spain, Italy, Germany, and the Netherlands. England and France were much less permissive, at times outlawing all forms of gambling. French king Louis IX prohibited gambling during his reign (1226–70) for religious reasons. Still, illegal gambling continued to thrive.

During this period Christian powers in Europe launched the Crusades—military expeditions against Muslim powers that controlled lands considered holy by Christians. They also permitted gambling, however, if only by knights and those of higher rank. Violators were subject to severe whippings. Even among the titled gamblers, there was a legal limit on how much money could be lost, a concept that later would come to be known as limited-stakes gambling.

English knights returned from the Crusades with long-legged Arabian stallions, which they bred with sturdy English mares to produce fine racehorses. Betting on private horse races became a popular pastime among the nobility. Card games also became popular in Europe around the end of the fourteenth century. According to the International Playing-Card Society, one of the earliest known references to playing cards in Europe dates from 1377. During the late 1400s and early 1500s, lotteries began to be used in Europe to raise money for public projects. Queen Elizabeth I established the first English state lottery in 1567.

Precolonial America and the Colonial Era

Native Americans played games of chance as part of tribal ceremonies and celebrations hundreds of years before America was colonized. One of the most common was a dice and bowl game in which five plum stones or bones carved with different markings were tossed into a bowl or basket. Wagers were placed before the game began, and scoring was based on the combination of markings that appeared after a throw. The Cheyenne people called the game *monshimout*. A similar game was called *hubbub* by the Arapaho and by New England tribes.

Colonists from Europe brought gambling traditions with them to the New World. Historical accounts report that people in parts of New England gambled on horse racing, cockfighting, and bull baiting. Bull baiting was a blood sport in which a bull was tethered in a ring or pit into which dogs were thrown. The dogs were trained to torment the bull, which responded by goring the dogs. Spectators gambled on how many of the dogs the bull would kill.

In 1612 England's King James I created a lottery to provide funds for Jamestown, Virginia, the first permanent British settlement in America. Lotteries were later held throughout the colonies to finance the building of towns, roads, hospitals, and schools and to provide other public services.

Many colonists, though, disapproved of gambling. The Pilgrims and Puritans fled to America during the 1620s and 1630s to escape persecution in Europe for their religious beliefs. They believed in a strong work ethic that considered labor morally redeeming and viewed gambling as sinful because it wasted time that might have been spent in productive endeavors.

Cockfighting, bear- and bull baiting, wrestling matches, and footraces were popular gambling sports throughout Europe during the sixteenth and seventeenth centuries. The predecessors of many modern casino games were also developed and popularized during this time. For example, the roulette wheel is often attributed to French mathematician Blaise Pascal.

Gambling among British aristocrats became so customary during the early years of the eighteenth century that it presented a financial problem for the country. Gentlemen gambled away their belongings, their country estates, even their titles. Large transfers of land and titles were disruptive to the nation's economy and stability, so the reigning monarch, Queen Anne, responded in 1710 with the Statute of Anne, which made large gambling debts "utterly void, frustrate, and of none effect, to all intents and purposes whatsoever" (9 Anne, c. 14). In other words, large gambling debts could not be legally enforced. This prohibition has prevailed in common law for centuries and is still cited in U.S. court cases. Queen Anne is also known for her love of horse racing, which became a popular betting sport (along with boxing) during her reign.

A surge of evangelical Christianity swept through England, Scotland, Germany, and the American colonies during the mid to late 1700s. Many historians refer to this as the "Great Awakening," a time when conservative moral values became more prevalent and widespread. Evangelical Christians considered gambling to be a sin and dangerous to society, and religion became a powerful tool for bringing about social change.

The Continental Congress of the American colonies issued an order, stating that the colonists "will discountenance and discourage every species of extravagance and dissipation, especially all horse racing, and all kinds of gaming, cockfighting, exhibitions of shews [*sic*], plays, and other expensive diversions and entertainments" (*The Articles of Association*, October 1774). The purpose of the directive was to "encourage frugality, economy, and industry."

Into the Nineteenth Century

In general, gambling was tolerated as long as it did not upset the social order. Georgia, Virginia, and South Carolina passed versions of the Statute of Anne during the colonial period to prevent gambling from getting out of hand, according to J. R. Westphal, L. J. Johnson, and their colleagues in "Gambling in the South: Implications for Physicians" (*Southern Medical Journal*, September 2000). New Orleans became a gambling mecca during the 1700s and 1800s, even though gambling was outlawed during much of that time. In the 1830s almost all southern states outlawed gambling in public places; some exceptions were made for "respectable gentlemen."

In 1823, eleven years after becoming a state, Louisiana legalized several forms of gambling and licensed several gambling halls in New Orleans. Even though the licensing act was repealed in 1835, casino-type gambling continued to prosper and spread to riverboats traveling the Mississippi River. Professional riverboat gamblers soon developed an unsavory reputation as cheats and scoundrels. Several historians trace the popularization of poker and craps in America to Louisiana gamblers of that period. Riverboat gambling continued to thrive until the outbreak of the Civil War in 1861.

From 1829 to 1837, Andrew Jackson was president of the United States. The Jacksonian era was associated with a new attention to social problems and a focus on morality. A new wave of evangelical Christianity swept the country. According to I. Nelson Rose of Whittier Law School, gambling scandals and the spread of a conservative view of morality led to an end to most legal gambling in the United States by the mid 1800s.

Frontier gambling, both legal and illegal, in the Old West peaked during the mid to late nineteenth century. Saloons and other gambling houses were common in towns catering to cowboys, traders, and miners. Infamous gamblers of the time included Bat Masterson, Doc Holliday, Poker Alice, and Wild Bill Hickok. Hickok was shot while playing poker in 1876. At the time he held a hand of two black aces and two black eights, which came to be known as the "dead man's hand."

Across the country, private and public lotteries were plagued by fraud and scandal and fell into disfavor. By 1862 only two states, Missouri and Kentucky, had legal lotteries. Objectionable to many southern legislators on moral grounds, lotteries had been banned in most southern states by the 1840s. However, they were reinstated after the Civil War to raise badly needed funds. In 1868 Louisiana implemented a lottery known as "the Great Serpent." Although it was extremely popular, the lottery was ridden with fraud and eventually outlawed by the state in 1895. Casino gambling, which had been legalized again in Louisiana in 1869, was outlawed at the same time.

Gambling in general fell into disfavor as the nineteenth century ended. In England, Queen Victoria's rule was characterized by concern for morality and by the spread of conservative values. These attitudes permeated American society as well. Gambling fell out of favor as a pastime for respectable people. Many eastern racetracks and western casinos were pressured to close for moral and ethical reasons. As new states entered the Union, many included provisions against gambling in their constitutions. By federal law, all state lotteries were shut down by 1900.

GAMBLING IN THE UNITED STATES SINCE 1900

As the twentieth century began, there were forty-five states in the Union. The territories of Oklahoma, New Mexico, and Arizona gained statehood between 1907 and 1912. According to Rose, whose particular area of study is gambling history and law, the closure of casinos in New Mexico and Arizona was a precondition for statehood. In 1910 Nevada outlawed casino gambling. That same year, horse racing was outlawed in New York, and almost all gambling was prohibited in the United States. The only legal gambling options at the time were horse races in Maryland and Kentucky and a few isolated card clubs.

Legalized Casinos in Nevada

The 1930s were a time of reawakening for legal gambling interests. Many states legalized horse racing and charitable gambling. Nevada went even further. In 1931 its legislature made casino gambling legal again. It seemed like a logical step: frontier gambling was widely tolerated in the state, even though gambling was officially illegal. More important, Nevada, like the rest of the country, was suffering from a deep recession, and it sought to cash in on two events. The state's divorce laws were changed in the early 1930s to allow the granting of a divorce after only six weeks of residency, so people from other states temporarily moved into small motels and inns to satisfy the residency requirement. At the same time, construction began on the massive Hoover Dam, only thirty miles from Las Vegas. Thousands of construction workers—like the people waiting for their divorces to become final—were all potential gamblers.

Although small legal gambling halls opened in Reno (in the northern part of the state), they catered mostly to cowboys and local residents and had a reputation for being raunchy and wild. In April 1931, however, the first gambling licenses were issued in Las Vegas. The first big casino, El Rancho Vegas, was opened in 1941 on what would later be known as the Strip.

Many in the business world doubted that casino gambling in Nevada would be successful. Most of the casino hotels were small establishments operated by local families or small private companies (some were dude ranches—western-style resorts that offered horseback riding). They were located in hot and dusty desert towns far from major cities, had no air-conditioning, and offered few amenities to travelers. There was little or no state and local oversight of gambling activities.

However, the end of Prohibition—which had made it illegal to import or sell alcoholic beverages in the United States—brought another element to Las Vegas. During the Prohibition Era (1920–33) organized crime syndicates operated massive bootlegging rings and became very powerful and wealthy. When Prohibition ended, they switched their focus to gambling. Organized criminals in New York and Chicago were among the first to see the potential of Nevada. Meyer Lansky and Frank Costello sent fellow gangster Benjamin "Bugsy" Siegel west to develop new criminal enterprises. Siegel invested millions of dollars of the mob's money in a big and lavish casino in Las Vegas that he was convinced would attract top-name entertainers and big-spending gamblers. The Flamingo, a hotel and casino, opened in 1946. It was a failure at first, and Siegel was soon killed by his fellow mobsters.

POST–WORLD WAR II. Nevada's casinos grew slowly until after World War II (1939–45). Postwar Americans were full of optimism and had spending money. Tourism began to grow in Nevada. Las Vegas casino resorts attracted Hollywood celebrities and famous entertainers. The state began collecting gaming taxes during the 1940s. The growing casinos in Las Vegas provided good-paying jobs to workers who brought their families with them, building a middle-class presence. In 1955 the state legislature created the Nevada Gaming Control Board within the Nevada Tax Commission. Four years later, the Nevada Gaming Commission was established.

CORPORATE GROWTH: THE 1960s. During the 1960s, the casinos of Las Vegas continued to grow. By that time, organized crime syndicates used respectable front men in top management positions while they manipulated the businesses from behind the scenes. Publicly held corporations had been largely kept out of the casino business by a provision in Nevada law that required every individual stockholder to be licensed to operate a casino.

One corporation that was able to get into the casino business was the Summa Corporation, a spin-off of the Hughes Tool Company, with only one stockholder: Howard Hughes. Hughes was a wealthy and eccentric businessman who owned the very profitable Hughes Aircraft Company. He spent a lot of his time in Las Vegas during the 1940s and 1950s and later moved there. In 1966 he bought the Desert Inn, a casino hotel on the Strip in Las Vegas. Later, he bought the nearby Sands, Frontier, Castaways, and Silver Slipper casinos.

Legend has it that mobsters threatened Hughes to get him out of the casino business in Las Vegas, but he refused to leave. He invested hundreds of millions of dollars in Las Vegas properties and predicted that the city would be an entertainment center by the end of the century. In 1967 the Nevada legislature changed the law to make it easier for corporations to own casinos.

To combat organized crime, federal statutes against racketeering were enacted in 1970, and Nevada officials overhauled the casino regulatory system, making it more difficult for organized crime figures to be involved. Corporations and legitimate financiers began to invest heavily in casino hotels in Las Vegas and other parts of the state.

The Development of Gambling beyond Nevada

During the 1970s the U.S. Commission on the Review of the National Policy toward Gambling studied Americans' attitudes about gambling and their gambling behavior. The commission found that 80% of Americans approved of gambling and 67% engaged in gambling activities. In its final report, *Gambling in America* (1976), the commission made recommendations to state governments that were considering the legalization of gambling and concluded that states should set gambling policy without interference from the federal government, unless problems developed from the infiltration of organized crime or from conflicts between states.

In 1978 the first legal casino outside of Nevada opened in Atlantic City, New Jersey. By the mid 1990s nine additional states had legalized casino gambling:

- Colorado (1990)
- Illinois (1990)
- Indiana (1993)
- Iowa (1989)
- Louisiana (1991)
- Michigan (1996)
- Mississippi (1990)
- Missouri (1993)
- South Dakota (1989)

STATE-SPONSORED LOTTERIES. In 1964 New Hampshire was the first state to make a lottery legal again. It was called the New Hampshire Sweepstakes and was tied to horse-race results to avoid laws prohibiting lotteries. New York established a lottery in 1967. Thirteen other states followed suit during the 1970s; most were concentrated in the Northeast:

- Connecticut (1972)
- Delaware (1975)
- Illinois (1974)
- Maine (1974)
- Maryland (1973)

- Massachusetts (1972)
- Michigan (1972)
- New Jersey (1970)
- Ohio (1974)
- Pennsylvania (1971)
- Rhode Island (1974)
- Vermont (1977)

Lotteries were legalized in twenty-three states and the District of Columbia during the 1980s and 1990s. The first multistate lottery game began operating in 1988 and included Iowa, Kansas, Oregon, Rhode Island, West Virginia and the District of Columbia. It went through several revisions before becoming the Powerball game in 1992.

South Carolina began operating a lottery in January 2002, following voter approval in a 2000 referendum. In November 2002 voters in Tennessee and North Dakota approved referendums allowing lotteries in their states. Both began operating in early 2004. Oklahoma started a state-controlled, institutionalized lottery in 2005, followed by North Carolina in 2006.

NATIVE AMERICAN GAMBLING ENTERPRISES. Native American tribes established bingo halls to raise funds for tribal operations, and these became highly popular during the 1970s. Some of the most successful were high-stakes operations in Maine and Florida, where most other forms of gambling were prohibited. However, as the stakes were raised, the tribes began to face legal opposition from state governments. The tribes argued that their status as sovereign (independent) nations made them exempt from state laws against gambling. Tribes in various states sued, and the issue was debated in court for years. Finally, the Supreme Court's landmark ruling in *California v. Cabazon Band of Mission Indians* (480 U.S. 202 [1987]) opened the door to tribal gaming when it found that gambling activities conducted on tribal lands did not fall within the legal jurisdiction of the state. The Indian Gaming Regulatory Act, passed by Congress in 1988, allowed federally recognized Native American tribes to open gambling establishments on their reservations if the states in which they were located already permitted legalized gambling.

In 2000 California voters passed Proposition 1A, which amended the state constitution to permit Native American tribes to operate lottery games, slot machines, and banking and percentage card games on tribal lands. Previously, the tribes were largely restricted to operating bingo halls. According to the National Indian Gaming Association, more than 224 tribes were engaged in Class II or III gaming in twenty-eight states in 2006 (http://www.indiangaming.org/library/indian-gaming-facts/

index.shtml). Class II and III gaming includes bingo, lotto, card and table games, slot machines, and pari-mutuel gambling.

INTERNET GAMBLING. During the mid 1990s Internet gambling sites began operating, most of them based in the Caribbean. By the end of the decade, between 600 and 700 Internet gambling sites were thought to be available online. The Internet gambling segment generated an estimated $12 billion dollars per year as of 2006 and was poised for explosive growth as cellular technologies and other innovations made it easier for patrons to log into gambling sites. However, while some countries, such as Great Britain, embraced Internet gambling and began to regulate the industry, the United States took action to interrupt online gambling activity by U.S. gamblers. Passage of the Unlawful Internet Gambling Enforcement Act of 2006 made it illegal for banks and credit card companies to process payments from U.S. customers to online gambling Web sites. Many sites immediately stopped accepting customers in the United States. Nielsen/Net Ratings reported a 67% drop in traffic at PartyPoker.com, the most popular online gambling Web site, between September 2006 and October 2006, the month in which the U.S. law was passed. Overall, Nielsen reported that the top ten online gaming sites experienced a 56% decline in traffic from September 2006 to October 2006.

THE MODERN INDUSTRY

Table 1.1 shows the legal gambling options offered in each state as of August 2006. Charitable gambling was the most common type, operating in forty-seven states and the District of Columbia. Gambling on horse races was also prevalent, both at live venues and at off-track betting sites. Lotteries operated in forty-two states and the District of Columbia during 2006. Although tribal casinos were less common, they were operating in more than half the states. Gambling on greyhound races occurred in a handful of states. A number of states that did not allow commercial casinos allowed card rooms instead, and a few states allowed slot machines at businesses other than casinos. Only Florida offered wagering on jai alai, a fast-paced ball game played on a walled court.

Industry analysts believe that many sectors of the American gambling market are reaching maturity. In other words, the growth spurt of the past few decades is likely over. Commercial casino gambling has not spread beyond the eleven states in which it operated in 1996. In November 2004 voters in Maine rejected a referendum that would have allowed tribal casinos in their state, and in 2004 the Alaskan legislature failed to pass a bill that would have paved the way for casinos in Anchorage. In 2005 Oklahoma installed its first slot machines at race tracks, and in 2006 Pennsylvania

TABLE 1.1

Legal gambling operations by state, 2006

State	Charitable gambling	Horse racing	Lottery	Tribal casinos	Greyhound racing	Card rooms (without commercial casinos)	Commercial casinos	Racinos	Slot machines at other businesses	Jai Alai
Alabama	Yes[a]	Yes		Yes[b]	Yes					
Alaska	Yes			Yes[b]						
Arizona	Yes	Yes	Yes	Yes	Yes					
Arkansas		Yes			Yes					
California	Yes	Yes	Yes	Yes		Yes				
Colorado	Yes	Yes	Yes	Yes	Yes		Yes			
Connecticut	Yes	Yes	Yes	Yes						
Delaware	Yes	Yes	Yes					Yes		
D.C.	Yes		Yes							
Florida	Yes	Yes	Yes	Yes	Yes	Yes		Yes[c]		Yes
Georgia	Yes		Yes							
Hawaii										
Idaho	Yes	Yes	Yes	Yes						
Illinois	Yes	Yes	Yes				Yes			
Indiana	Yes	Yes	Yes							
Iowa	Yes	Yes	Yes	Yes	Yes		Yes	Yes		
Kansas	Yes	Yes	Yes	Yes	Yes		Yes			
Kentucky	Yes	Yes	Yes							
Louisiana	Yes	Yes	Yes	Yes			Yes	Yes	Yes	
Maine	Yes	Yes	Yes					Yes		
Maryland	Yes	Yes	Yes							
Massachusetts	Yes	Yes	Yes		Yes					
Michigan	Yes	Yes	Yes	Yes			Yes			
Minnesota	Yes	Yes	Yes	Yes		Yes				
Mississippi	Yes			Yes			Yes			
Missouri	Yes	Yes	Yes				Yes			
Montana	Yes	Yes	Yes	Yes		Yes			Yes	
Nebraska	Yes	Yes	Yes	Yes						
Nevada	Yes	Yes		Yes			Yes		Yes	
New Hampshire	Yes	Yes	Yes		Yes					
New Jersey	Yes	Yes	Yes				Yes			
New Mexico	Yes	Yes	Yes	Yes				Yes		
New York	Yes	Yes	Yes					Yes		
North Carolina	Yes	Yes	Yes	Yes						
North Dakota	Yes	Yes	Yes	Yes						
Ohio	Yes	Yes	Yes							
Oklahoma	Yes	Yes	Yes	Yes				Yes		
Oregon	Yes	Yes	Yes	Yes					Yes	
Pennsylvania	Yes	Yes	Yes					Yes[c]		
Rhode Island	Yes	Yes	Yes		Yes			Yes		
South Carolina	Yes		Yes							
South Dakota	Yes	Yes	Yes	Yes			Yes			
Tennessee	Yes		Yes							
Texas	Yes	Yes	Yes	Yes	Yes					
Utah[d]										
Vermont	Yes	Yes	Yes							
Virginia	Yes	Yes	Yes							
Washington	Yes	Yes	Yes	Yes		Yes				
West Virginia	Yes	Yes	Yes		Yes			Yes	Yes	
Wisconsin	Yes	Yes	Yes	Yes	Yes					
Wyoming	Yes	Yes		Yes[b]						

[a]Certain counties only
[b]Bingo only
[c]Under construction in summer 2006
[d]No gambling operations of any kind

SOURCE: Created by John Weier for Thomson Gale, 2006

and Florida were constructing facilities for slot machines at racetracks. Allowing machine gambling at existing gambling venues such as racetracks is generally more acceptable to voters and politicians than full-fledged casino gambling. However, this is not true in all states. Kentucky and Maryland legislators have continually rejected bills that would have expanded gambling at the state's racetracks.

GAMBLING ISSUES AND SOCIAL IMPACT

In 1957 two men with gambling obsessions decided to meet regularly to discuss the problems gambling had caused them and the changes they needed to make in their lives to overcome it. After meeting for several months, each realized that the moral support offered by the other was allowing them to control their desire to gamble. They started an organization based on the spiritual principles used by Alcoholics Anonymous and similar groups to control addictions. The first group meeting of Gamblers Anonymous was held on September 13, 1957, in Los Angeles.

As gambling became more widespread throughout the country, efforts were undertaken to help those whose lives had been negatively affected by gambling. In recognition of the wide social impact of the industry, the American Psychiatric Association officially recognized pathological gambling as a mental health disorder in 1980. Pathological gambling was listed under disorders of impulse control and described as a "chronic and progressive failure to resist impulses to gamble." During the 1980s many states began setting up programs to offer assistance to compulsive gamblers. Harrah's Entertainment became the first commercial casino company to officially address problem gambling when it instituted the educational campaigns Operation Bet Smart and Project 21 to promote responsible gaming and raise awareness about problems associated with underage gambling.

In 1996 Congress authorized the National Gambling Impact Study Commission (NGISC) to investigate the social and economic consequences of gambling in the country. The federally funded group included nine commissioners representing pro- and antigambling positions. Existing literature was reviewed, and new studies were ordered. The commission held hearings around the country at which a variety of people involved in and affected by the gambling industry testified. The commission's final report in 1999 concluded that, with the exception of Internet gambling, gambling policy decisions were best left up to state, tribal, and local governments. The commission also recommended that legalized gambling not be expanded further until all related costs and benefits were identified and reviewed.

Also during 1999, *Pathological Gambling: A Critical Review*, published by National Academies Press, identified and analyzed all available scientific research studies dealing with pathological and problem gambling. The researchers estimated that about 1.5% of American adults had been pathological gamblers at some point in their lives, with about 1.8 million compulsive gamblers actively gambling during a given year. Although the researchers were able to draw some general conclusions about the prevalence of pathological gambling in the United States, they cited a lack of scientific evidence as a limiting factor in their ability to draw more specific conclusions. For example, they found that men were more likely than women to be pathological gamblers, but they lacked data to estimate the prevalence of problem gambling among such demographic subgroups as the elderly or those with low incomes.

As the century closed, *The WAGER* (a public education project of the Division on Addictions at Harvard Medical School) asked its readers to rank thirteen gambling events of the twentieth century in order of importance. The results are shown in Figure 1.1. The legalization of gambling in Nevada in 1931 was voted the most important gambling event of the century, followed by the introduction of the first modern state lottery in New Hampshire in 1964. Publication of *Pathological Gambling: A Critical Review* in 1999 was ranked third.

PUBLIC OPINION

In May 2006 the Gallup Organization conducted a nationwide poll to determine the moral acceptability of a variety of social issues. Pollsters interviewed 1,000 adults aged eighteen and older regarding their opinions. The results are shown in Table 1.2. Overall, gambling was considered morally acceptable by 60% of those asked. Roughly the same percentage of people (61%) saw medical testing on animals and embryonic stem cell research as morally acceptable. The acceptability of gambling had declined slightly since 2004 when 66% of Americans polled pronounced it morally acceptable.

The top five issues considered morally acceptable by Democrats and Republicans are detailed in Figure 1.2 and Figure 1.3. Gambling was considered morally acceptable by 54% of self-described Republicans and 65% of self-described Democrats, a difference of eleven percentage points.

In February and March 2006 Pew Research Center polled 2,250 adults and asked them about their attitudes towards legalized gambling. The results were released in the May 2006 report, *Gambling: As the Take Rises, So Does Public Concern*, by Paul Taylor, Cary Funk, and Peyton Craighill. In 2006, 71% of adults approved of cash lotteries and 66% approved of bingo for cash prizes. Casino gambling and off-track betting on horse races received less support. Legalized betting on professional sports received the lowest approval rating. (See Figure 1.4.)

Overall, a smaller percentage of respondents approved of gambling in the 2006 Pew poll than did in a similar survey conducted by the Gallup Organization in April 1989. (See Figure 1.4.) Approval of legalized lotteries and bingo dropped the most between 1989 and 2006. The authors of the Pew report suggest that the change in Americans' attitudes about gambling had less to do with moral values and more to do with economic values. Less than one-third (28%) of respondents to the 2006 Pew poll thought gambling was immoral, but 70% of respondents did believe that legalized gambling caused people to spend money they did not have. This represented an 8% increase from the 62% of respondents who felt the same way in the earlier poll by Gallup. (See Figure 1.5.)

According to a January 2006 Harris Poll (http://www.harrisinteractive.com), adults showed far less support

FIGURE 1.1

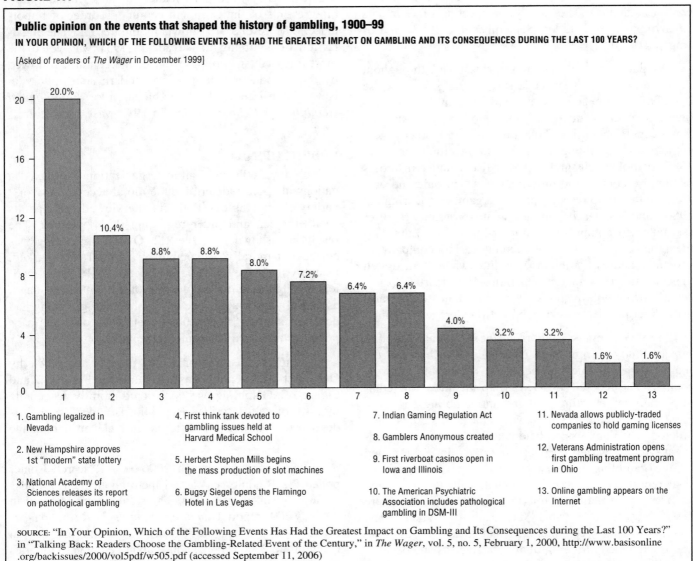

Public opinion on the events that shaped the history of gambling, 1900–99

IN YOUR OPINION, WHICH OF THE FOLLOWING EVENTS HAS HAD THE GREATEST IMPACT ON GAMBLING AND ITS CONSEQUENCES DURING THE LAST 100 YEARS?

[Asked of readers of *The Wager* in December 1999]

1. Gambling legalized in Nevada
2. New Hampshire approves 1st "modern" state lottery
3. National Academy of Sciences releases its report on pathological gambling
4. First think tank devoted to gambling issues held at Harvard Medical School
5. Herbert Stephen Mills begins the mass production of slot machines
6. Bugsy Siegel opens the Flamingo Hotel in Las Vegas
7. Indian Gaming Regulation Act
8. Gamblers Anonymous created
9. First riverboat casinos open in Iowa and Illinois
10. The American Psychiatric Association includes pathological gambling in DSM-III
11. Nevada allows publicly-traded companies to hold gaming licenses
12. Veterans Administration opens first gambling treatment program in Ohio
13. Online gambling appears on the Internet

SOURCE: "In Your Opinion, Which of the Following Events Has Had the Greatest Impact on Gambling and Its Consequences during the Last 100 Years?" in "Talking Back: Readers Choose the Gambling-Related Event of the Century," in *The Wager*, vol. 5, no. 5, February 1, 2000, http://www.basisonline.org/backissues/2000/vol5pdf/w505.pdf (accessed September 11, 2006)

for legalized Internet gambling. Some 53% of adults who were online believed that Internet gambling should continue to be illegal. Attitudes towards Internet gambling were more negative among older adults than younger adults. Seventy-six percent of those sixty-five and older who were online believed that Internet gambling should remain illegal, as opposed to only 38% of those aged twenty-five to twenty-nine who were online.

TABLE 1.2

Public opinion on the moral acceptability of sixteen issues, May 2006

	Morally acceptable %	Morally wrong %
The death penalty	71	22
Divorce	67	24
Buying and wearing clothing made of animal fur	62	32
Medical research using stem cells obtained from human embryos	61	30
Medical testing on animals	61	32
Gambling	60	34
Sex between an unmarried man and woman	59	37
Having a baby outside of marriage	51	43
Doctor-assisted suicide	50	41
Homosexual relations	44	51
Abortion	43	44
Cloning animals	29	65
Suicide	15	78
Cloning humans	8	88
Polygamy—one husband has more than one wife at the same time	5	93
Married men and women having an affair	4	93

SOURCE: Joseph Carroll, "Moral Acceptability of Issues" in *Republicans, Democrats Differ on What Is Morally Acceptable,* Gallup News Service, The Gallup Organization, May 24, 2006, http://poll.gallup.com/content/default .aspx?CI=22915 (accessed September 6, 2006). Copyright © 2006 by The Gallup Organization. Reproduced by permission of The Gallup Organization.

FIGURE1.2

Democrats' opinion on the moral acceptability of sixteen issues, May 2006

[In percentages]

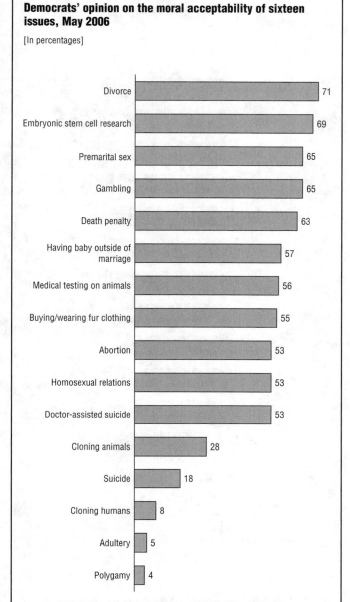

SOURCE: Joseph Carroll, "Moral Acceptability of Issues Among Democrats (Including 'Leaners')" in *Republicans, Democrats Differ on What Is Morally Acceptable*, Gallup News Service, The Gallup Organization, May 24, 2006, http://poll.gallup.com/content/default .aspx?CI=22915 (accessed September 6, 2006). Copyright © 2006 by The Gallup Organization. Reproduced by permission of The Gallup Organization.

FIGURE 1.3

FIGURE 1.4

Republicans' opinion on the moral acceptability of sixteen issues, May 2006

[In percentages]

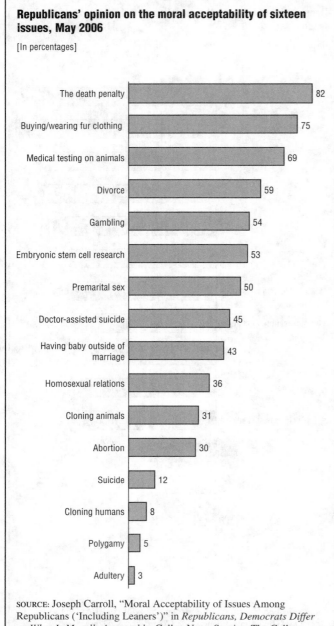

The death penalty — 82
Buying/wearing fur clothing — 75
Medical testing on animals — 69
Divorce — 59
Gambling — 54
Embryonic stem cell research — 53
Premarital sex — 50
Doctor-assisted suicide — 45
Having baby outside of marriage — 43
Homosexual relations — 36
Cloning animals — 31
Abortion — 30
Suicide — 12
Cloning humans — 8
Polygamy — 5
Adultery — 3

SOURCE: Joseph Carroll, "Moral Acceptability of Issues Among Republicans ('Including Leaners')" in *Republicans, Democrats Differ on What Is Morally Acceptable*, Gallup News Service, The Gallup Organization, May 24, 2006, http://poll.gallup.com/content/default .aspx?CI=22915 (accessed September 6, 2006). Copyright © 2006 by The Gallup Organization. Reproduced by permission of The Gallup Organization.

Public approval of legalized gambling, 1989 and 2006

[By percentage]

■ *Pew poll 2006*   □ *Gallup poll 1989*

Lotteries for cash prizes — 71 / 78
Bingo for cash prizes — 66 / 75
Casino gambling — 51 / 54
Offtrack betting on horse races — 50 / 54
Betting on pro sports — 42 / 42

SOURCE: Paul Taylor, Cary Funk, and Peyton Craighill, "Approval of Legalized Gambling Down Slightly," in *Gambling: As the Take Rises, So Does Public Concern*, Pew Research Center, May 23, 2006, http:// pewresearch.org/assets/social/pdf/Gambling.pdf (accessed September 6, 2006). Data from The Gallup Organization. Copyright © 1989 by The Gallup Organization. Reproduced by permission of The Gallup Organization.

FIGURE 1.5

Poll respondents who say legalized gambling encourages people to gamble more than they can afford, 1989 and 2006

[By percentage]

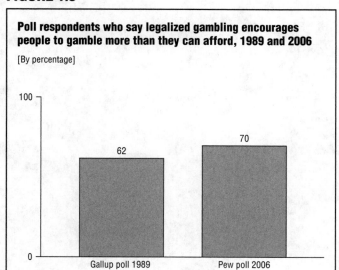

SOURCE: Paul Taylor, Cary Funk, and Peyton Craighill, "More See a Downside to Gambling," in *Gambling: As the Take Rises, So Does Public Concern*, Pew Research Center, May 23, 2006, http://pewresearch.org/assets/social/pdf/Gambling.pdf (accessed September 6, 2006). Data from The Gallup Organization. Copyright © 1989 by The Gallup Organization. Reproduced by permission of The Gallup Organization.

CHAPTER 2

SUPPLY AND DEMAND: WHO OFFERS GAMBLING? WHO GAMBLES?

Like any business in a capitalist society, the gambling industry is driven by the principles of supply and demand. Gambling proponents say that demand drives supply. In other words, the industry grows and spreads into new markets because the public is eager to gamble. Illegal gambling has always flourished, and opinion polls show that most Americans support legal gambling opportunities, particularly lotteries and casinos. Gambling is one of the most popular leisure activities in the country. Casinos alone took in nearly $52.6 billion in 2005, dwarfing box office sales of the U.S. motion picture industry, for example, which earned $9 billion in the domestic market and $23.2 billion worldwide (Motion Picture Association of America, (http://www.mpaa.org/research Statistics.asp).

Gambling opponents say that supply drives demand. They argue that people would not be tempted to gamble or to gamble as often if opportunities were not so prevalent and widespread. They see gambling as an irresistible temptation with potentially dangerous consequences. It bothers them that gambling opportunities are presented, promoted, and supported not only by the business world but also by government leaders and politicians—people who are supposed to represent the best interests of the public they serve.

Whatever the driving reason, gambling has become a big business and a popular pastime for many Americans.

SUPPLY—GAMBLING OPPORTUNITIES AND OPPORTUNISTS

A variety of gambling opportunities are available in this country, both legal and illegal. Gambling is a money-making activity for corporations, small businesses, charities, governments, and in some cases, criminals. The legal gambling industry employs hundreds of thousands of people across the country. In addition, it generates business in a variety of related industries, including manufacturing companies that provide slot machines and other supplies, travel and tourism operators that provide transportation, food, and lodging for gamblers, advertising agencies that promote gambling enterprises, breeders that raise and train racehorses, and many more.

According to the American Gaming Association (AGA), the legal gambling industry's gross revenues increased from $3 billion per year in 1975 to nearly $84.7 billion per year in 2005 (October 2006, http://www.americangaming.org/Industry/factsheets/statistics_detail.cfv?id=7). A significant portion of this growth took place during the 1990s, when gross gambling revenues doubled. Gross gambling revenue is the money taken in by the industry minus the winnings paid out. In other words, it is equivalent to sales. From this number, then, such operating expenses as wages, benefits, and taxes must be subtracted in order to gauge the profits realized by the industry. The AGA estimated in its 2006 *State of the States: The AGA Survey of Casino Entertainment* survey that gross revenues for the commercial casino industry in 2005 were about $30.3 billion; of that, $12.6 billion was paid out in wages and $4.9 billion was paid in taxes (http://www. americangaming. org/assets/files/2006_Survey_for_Web.pdf).

Corporations

CASINO OWNERS AND OPERATORS. Corporations have profited the most from legalized gambling since they took over the small casinos of Las Vegas during the late 1960s. Organized crime had been pushed out by the government, so the corporations could bring their management practices to an increasingly profitable business. They invested money in new and bigger properties in Las Vegas and throughout the state of Nevada and then, in 1978, opened the first casino hotel in Atlantic City, New Jersey. Today, most corporations in the industry own and/or operate several commercial casinos. Casino City's *North American Gaming Almanac* estimates that commercial casinos and card rooms control 39% of the legal gambling revenue pie, compared with 25% controlled by tribal casinos and 28% by lotteries (http://

casinocitypress.com/Advertising/PocketDirectory/PGD2006_ IndustryOverviewPages.pdf) Some companies, such as Harrah's Entertainment, also manage casinos for Native American tribes. The tribes are increasingly partnering with large, well-known corporations to take advantage of their name recognition and corporate experience.

Many of the nation's gambling properties are controlled by five well-known public corporations:

- Harrah's Entertainment was the largest gambling and gaming corporation in 2005 with nearly forty casinos in three countries. According to its annual report, Harrah's employed more than 85,000 people and had net revenues of $7.1 billion in 2005, up from $4.5 billion in 2004. (The increase in its revenues reflected its acquisition of Horseshoe Gaming Holding Corporation in July 2004 and Caesars Entertainment in June 2005.) In Las Vegas, the company owned Harrah's, Rio, Caesars Palace, Paris, Bally's, Flamingo, and the Imperial Palace. Other properties in Nevada included Harrah's and Flamingo in Laughlin; Harrah's and the Reno Hilton in Reno; and Harrah's, Harveys, and Bill's in Lake Tahoe. In Atlantic City, Harrah's owned Bally's, Harrah's, Showboat, and Caesars. The corporation also owned Harrah's Joliet and Harrah's Metropolis in Illinois; Horseshoe Hammond and Caesars in Indiana; Harrah's Council Bluffs in Iowa; the Horseshoe Tunica, Grand Casino Resort Tunica, the Sheraton Casino and Hotel, and the Grand Biloxi in Mississippi; Harrah's St. Louis and Harrah's North Kansas City in Missouri; and Harrah's New Orleans and Horseshoe Bossier City in Louisiana. (Harrah's Lake Charles closed indefinitely after Hurricane Rita.) Four tribal casinos were operated by the company in 2005: Harrah's Cherokee in Cherokee, North Carolina; Harrah's Phoenix Ak-Chin in Maricopa, Arizona; Harrah's Prairie Band Casino in Mayetta, Kansas; and Harrah's Rincon–San Diego in Valley Center, California. In addition, the corporation operated the Louisiana Downs Thoroughbred horseracing track and casino in Bossier City, Louisiana, and the Bluffs Run greyhound-racing track and casino in Council Bluffs, Iowa. Harrah's also had casinos in Canada and Uruguay as well as two cruise-ship casinos.

- MGM Mirage owned twenty-four casinos resorts in 2005, including the Bellagio, Circus Circus, Excalibur, Luxor, Mandalay Bay, the Mirage, MGM Grand, Monte Carlo, New York–New York, Slots-A-Fun, and Treasure Island in Las Vegas; the Colorado Belle and Edgewater in Laughlin; Whiskey Pete's, Buffalo Bill's, and Primm Valley Casino along the Nevada/ California state line; Circus Circus in Reno; Gold Strike and Nevada Landing in Jean, Nevada; Railroad Pass in Henderson, Nevada; Beau Rivage in Biloxi, Mississippi; the Gold Strike in Tunica, Mississippi;

and MGM Grand in Detroit, Michigan. The company owned 50% of the Borgata casino resort in Atlantic City, the Grand Victoria in Elgin, Illinois, and the Silver Legacy in Reno. The company also had interests in the Shadow Creek golf course in North Las Vegas and two golf courses in Primm Valley, Nevada. According to the company's annual report, it employed nearly 70,000 people and had revenues of $6.5 billion in 2005, up from $4.2 billion in 2004, an increase of 53%. Most of the increase in revenue resulted from the company's purchase of Mandalay Resort Group in 2005 for approximately $7.3 billion.

- Boyd Gaming Corporation has nineteen casinos, including Par-A-Dice Casino in East Peoria, Illinois; Blue Chip Casino in Michigan City, Indiana; Treasure Chest Casino, Sam's Town, and Delta Downs racetrack casino in Louisiana; Sam's Town in Robinsonville, Mississippi; and the California, Barbary Coast, El Dorado, Fremont, Gold Coast, Jokers Wild, Main Street Station, Orleans, Sam's Town, South Coast, and Stardust in and around Las Vegas. Boyd is a joint-venture partner with MGM Mirage in the Borgata Casino in Atlantic City. According to the corporation's annual report, it employed more than 23,000 people and had net corporate revenue of $2.2 billion in 2005.

- Penn National Gaming ran thirteen gaming properties in the United States in 2005, according to its annual report. It acquired several of those establishments from Argosy Gaming Corporation in October 2005 for $2.3 billion. It owned seven riverboat casinos, including the Boomtown in Biloxi, Mississippi; Argosy Casino Alton in Illinois; Argosy Casino Riverside near Kansas City, Missouri; Casino Rouge in Baton Rouge, Louisiana; Argosy Casino Sioux City in Iowa; Argosy Casino Lawrenceburg in Indiana; and the Empress Casino in Joliet, Illinois. The company's land-based casinos included Bullwhackers Casino in Black Hawk, Colorado; Hollywood Slots in Bangor, Maine; Hollywood Casino in Aurora, Illinois; and Hollywood Casino Bay St. Louis and Hollywood Casino Tunica in Mississippi. The company also owned a casino in Ontario, Canada, and several racetracks. In 2005, Penn National Gaming employed nearly 14,000 people and had net revenue of $1.4 billion.

- In 2005 Station Casinos, Inc., had full or part ownership of fifteen casinos in and around Las Vegas that catered to local markets. The properties included Palace Station, Boulder Station, Fiesta Rancho, the Gold Rush, the Magic Star, Santa Fe Station, Texas Station, the Wildfire, the Wild Wild West, Fiesta Henderson, Sunset Station, Barley's Casino and Brewery (joint venture), Green Valley Ranch (joint venture), and the

Greens (joint venture in Henderson). In addition, the company managed the Thunder Valley Casino for the United Auburn Indian Community in Lincoln, California. A new casino resort, Red Rock, opened in April 2006 in Las Vegas. The company employed more than 14,000 people and had net corporate revenue of $1.1 billion in 2005, according to its financial statements.

Most corporations involved in gambling enterprises, including those listed above, are publicly held, meaning that investors can buy shares in the companies on the stock market. In return, investors receive a portion of the profits, if any, made by the company. Publicly held companies are answerable to their shareholders. The U.S. Securities and Exchange Commission requires publicly held companies to disclose certain financial and other information to the public. Some casino companies are privately owned, which means they do not offer shares of stock to the public on a stock exchange and therefore do not have to meet the strict disclosure requirements of public companies. For example, the Columbia Sussex company, headquartered in Kentucky, owned eight casinos in three states in 2006 and did not disclose its revenue. In late 2006 the company was seeking regulatory approval for a $2.8 billion takeover of Aztar Corporation, a Phoenix-based casino operator with 2005 revenues of $915 million.

OTHER GAMBLING CORPORATIONS. Different companies play major roles in other realms of the gambling industry. Two publicly traded companies, Churchill Downs and Magna Entertainment, are major organizations in the Thoroughbred horse racing business. In 2005 Churchill Downs operated tracks in Florida, Illinois, Indiana, Louisiana, and Kentucky. Magna Entertainment, a Canadian-based corporation, operated fourteen racetracks throughout North America in 2005. In 2005 Churchill Downs had revenues of $409 million, and Magna Entertainment had revenues of $625 million.

Lottery tickets were available at more than 240,000 retail locations throughout the United States and Canada as of 2006, according to the North American Association of Provincial and State Lotteries (NASPL; http://www. naspl. org/index. cfm?fuseaction=content&PageID=41&PageCategory =38). These locations included most supermarkets, gas stations, and convenience stores in states with lotteries. The National Association of Convenience Stores estimated in 2006 that half of all lottery tickets sold in North America each year are sold in convenience stores (http://www.nacsonline.com/nacs/resource/prtoolkit/factsheets/prtk_fact_lottery.htm). 7-Eleven, the largest convenience store operator, franchisor, and licensor in the world, had approximately 5,800 stores in the United States and Canada in 2006 and most sold lottery tickets. Other large corporations in the convenience store business included Couche-Tard (the parent company of Circle K and Mac's), QuikTrip, and Amerada Hess Corporation.

Many corporations directly support the gambling industry by providing equipment, goods, supplies or services. They may be members of the Gaming Standards Association, an international organization devoted to the development of uniform standards for communication and computer technology used in gambling machines. Some examples of these corporations are:

- GTECH Corporation, which introduced the first lottery terminal in 1982 and now provides technology services to lotteries in twenty-five states
- Bally Technology, which introduced its first slot machine in 1936 and is now a successful machine manufacturer and distributor
- Konami Gaming, a leading producer of high-tech video slot machines and multisite casino management systems
- WMS Gaming, which is engaged entirely in the manufacture, sale, leasing, and licensing of gambling machines

GAMBLING AS AN INVESTMENT. The investment firm MUTUALS.com sells shares in the Vice Fund, a mutual fund composed entirely of companies in the alcohol, tobacco, gambling, and defense industries. In 2006, according to the fund's Web site (http://www.vicefund. com), gambling companies made up 27% of the fund's investments. For the one-year period ending March 31, 2006, the fund had a 19% return on investments, which compared with an 11.7% gain for companies in the Standard & Poor's 500 Index. Companies such as Boyd Gaming Corp., Scientific Games Corp., CryptoLogic, Inc., Shuffle Master, Inc., Monarch Casino & Resort, Inc., and International Game Technology were major contributors to the Vice Fund's growth.

Small Businesses

Many small casinos and racetracks, mini casinos, and card rooms around the country are owned and/or operated by small companies, families, and entrepreneurs. Other ways in which small businesses are engaged in or serve the gambling industry include:

- selling lottery tickets and operating electronic gaming devices at independently owned convenience stores, markets, service stations, bars, restaurants, bowling alleys, and newsstands
- manufacturing and distributing equipment such as slot machines, roulette wheels, lottery tickets, dice, and cards
- providing services such as advertising, marketing, public relations, accounting, information technology, and food
- breeding, training, and caring for horses and greyhounds

Gambling

Supply and Demand: Who Offers Gambling? Who Gambles? **15**

Most small businesses that offer gambling do so through lottery ticket sales and/or electronic gaming devices, such as slot machines. These are considered forms of convenience gambling, because patrons do not have to travel to special destinations, such as casinos and racetracks. Convenience gambling has been more controversial than destination gambling. Critics say that allowing gambling in stores and restaurants and other places that people visit as part of their everyday routine makes it too easy for them to gamble. The same criticism is leveled against Internet gambling, which patrons can do at home.

INTERNET GAMBLING BUSINESSES. Internet gambling is illegal in the United States, so the majority of Internet gambling sites are operated by small companies located offshore, many in the Caribbean. Little is known about these companies, which operate without regulatory oversight. However, the American Gaming Association has estimated that more than 2,500 Internet gambling sites operated around the world at the end of 2005. Christiansen Capital Advisors, which provides analysis and management for the gaming industry, estimated that Internet gambling generated nearly $12 billion in 2005. (See Chapter 9.)

Criminals

Gambling in America has had a checkered legal history. At various times it has been legal, illegal but tolerated, or illegal and actively prosecuted. During times when gambling opportunities have been outlawed, entrepreneurs have stepped in to offer them anyway. These entrepreneurs range from mobsters running million-dollar betting rings to grandmothers running neighborhood bingo games. Either way, the illegal nature of the activity makes these entrepreneurs criminals.

Organized crime groups have often been associated with gambling, a cash business with high demand and good profits. Eastern crime syndicates were among the first to see the potential of Las Vegas, invest in it, and profit from it. At times they have infiltrated other segments of the legal gambling industry, such as horse racing. Strict regulations and crackdowns by law enforcement have been put into place to push them out. The federal Racketeer Influenced and Corrupt Organizations (RICO) Act enacted in 1970 was designed to combat infiltration by organized crime into legitimate businesses, including gambling. Most analysts believe those efforts have been largely successful at keeping mobsters from establishing or taking over legal gambling businesses.

However, while they have been denied casino ownership and management roles, some organized crime figures have infiltrated casinos in other ways, such as through labor unions and maintenance or food services. Law enforcement officials also believe that organized

crime families have been involved in bribing state officials who were considering the extension or expansion of gambling options, particularly relating to electronic gambling machines.

The Nevada Gaming Commission and State Gaming Control Board maintain a list of people who are prohibited from gambling in Nevada. The List of Excluded Persons, more commonly known as "Nevada's Black Book," includes known cheaters, crime family bosses, mob associates, and others linked in some way to organized crime. These people are considered so dangerous to the integrity of legal gambling that they are not allowed to set foot in Nevada casinos. The Nevada Gaming Commission and State Gaming Control Board publish photographs of the excluded people on their Web site (http://gaming.nv.gov/loep_main.htm).

The most lucrative sector of the gambling industry for organized crime has been and continues to be illegal bookmaking and numbers games. Bookmaking is a gambling activity in which a bookmaker takes bets on the odds that a particular event will occur or that an event will have a particular outcome. The vast majority of bookmaking revolves around sporting events, such as college and professional football and basketball games. Such wagering is extremely popular in the United States. Because sports bookmaking is legal only in Nevada, there is a large illegal market for it across the country. Gaming industry and sports analysts say gamblers illegally wager $100 billion to $300 billion each year on sports in the United States, according to Michael McCarthy in "Football Bettors Put Billions on the Line" (*USA Today*, http://www.usatoday.com/sports/football/nfl/2005-09-07-betting_x. htm).

Illegal numbers games are similar to lottery games in that players wager money on particular numbers to be selected in a drawing or by other means. Illegal numbers operators thrive in many parts of the country, especially large cities—even those where legal lotteries are offered.

Not all bookmaking is done through mobsters. Many enterprising entrepreneurs run small-time illegal gambling books, mostly related to sporting events. Office pools, in which coworkers pool small wagers on sports or office events—for example, when a baby is going to be born—are common. Although society does not generally consider private wagers and small-stakes office pools to be illegal gambling, the laws in most states do.

Despite widespread illegal gambling, few people are actually arrested for engaging in it. According to *Crime in the United States 2004* (U.S. Department of Justice, 2005), in 2004 authorities made only 10,755 arrests for gambling out of nearly 14 million total arrests. (See Table 2.1.) This was down slightly from 10,954 arrests in 2003.

16   Supply and Demand: Who Offers Gambling? Who Gambles?

Gambling

TABLE 2.1

Estimated arrests by type of crime, 2004

Total[a]	13,938,071
Murder and nonnegligent manslaughter	13,467
Forcible rape	26,066
Robbery	108,992
Aggravated assault	438,033
Burglary	294,645
Larceny-theft	1,185,619
Motor vehicle theft	148,429
Arson	15,504
Violent crime[b]	586,558
Property crime[b]	1,644,197
Other assaults	1,284,858
Forgery and counterfeiting	119,518
Fraud	282,938
Embezzlement	17,332
Stolen property; buying, receiving, possessing	128,529
Vandalism	272,522
Weapons; carrying, possessing, etc.	175,776
Prostitution and commercialized vice	87,872
Sex offenses (except forcible rape and prostitution)	90,913
Drug abuse violations	1,746,570
Gambling	10,755
Offenses against the family and children	124,936
Driving under the influence	1,433,382
Liquor laws	612,528
Drunkenness	552,671
Disorderly conduct	657,637
Vagrancy	36,404
All other offenses	3,815,435
Suspicion	3,554
Curfew and loitering law violations	137,398
Runaways	119,342

[a]Does not include suspicion.
[b]Violent crimes are offenses of murder, forcible rape, robbery, and aggravated assault. Property crimes are offenses of burglary, larceny-theft, motor vehicle theft, and arson.

SOURCE: "Table 29. Estimated Number of Arrests, United States, 2004," in *Crime in the United States, 2004*, U.S. Department of Justice, Federal Bureau of Investigation, October 2005, http://www.fbi.gov/ucr/cius_04/documents/CIUS2004.pdf (accessed September 6, 2006)

Charities

Charitable gambling is the most widely practiced form of gambling in the United States. As shown in Table 1.1 in Chapter 1, it was legal in forty-seven states and the District of Columbia in 2006 (prohibited only in Arkansas, Hawaii, and Utah). In charitable gambling, a specified portion of the money raised (less prizes, expenses, and any state fees and taxes) goes to qualified charitable organizations. Such organizations, include religious groups, fraternal organizations, veterans' groups, volunteer fire departments, parent-teacher organizations, civic and cultural groups, booster clubs, and other nonprofit organizations.

Generally, a charitable organization has to have been in existence for several years and has to obtain a state license for the gambling activity. Most states will only issue licenses to organizations that have been recognized by the Internal Revenue Service as exempt from federal income tax under Tax Code section 501(c). Thousands of charitable organizations are registered to conduct gambling throughout the country.

Most charitable gambling is regulated by state governments, although not uniformly by the same department—it may be the department of revenue, the state police, the alcohol control board, or the lottery, gaming, or racing commission. Administrative fees and taxes are levied in most states. In some states charitable gambling activity is unregulated.

Typical games allowed included bingo (the most common), pull tabs (lottery tickets with tabs that gamblers pull open to reveal cash prizes), raffles, and card games such as poker or blackjack. Slot machines and table games such as roulette and craps are generally not permitted. Limits are usually placed on the size of cash prizes that can be awarded. States allow different games for charity fundraising. For example, California only allows bingo games.

Because of the inconsistencies in state oversight it is difficult to determine the complete extent of charitable gambling in the United States. The American Gaming Association estimates that revenues from charitable gaming totaled $1.9 billion in 2004.

According to the National Association of Fundraising Ticket Manufacturers (http://www.naftm.org), a trade association representing companies that manufacture bingo paper, pull tabs, and other supplies used in the charitable gambling industry, in 2004 $7.5 billion was wagered on charitable gaming in the twenty-six states for which it compiled statistics (*Charity Gaming in North America 2004 Annual Report*, 2005). The top five states were Minnesota ($1.4 billion), Washington ($870 million), Texas ($603 million), Kentucky ($571 million), and Indiana ($539 million). (See Figure 2.1.) On average, about 71% of gross receipts went to prize payouts, 16% to expenses, and 3% to taxes and fees. The remaining 10% was net profit for charitable organizations.

According to the trade association, nearly all states charge licensing fees to conduct charitable gambling events. For example, South Carolina charges a onetime fee of $1,000. Other states charge a fee per event or set weekly, monthly, or yearly fees, which generally run from $10 to $100. A handful of states base licensing fees on the amount of gross receipts, so the fees can be thousands of dollars. Most states also impose a gaming tax on the proceeds from charitable gambling and/or collect administrative fees. Most states allocate all or a portion of these revenues to their general funds or to the agencies that oversee charitable gambling. A few states split the money with local law enforcement agencies.

Minnesota is believed to have the highest gross receipts from charitable gambling of any state—probably half of all money wagered in the United States for this purpose. According to the *Annual Report of the Minnesota Gambling Control Board: Fiscal Year 2005*, charity gambling brought

Gambling

Supply and Demand: Who Offers Gambling? Who Gambles? **17**

FIGURE 2.1

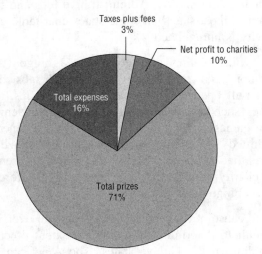

Gross receipts and proceeds from charitable gaming in top ten participating states, 2004

Taxes plus fees 3%

Net profit to charities 10%

Total expenses 16%

Total prizes 71%

State	Gross receipts	State	Proceeds
Minnesota	$1,402,373,000	Minnesota	$127,293,000
Washington	$870,279,763	Washington	$90,226,167
Texas	$602,907,777	Michigan	$79,088,250
Kentucky	$570,688,422	Indiana	$75,735,668
Indiana	$538,824,604	New York	$66,816,456
Michigan	$432,910,341	Kentucky	$52,001,929
New York	$397,369,504	Virginia	$45,711,700
Alaska	$355,290,436	New Jersey	$44,841,032
Virginia	$328,178,400	Wisconsin	$38,020,808
N. Dakota	$272,121,369	Alaska	$31,913,617

SOURCE: "Distribution/Top 10 States," in *Charity Gaming in North America: 2004 Annual Report*, National Association of Fundraising Ticket Manufacturers, 2005, http://www.naftm.org/vertical/Sites/{10B16680-A509-4D78-B468-8A1901FC0CF7}/uploads/{48BF2972-BC96-4864-BBC4-F4AABB5B9204}.PDF (accessed September 6, 2006)

TABLE 2.2

Gambling winnings that must be reported to the Internal Revenue Service (IRS), 2006

Type of game	Amount of prize paid is equal to or greater than:
Lotteries, sweepstakes, horse races, dog races, instant bingo game prizes/pull-tabs, jai alai and other wagering transactions	$600 and prize is at least 300 times wager
Bingo	$1,200
Slot machines	$1,200
Keno	$1,500

SOURCE: Adapted from *2006 Instructions for Forms W-2G and 5754*, Internal Revenue Service, 2006, http://www.irs.gov/pub/irs-pdf/iw2g.pdf (accessed September 6, 2006)

THE FEDERAL GOVERNMENT. The primary means by which the federal government makes money from the gambling industry is by taxing winning gamblers and gambling operators. Gamblers must declare gambling earnings when they file their personal income taxes. They get to subtract their gambling losses, but they must keep thorough records and have receipts, if possible, to prove their losses. For racetrack gamblers, this means saving losing betting slips and keeping a gambling diary of dates, events, and amounts. Casino gamblers who join "slot clubs" can get a detailed printout of their gambling history from the casino.

Gambling operators, like all companies, are subject to corporate taxes. They are required to report winnings that meet certain criteria to the Internal Revenue Service. (See Table 2.2.) The gambling operator must withhold income tax from winnings of more than $5,000, usually at a withholding rate of 25%. However, 28% is withheld from the winnings of gamblers who do not provide the gambling operator with their Social Security numbers or if the winnings are from bingo, keno, or slots. Gamblers who win noncash prizes, such as cars or other merchandise, have to pay taxes on the fair market value of the item.

The federal government is itself in the gambling business as well. The four branches of the U.S. armed forces operated 4,150 modern video slot machines at U.S. military bases in nine countries overseas in 2005, according to Diana B. Henriques in "Temptation to Gamble Is Near for Troops Overseas" (*New York Times*, October 19, 2005). Revenue from the machines totaled about $120 million. Based on an average payout of 94%, the total amount wagered in military slot machines was around $2 billion per year. In addition, the Army ran bingo games at military bases. Revenue totaled $7 million.

STATE GOVERNMENTS. State governments make money from legal gambling enterprises operated within their borders, including lotteries, commercial casinos, horse and dog races, jai alai games, card rooms, charitable

in gross receipts of almost $1.4 billion during fiscal year 2005, down slightly from 2004. Total prizes paid out amounted to $1.1 billion in 2005, or 82% of gross receipts. About 9% went to expenses, while 4% went to pay state taxes. About 5% ($13 million) went to the charities.

The Government

Federal, tribal, state, and local agencies collect money from gambling operations through the assessment of taxes and fees and, in some cases, by directly supplying gambling opportunities. Because the money raised is spent on public programs, many Americans are ultimately affected by the government's involvement in gambling. In states facing budget deficits, the expansion of gambling often seems an attractive solution. As Alabama State Representative John Rogers (D-Jefferson) put it, "Given the choice, people will take gambling over tax increases any day" (Mandy Rafool, "Gambling on Gaming," *State Legislatures*, January 2005).

gambling, and video machine gambling. Only lotteries are operated by state governments. All other gambling options are operated by other parties. As of August 2006, there were no state-owned casinos in the United States; proposals for such establishments have been offered in several states, but all have failed to become law.

Forty-two states and the District of Columbia operated lotteries as of mid 2006; Alabama, Alaska, Arkansas, Hawaii, Mississippi, Nevada, Utah, and Wyoming did not. (See Table 1.1 in chapter 1.) They had approximately $53.2 billion in sales for fiscal year 2005, according to the North American Association of State and Provincial Lotteries. Generally, after paying expenses and the winners and retailers who sell the tickets, states have a 30% to 40% profit to spend on government programs, such as education.

TRIBAL GOVERNMENTS. Native American tribes that have been officially recognized by the U.S. government are considered sovereign nations, which means that, to a certain extent, they govern themselves. In 1988 the U.S. Congress passed the Indian Gaming Regulatory Act, which allowed federally recognized tribes to open gambling establishments if the state in which they were located already permits certain types of legalized gambling.

According to the National Indian Gaming Commission, Native American tribes operated 391 gambling locations and made $22.6 billion during 2005 (http://www.nigc.gov/Portals/0/NIGC%20Uploads/Tribal%20Data /tribalgaming revenues05.pdf). Three-fourths of the 224 tribes operating casinos in 2005 allocated all gambling revenue to tribal governmental services, economic and community development, neighboring communities, and charitable purposes, according to the National Indian Gaming Association (http://www.indiangaming.org/library/indian-gaming-facts/index.shtml). Tribal governments have used gambling revenues to build health clinics, schools, houses, and community centers and to provide educational scholarships and social services for their members.

LOCAL GOVERNMENTS. Local governments in some states collect taxes and fees from gambling activities operated within their jurisdictions. This is particularly true for casinos and racetracks.

New York City is particularly active in the gambling industry. The New York City Off-Track Betting Corporation was founded in 1970 to provide a legal alternative to the widespread off-track wagering that was offered by organized crime syndicates. Although the corporation is a government entity, it operates as a private enterprise that turns profits over to state and local governments. During the 2006 fiscal year, the OTB reported handling more than $1 billion in off-track wagers (http://www.nycotb.com/viewPage.cfm?pageId=18).

DEMAND—THE GAMBLERS

Gambling is a leisure activity—people gamble because they enjoy it. Proponents say there is no difference between spending money at a theme park and spending it at a casino: the money is exchanged for a good time in either case. Gambling has a powerful allure in addition to fun, though: the dream of wealth, a very strong motivator. Some options, such as lotteries, offer the chance to risk a small investment for an enormous payoff. This potential is too appealing for many people to pass up.

Adults

In May 2006 the Pew Research Center released *Gambling: As the Take Rises, So Does Public Concern*, a nationwide poll by Paul Taylor, Cary Funk, and Peyton Craighill that examined gambling participation in the United States. The survey showed that 67% of adults had gambled during the previous twelve months. (See Figure 2.2.) Lottery play was the most popular gambling activity—more than half of those asked (52%) had engaged in it—while 29% had visited a casino and 24% had played a slot machine. Other forms of gambling were far less common. Overall, the popularity of gambling had dropped since the Gallup Organization conducted a similar survey seventeen years earlier. Seventy-one percent of people in the Gallup survey reported gambling in 1989. Some forms of gambling were more popular in 2006 than in 1989. Figure 2.3 reveals that a higher percentage of people gambled at casinos and played slot machines in 2006 than in 1989, most likely because of the increase in the number of casinos. A higher percentage of people bet on professional sports and horse racing in 1989 than in 2006.

About seven out of ten men (72%) had gambled in the past year, according to the Pew survey, while six out of ten women had. (See Table 2.3.) Those with a college education were slightly less likely to have gambled than those with only some college or with a high school degree or less. The participation rate for people with higher incomes (greater than $100,000 per year) was higher than for other income groups. Only 59% of those making less than $30,000 per year reported gambling during the previous twelve months, compared with 79% of those making more than $100,000 per year.

The researchers discovered that gambling participation rates varied with religion as well. Protestants reported less gambling activity than Catholics or those who were identified as "secular." Among Protestants, members of mainline denominations, such as Methodists, gambled far more than those who identified with evangelical denominations. Northeasterners were more active gamblers than those living in other regions of the country. A larger percentage of white people than nonwhite people reported

Gambling

Supply and Demand: Who Offers Gambling? Who Gambles?   **19**

FIGURE 2.2

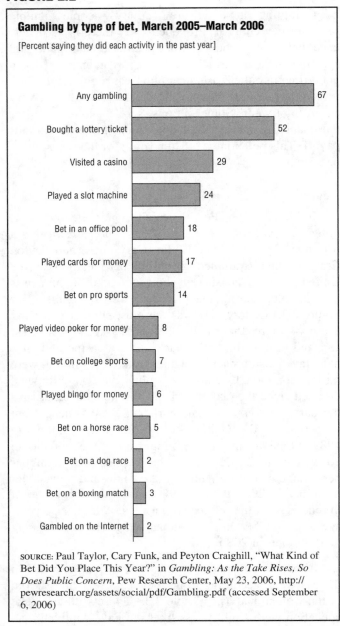

Gambling by type of bet, March 2005–March 2006

[Percent saying they did each activity in the past year]

Activity	Percent
Any gambling	67
Bought a lottery ticket	52
Visited a casino	29
Played a slot machine	24
Bet in an office pool	18
Played cards for money	17
Bet on pro sports	14
Played video poker for money	8
Bet on college sports	7
Played bingo for money	6
Bet on a horse race	5
Bet on a dog race	2
Bet on a boxing match	3
Gambled on the Internet	2

SOURCE: Paul Taylor, Cary Funk, and Peyton Craighill, "What Kind of Bet Did You Place This Year?" in *Gambling: As the Take Rises, So Does Public Concern*, Pew Research Center, May 23, 2006, http:// pewresearch.org/assets/social/pdf/Gambling.pdf (accessed September 6, 2006)

FIGURE 2.3

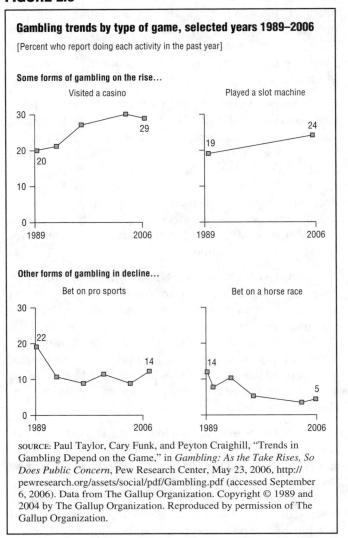

Gambling trends by type of game, selected years 1989–2006

[Percent who report doing each activity in the past year]

Some forms of gambling on the rise...

Visited a casino: 20 (1989) ... 29 (2006)

Played a slot machine: 19 (1989) ... 24 (2006)

Other forms of gambling in decline...

Bet on pro sports: 22 (1989) ... 14 (2006)

Bet on a horse race: 14 (1989) ... 5 (2006)

SOURCE: Paul Taylor, Cary Funk, and Peyton Craighill, "Trends in Gambling Depend on the Game," in *Gambling: As the Take Rises, So Does Public Concern*, Pew Research Center, May 23, 2006, http:// pewresearch.org/assets/social/pdf/Gambling.pdf (accessed September 6, 2006). Data from The Gallup Organization. Copyright © 1989 and 2004 by The Gallup Organization. Reproduced by permission of The Gallup Organization.

gambling during the previous year. Differences in participation by age were minor, although poll participants aged eighteen to twenty-nine were slightly more active in gambling than those of other ages.

Younger gamblers in the Pew survey also thought they were more successful: almost half (49%) believed that they had made more money than they had lost money gambling in the year prior to the survey. By contrast, 26% of those aged thirty to forty-nine felt they were financially ahead and only 23% of those aged sixty-five and older believed they were ahead.

SENIOR CITIZENS. The 2006 Pew poll showed that 58% of people aged sixty-five and older reported gambling during the previous year. Other studies have shown similar, or even higher rates, of participation. For example, a 2005 study conducted by researchers at the University of Pennsylvania and the Pennsylvania State College of Medicine (Suzi Levens et al., "Gambling among Older, Primary-Care Patients," *American Journal of Geriatric Psychiatry*, January 2005) revealed that nearly 70% of Americans older than sixty-five reported gambling in the previous twelve months. That study, which was based on a survey of 843 elderly patients, also found that nearly 11% of those questioned were "at risk" for problem gambling.

For older adults not at risk for gambling problems, the activity may have a positive impact. A 2004 Yale School of Medicine study (Rani Desai et al., "Health Correlates of Recreational Gambling in Older Adults," *American Journal of Psychiatry*, September 2004) revealed that a correlation existed between gambling and good health among people older than age sixty-five.

TABLE 2.3

Gamblers by demographic characteristics, March 2005–March 2006

	Any type of gambling	Bought lottery ticket	Visited casino	Bet[a] on sports	Played cards for money
	%	%	%	%	%
All adults	67	52	29	23	17
Gender					
Men	72	56	31	32	25
Women	62	48	27	15	10
Race/ethnicity					
White	68	53	30	23	18
Black	62	45	24	24	14
Hispanic[b]	62	47	22	16	12
Age					
18–29	71	48	30	30	32
30–49	69	56	30	25	17
50–64	68	55	31	22	11
65+	58	43	22	13	10
Education					
College grad	65	48	31	25	15
Some college	71	55	32	23	21
H.S. grad or less	66	52	27	22	17
Family income					
$100,000+	79	57	40	39	24
$50K–$99K	74	60	37	27	22
$30K–$49K	67	54	27	22	21
Less than $30K	59	44	21	16	11
Region					
Northeast	77	63	31	26	20
Midwest	64	52	26	23	18
South	62	48	24	21	15
West	68	47	38	23	17
Religion					
Protestant	61	48	24	19	13
Catholic	77	62	39	30	23
Secular	72	52	29	24	23
White Protestants					
Evangelical	50	40	19	14	11
Mainline	73	58	29	24	17

[a]Betting on sports includes professional sports, college sports or an office pool.
[b]Hispanics are of any race.

SOURCE: Paul Taylor, Cary Funk, and Peyton Craighill, "Profile of Gamblers," in *Gambling: As the Take Rises, So Does Public Concern*, Pew Research Center, May 23, 2006, http://pewresearch.org/assets/social/pdf/Gambling.pdf (accessed September 6, 2006)

The researchers did not find a similar correlation in those aged eighteen to sixty-four. The study, which was based on interviews with 2,417 older adults, focused only on recreational gamers and did not include subjects who exhibited gambling addiction.

Young People

The minimum legal age for placing a legal bet ranges from eighteen to twenty-one, depending on the state and the activity. For example, the majority of states limit the sale of lottery tickets to those eighteen or older, although most allow minors to receive lottery tickets as gifts. All commercial casinos have a minimum gambling age of twenty-one as set by state law. Tribal casinos are allowed to set their own minimum gambling age as long as it is at least eighteen. The minimum age to participate in charitable gambling activities, such as bingo games, is eighteen in most states. A few states allow people as young as sixteen to participate.

Each year the Annenberg Public Policy Center at the University of Pennsylvania releases the National Annenberg Risk Survey of Youth. In 2005, researchers interviewed nine hundred young people ages fourteen to twenty-two and asked them about their gambling habits, specifically with regard to poker playing and Internet gambling. The survey found that some 16% of young people gambled on a weekly basis and 44.2% gambled on a monthly basis. When asked about poker, 7.9% of young people (2.9 million people fit into this age group nationwide) responded that they gambled on cards on a weekly basis. Roughly 80% of those who played card games were male, which equates to 12.5% of the country's male population between ages fourteen and twenty-two. About 1.6% gambled online on a weekly basis in 2005, which was up considerably from 0.9% in 2004. A much higher percentage (14.2%) gambled online on a monthly basis.

Problem Gamblers

Problem gambling is a broad term that covers all gambling behaviors that are harmful to people in some way—financially, emotionally, socially, and/or legally. The harmful effects of problem gambling include:

- financial difficulties, such as unpaid bills, loss of employment, large debts, and even bankruptcy

- emotional problems, such as depression, anxiety, addictions, and thoughts of suicide

- social problems, as evidenced by strained or broken relationships with spouses, family, friends, and co-workers

- legal problems related to neglect of children or commission of criminal acts to obtain money

In the 2006 Pew survey, 6% of those asked said gambling had been a source of problems for their families. (See Table 2.4.) This percentage was up slightly from those reported by the Gallup polling organization in 1989, 1992, and 1996, but down slightly from the percentage reported in 1999. The 2006 Pew survey showed a marked difference in answers by age. Only 5% of those aged fifty and older said gambling had been a problem for their families, compared with 11% of adults younger than fifty.

In general, scientists characterize gambling behavior by the level of harm that it causes. People who experience

Gambling

Supply and Demand: Who Offers Gambling? Who Gambles? **21**

TABLE 2.4

Poll respondents who have experienced family problems related to gambling, selected years April 1989–March 2006

DO YOU SOMETIMES GAMBLE MORE THAN YOU THINK YOU SHOULD?

	Yes	No	Don't know
All gamblers	%	%	%
March 2006	9	90	1 = 100
December 2003	10	90	0 = 100
May 1999	11	88	1 = 100
June 1996	7	93	= 100
November 1992	9	91	0 = 100
April 1989	10	90	0 = 100

HAS GAMBLING EVER BEEN A SOURCE OF PROBLEMS WITHIN YOUR FAMILY?

All adults

	Yes	No	Don't know
March 2006	6	93	1 = 100
December 2003	6	94	= 100
May 1999	9	91	= 100
June 1996	5	95	= 100
November 1992	5	94	1 = 100
April 1989	4	96	= 100

Note: Based on people who gambled in past year. March 2006 figures are from Pew Research Center; data from all other years are from the Gallup Organization.

SOURCE: Paul Taylor, Cary Funk, and Peyton Craighill, "Gamble too much? Has gambling ever been a source of problems within your family?" in *Gambling: As the Take Rises, So Does Public Concern*, Pew Research Center, May 23, 2006, http://pewresearch.org/assets/social/pdf/Gambling.pdf (accessed September 6, 2006). Data from The Gallup Organization. Copyright © 1989–2003 by The Gallup Organization. Reproduced by permission of The Gallup Organization.

TABLE 2.5

Twenty questions designed to determine whether a person is a compulsive gambler

Gamblers Anonymous offers the following questions to anyone who may have a gambling problem. These questions are provided to help the individual decide if he or she is a compulsive gambler and wants to stop gambling.

1. Did you ever lose time from work or school due to gambling?
2. Has gambling ever made your home life unhappy?
3. Did gambling affect your reputation?
4. Have you ever felt remorse after gambling?
5. Did you ever gamble to get money with which to pay debts or otherwise solve financial difficulties?
6. Did gambling cause a decrease in your ambition or efficiency?
7. After losing did you feel you must return as soon as possible and win back your losses?
8. After a win did you have a strong urge to return and win more?
9. Did you often gamble until your last dollar was gone?
10. Did you ever borrow to finance your gambling?
11. Have you ever sold anything to finance gambling?
12. Were you reluctant to use "gambling money" for normal expenditures?
13. Did gambling make you careless of the welfare of yourself or your family?
14. Did you ever gamble longer than you had planned?
15. Have you ever gambled to escape worry or trouble?
16. Have you ever committed, or considered committing, an illegal act to finance gambling?
17. Did gambling cause you to have difficulty in sleeping?
18. Do arguments, disappointments or frustrations create within you an urge to gamble?
19. Did you ever have an urge to celebrate any good fortune by a few hours of gambling?
20. Have you ever considered self destruction or suicide as a result of your gambling?

Most compulsive gamblers will answer yes to at least seven of these questions.

SOURCE: "Twenty Questions," in *Gamblers Anonymous Combo Book*, Gamblers Anonymous International Service Office, 1999, http://www .gamblersanonymous.org/20questions.html (accessed September 12, 2006)

no harmful effects are called "nonproblem gamblers," or social, casual, or recreational gamblers. Those who gamble regularly and may be prone to a gambling problem are called "at-risk gamblers," while those who experience minor to moderate harm from their gambling behavior are called "problem gamblers." "Pathological gamblers" are severely harmed by their gambling activities.

Scientists use a screening process to determine which category fits a particular gambler. One of the most common is the South Oaks Gambling Screen (SOGS), a sixteen-item questionnaire developed in the 1980s by Dr. Henry Lesieur and Dr. Sheila Blume. A detailed description of the questionnaire and its development was first presented in "SOGS: A New Instrument for the Identification of Pathological Gamblers" (*American Journal of Psychiatry*, September 1987). The authors used information from 1,616 subjects to develop the SOGS screen, including patients with substance abuse and pathological gambling problems, members of Gamblers Anonymous, university students, and hospital employees. Because the questionnaires are filled out by potential problem gamblers themselves, scores depend entirely on the truthfulness of the people answering the questions.

Another means of defining "problem gamblers" was created by Gamblers Anonymous, the self-help organization, which prefers the term *compulsive gambling*. According to the group's Web site, compulsive gamblers exhibit certain characteristic behaviors (http://www.gamblersanonymous. org/qna.html):

- an "inability and unwillingness to accept reality"
- a belief that they have a "system" that will eventually pay off
- a lot of time spent daydreaming about what they will do when they finally make a big win
- feelings of emotional insecurity when they are not gambling
- immaturity and a desire to escape from responsibility
- wanting all the good things in life without expending much effort for them
- desire to be a "big shot" in the eyes of other people

Gamblers Anonymous has a list of twenty questions that gamblers can use to determine if they have a gambling problem. (See Table 2.5.) The organization indicates that compulsive gamblers are likely to answer yes to at least seven of the questions.

PATHOLOGICAL GAMBLERS. In general, pathological gambling is a disorder characterized by irrational thinking in which people continuously (or periodically) lose

22 Supply and Demand: Who Offers Gambling? Who Gambles?

Gambling

FIGURE 2.4

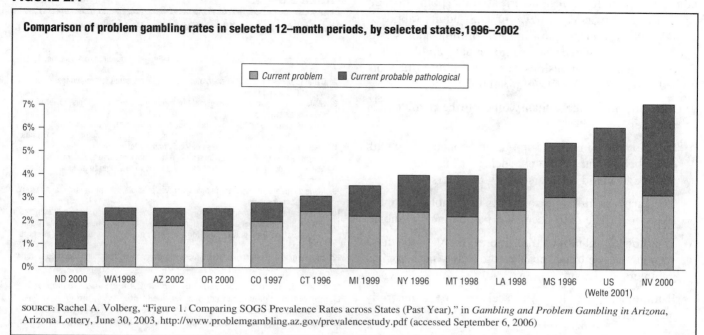

Comparison of problem gambling rates in selected 12–month periods, by selected states,1996–2002

□ *Current problem* ■ *Current probable pathological*

SOURCE: Rachel A. Volberg, "Figure 1. Comparing SOGS Prevalence Rates across States (Past Year)," in *Gambling and Problem Gambling in Arizona*, Arizona Lottery, June 30, 2003, http://www.problemgambling.az.gov/prevalencestudy.pdf (accessed September 6, 2006)

control over their gambling behavior. Pathological gamblers become preoccupied with gambling, constantly thinking about their next bet or how to raise more money with which they can gamble. This behavior continues even if the gambler suffers adverse consequences, such as financial difficulties or strained relationships with family and friends.

In 1975 the first nationwide study on gambling in the United States was conducted by researchers at the University of Michigan for the Commission on the Review of the National Policy Toward Gambling. Responses were obtained from 1,736 adults. As there was no scientific basis at the time for determining whether someone was a problem gambler, researchers used a questionnaire based on the twenty questions of Gamblers Anonymous. Results indicated that about 0.8% of Americans were "probable compulsive gamblers" and slightly more than 2.3% were "potential compulsive gamblers." The percentages for Nevada residents were approximately three times higher than for the national sample. A later comparison of problem gambling rates in various states showed that Nevada continued to have the highest percentage of problem gamblers in 2000—about 6.4% of all gamblers—as well as the highest percentage of probable pathological gamblers—3.5%. (See Figure 2.4.)

The American Psychiatric Association officially recognized pathological gambling as a mental health disorder in 1980 and listed it in its publication *Diagnostic and Statistical Manual of Mental Disorders*. The latest edition of the manual, published in 2000, is known as DSM-IV-

TR. The SOGS questionnaire was designed to correlate with those criteria.

In 1996 the National Center for Responsible Gaming provided a grant to researchers at Harvard Medical School to perform another large-scale study of the prevalence of problem gambling. The results were published in *Estimating the Prevalence of Disordered Gambling in the U.S. and Canada: A Meta-Analysis* (1997). A meta-analysis is an analysis of previously collected data. After examining hundreds of scientific studies on gambling in the United States and Canada, the researchers developed a ranking system for problem gambling:

- Level 0—nongamblers

- Level 1—social gamblers with no gambling problems

- Level 2—problem gamblers

- Level 3—pathological gamblers

The researchers calculated the lifetime prevalence rate of Level 3, or pathological, gambling in the adult North American population to be 1.6%.

In 1999 *Pathological Gambling: A Critical Review* was published by National Academies Press. The book identified and analyzed all available scientific research studies dealing with pathological and problem gambling. The studies were reviewed by dozens of researchers on behalf of the National Research Council, an organization administered by the National Academy of Sciences, the National Academy of Engineering, and the Institute of Medicine. The researchers estimated that 1.5% of U.S.

Gambling

Supply and Demand: Who Offers Gambling? Who Gambles? **23**

adults are pathological gamblers at some point in their lives. In any given year, 0.9% of U.S. adults (approximately 1.8 million people) and 1.1 million adolescents aged twelve to eighteen are pathological gamblers. The following general conclusions were drawn (http://newton.nap.edu/books/0309065712/html/4.html):

- Men are more likely than women to be pathological gamblers.

- Pathological gambling often occurs concurrently with other behavioral problems, such as drug and alcohol abuse and mood and personality disorders.

- The earlier in life a person starts to gamble, the more likely he or she is to become a pathological gambler.

- Pathological gamblers are more likely than those without a gambling problem to have pathological gamblers as parents.

- Pathological gamblers who seek treatment generally get better.

However, the researchers were unable to determine from available studies whether any particular treatment technique was more effective than most others or even if some pathological gamblers are able to recover on their own. They were also unable to determine whether particular groups, such as the elderly and the poor, have disproportionately high rates of pathological gambling. The researchers concluded that further studies are needed to provide a detailed understanding of pathological gambling.

TREATMENT ORGANIZATIONS. A variety of treatment methods are available to problem gamblers through organizations and private counselors. Gamblers Anonymous, for example, is open to all people who want to stop gambling. At its meetings, which are held throughout the United States, gamblers remain anonymous by using only their first names. The group method offers compulsive gamblers moral support and an accepting environment where they can talk about their past experiences and the problems in their lives caused by gambling. Gambling is not treated as a vice but as a progressive illness.

Gamblers Anonymous regards compulsive gamblers as people with an illness who can recover by following the organization's twelve-step recovery program. (See Table 2.6.) These steps are similar to those employed by such support groups as Alcoholics Anonymous. Although the steps have a spiritual aspect, Gamblers Anonymous is not affiliated with any religious group or institution, and the organization is funded by donations. The premise of Gamblers Anonymous is that a recovering compulsive gambler cannot gamble at all without succumbing to the gambling compulsion, so it advocates a "cold turkey" approach to quitting—the gambler just stops gambling—rather than a gradual reduction in gambling activity.

TABLE 2.6

Gamblers Anonymous 12–step program of recovery

1. We admitted we were powerless over gambling—that our lives had become unmanageable.
2. Came to believe that a Power greater than ourselves could restore us to a normal way of thinking and living.
3. Made a decision to turn our will and our lives over to the care of this Power of our own understanding.
4. Made a searching and fearless moral and financial inventory of ourselves.
5. Admitted to ourselves and to another human being the exact nature of our wrongs.
6. Were entirely ready to have these defects of character removed.
7. Humbly asked God (of our understanding) to remove our shortcomings.
8. Made a list of all persons we had harmed and became willing to make amends to them all.
9. Made direct amends to such people wherever possible, except when to do so would injure them or others.
10. Continued to take personal inventory and when we were wrong, promptly admitted it.
11. Sought through prayer and meditation to improve our conscious contact with God as we understood Him, praying only for knowledge of His will for us and the power to carry that out.
12. Having made an effort to practice these principles in all our affairs, we tried to carry this message to other compulsive gamblers.

SOURCE: "The Recovery Program," in *Gamblers Anonymous Combo Book*, Gamblers Anonymous International Service Office, 1999, http://www.gamblersanonymous.org/recovery.html (accessed September 12, 2006)

The National Council on Problem Gambling is a nonprofit organization founded to increase public awareness about pathological gambling and to encourage development of educational, research, and treatment programs. It sponsors the *Journal of Gambling Studies,* an academic journal dedicated to scientific research. It has thirty-five state affiliate chapters and operates a confidential hotline (1-800-522-4700) for problem gamblers who need help.

The council also operates the National Certified Gambling Counselor program and offers a database of more than two hundred counselors throughout the United States who have completed its certification program (http://www.ncpgambling.org/resources/resources_counselor.asp). Other organizations that certify gambling counselors include the American Compulsive Gambling Certification Board and the American Academy of Health Care Providers in the Addictive Disorders.

TREATMENT METHODS. Many problem gamblers seek professional counseling. The most common treatment method, in both group and individual counseling sessions, is called *cognitive behavior therapy.* The cognitive portion of the therapy focuses attention on the person's thoughts, beliefs, and assumptions about gambling. The primary goal is recognizing and changing faulty thinking patterns, such as a belief that gambling could lead to great riches. Behavior therapy focuses on changing harmful behaviors. Most counselors favor complete abstinence from gambling during treatment. For those with mild to moderate gambling problems, treatment usually involves weekly meetings with a support group and/or individual counseling sessions. Those with severe gambling problems often must check into addiction treatment centers to curb their addiction. Such treatment centers isolate patients from the outside world so they can focus on overcoming their addiction. Some treatment centers even forbid patients from keeping cash on them or from using laptops, phones, or any device that could allow them to gamble.

More and more, mental health professionals and gambling treatment centers are using antidepressants along with cognitive therapy to treat compulsive gambling. Researchers have speculated that some compulsive gamblers experience highly elevated levels of euphoria-causing chemicals, such as dopamine, in the brain when they gamble. A number of antidepressant drugs have been proven to prevent such chemicals from interacting with the brain. For years, however, no one had conclusive evidence that antidepressants specifically reduced gambling urges. In 2006 scientists reported that the antidepressant nalmefene significantly lowered the need to gamble among people diagnosed with compulsive gambling (Jon E. Grant et al., "Multicenter Investigation of the Opiod Antagonist Nalmefene in the Treatment of Pathological Gambling," *American Journal of Psychiatry*, February 2006.) As of late 2006 a number of studies were underway to test the ability of other antidepressants, such as Zoloft, to suppress gambling urges.

CHAPTER 3
AN INTRODUCTION TO CASINOS

When most people think about gambling, they think about a casino. But what is a casino? According to *Merriam-Webster's Dictionary*, a casino is a "building or room used for social amusements; specifically, one used for gambling." This definition is much broader than what the average American would consider a casino to be. Most people would picture one of the megaresorts in Las Vegas—a massive hotel and entertainment complex, blazing with neon lights, games, and fun. While this description does fit some casinos, many others are small businesses defined more by the types of gambling they offer than by glitz and glamour.

The federal government classifies all businesses and industries operated within the United States with a six-digit code called the North American Industry Classification System code. The code for casinos, 713210, is defined as follows: "This industry comprises establishments primarily engaged in operating gambling facilities that offer table wagering games along with other gambling activities, such as slot machines and sports betting. These establishments often provide food and beverage services. Included in this industry are floating casinos (i.e., gambling cruises, riverboat casinos)." Casino hotels—that is, hotels with a casino on the premises—fall under code 721120. They typically offer a variety of amenities, including dining, entertainment, swimming pools, and conference and convention rooms.

For practical purposes, casino gambling encompasses games of chance and skill played at tables and machines. Therefore, casino games take place in massive resorts as well as in small card rooms. There are floating casinos operating on boats and barges on waterways across the country. Casino game machines have been introduced at racetracks to create *racinos*. In some states, casino-type game machines are also allowed in truck stops, bars, grocery stores, and other small businesses.

Successful casinos take in billions of dollars each year for the companies, corporations, investors, and Native American tribes that own and operate them. State and local governments also reap casino revenues in the form of taxes, fees, and other payments.

THE HISTORICAL AND CURRENT STATUS OF CASINOS

Gambling was illegal for most of the nation's history. This did not keep casino games from occurring, sometimes openly and with the complicity of local law enforcement, but it did keep them from developing into a legitimate industry. Even after casino gambling was legalized in Nevada in 1931, its growth outside that state was stifled for decades. It took forty-five years before a second state, New Jersey, decided to allow casino gambling within its borders.

As Atlantic City, New Jersey, opened casinos during the late 1970s, gambling change swept across the country, much of it generated by Native American tribes. A string of legal victories allowed the tribes to convert the small-time bingo halls they had been operating into full-scale casinos. Suddenly, other states wanted to get in on the action. Between 1989 and 1996, nine states authorized commercial casino gambling: Colorado, Illinois, Indiana, Iowa, Louisiana, Michigan, Mississippi, Missouri, and South Dakota.

Commercial and tribal casinos had revenues of about $53 billion in 2005. The American Gaming Association (AGA) estimated that commercial casinos had revenues of $30.3 billion, up from $28.9 billion in 2004 (see Figure 3.1), while the National Indian Gaming Commission (NIGC) estimated that tribal casino revenue totaled $23 billion in 2005. According to AGA, nine hundred commercial, racetrack, and tribal casinos operated nationwide in 2005. Slightly more than half (455) were commercial and racetrack operations. These statistics did not include card rooms, which numbered 545 in five states. (See Figure 3.2.)

FIGURE 3.1

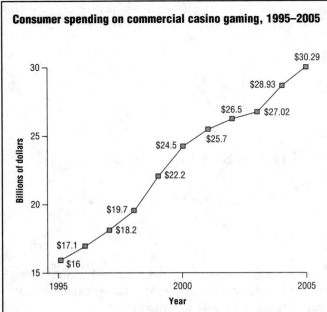

Consumer spending on commercial casino gaming, 1995–2005

SOURCE: "U.S. Consumer Spending on Commercial Casino Gaming, 1995–2005," in *2006 State of the States: The AGA Survey of Casino Entertainment*, American Gaming Association, 2006, http://www.americangaming.org/assets/files/2006_Survey_for_Web.pdf (accessed September 12, 2006). Data from Christiansen Capital Advisors, 1995–99, and State Gaming Regulatory Agencies, 2000–05. Reprinted with permission from the American Gaming Association. All rights reserved.

In August 2006 commercial casinos operated in Colorado, Illinois, Indiana, Iowa, Louisiana, Michigan, Mississippi, Missouri, Nevada, New Jersey, and South Dakota, while Native American casinos operated in twenty-eight states. Besides the full-scale casinos, there were racetrack casinos, in nine states—Delaware, Iowa, Louisiana, Maine, New Mexico, New York, Oklahoma, Rhode Island, and West Virginia. These facilities are racetracks that also offer slot machines. Both Florida and Pennsylvania were constructing facilities at racetracks that would house slot machines.

CASINO ACCEPTABILITY

Each year the AGA, the trade organization that represents the commercial casino industry, releases results of a survey on the attitudes of Americans towards casino gambling. To prepare *2006 State of the States: The AGA Survey of Casino Entertainment*, Peter D. Hart Research Associates and Luntz, Maslansky Strategic Research interviewed 1,250 adults across the United States. A vast majority of those surveyed considered casino gambling acceptable: 50% of respondents found casino gambling to be acceptable for anyone, and 29% considered it acceptable for others, but not for themselves. Only 18% of respondents thought casino gambling was not acceptable for anyone. These percentages had changed very little since 2001. (See Figure 3.3.)

According to the survey, more men than women believe that casino gambling is acceptable for anyone. However, women interviewed were more likely to see casino gambling as acceptable for others, if not themselves. Acceptability was highest among those living in the Northeast and Pacific states (87%) and lowest among those living in southern states (76%). It was highest among those in upper income brackets, as well as those who attend church rarely or not at all. Weekly churchgoers were far less accepting of casino gambling, with 27% saying it was unacceptable for anyone.

CASINO GAMES

Casinos offer a variety of games, including card games, dice games, domino games, slot machines, and gambling devices (such as the roulette wheel). Some games are banked games, meaning that the house has a stake in the outcome of the game and bets against the players. Banked games include blackjack, craps, keno, roulette, and traditional slot machines. A nonbanked game is one in which the payout and the house's cut depend on the number of players or the amount that is bet, not the outcome of the game. In percentage games, the house collects a share of the amount wagered.

For example, in traditional poker, players bank their own games. Each player puts money into the "pot" and competes against the other players to win the pot. A portion of the pot is taken by the house. In house-banked games, the players compete against the house rather than each other. Another type of house-banked game is one in which there is a posted payout schedule for winning hands rather than a pot.

Gaming machines are by far the most popular type of casino activity. They are simple to operate and can offer large payouts for small wagers. The first commercial gambling machines, introduced in 1896, were called *slot machines* because the gambler inserted a coin into a slot to begin play. Each slot machine consisted of a metal box housing three reels, each of which was decorated all around with symbols (usually types of fruit or spades, hearts, diamonds, and clubs). When the player moved the handle on the machine, the reels spun randomly until they were slowed by stoppers within the machine. If a matching sequence of symbols appeared when the reels stopped, the player won. Each reel had many symbols, so literally thousands of outcomes were possible. Because of they were easy to play, the odds of winning were low, and only a single handle was used to activate them, slot machines came to be known as "one-armed bandits."

Some casinos still offer old-fashioned slot machines, but most gaming machines today are electronic and computer controlled. They are manufactured to strict technical specifications and use a computer programming technique called *random number generation*. A computer chip in each machine determines the percentage of

FIGURE 3.2

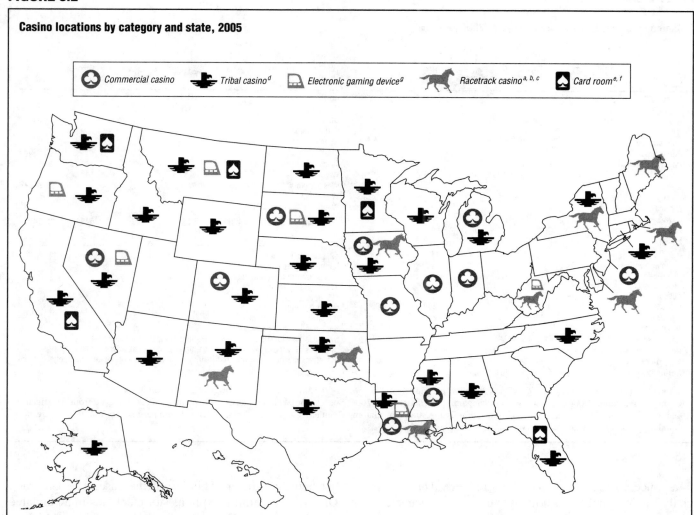

Casino locations by category and state, 2005

[Legend:] Commercial casino — Tribal casino[d] — Electronic gaming device[g] — Racetrack casino[a, b, c] — Card room[e, f]

[a]In Rhode Island, there are video lottery terminals operating at a closed jai alai fronton, not considered a racetrack casino, but a pari-mutuel facility.
[b]Racetrack casinos in Florida and Pennsylvania are legal but not yet operational. Pennsylvania also has legalized stand-alone slot facilities, but there are none operating.
[c]The states with racetrack casinos operate class III gaming machines. There are two racinos in Alabama—not indicated on this map—that have class II machines only, which are legal only in the counties where they operate.
[d]Native American casinos noted here include both class II and class III facilities. States with class II gaming only are Alabama, Alaska, Florida, Nebraska, Texas and Wyoming.
[e]The states with card rooms indicated here do not include states that have commercial casinos with poker facilities.
[f]The card rooms in Washington operate blackjack and other house- or player-banked card games in addition to poker.
[g]The electronic gaming devices operating in the states indicated on this map are recognized as legal operations. There are some states with similar facilities, but the machines may not be authorized.

payout. The machines are similar to high-tech video games, offering sophisticated graphics and sound. Some are even designed to mimic the look and feel of reel-type machines. Patrons may have a choice of a modern push button or an old-fashioned handle to activate play.

Electronic slot machines offer many different games (poker is one of the most popular) and are called by a variety of names: electronic gaming devices, video gaming terminals, video gaming devices, video poker machines, or just slots. Slot machines can be played for a variety of denominations—from a penny up to hundreds of dollars. The quarter machine is the most popular.

Some casinos have slot machines with progressive jackpots—in other words, the jackpot grows with continued play. Most progressive jackpot machines are connected to others in a computerized network. Play on any one machine within the group causes the jackpot to increase. On March 21, 2003, a man playing a progressive slot machine at the Excalibur Hotel–Casino in Las Vegas won $38.7 million, the largest slot machine payout in U.S. history (as of July 2006).

Odds against Gamblers

Because casinos are businesses and must make money to survive, the mathematical odds are always against players in casino games. For example, according to *Frontline* (PBS, http://www.pbs.org/wgbh/pages/front line/shows/gamble/), a person betting $100 an hour on roulette will lose an average of $5.26 per hour in the long run. The "long run"

FIGURE 3.2

Casino locations by category and state, 2005 [CONTINUED]

State	♣	🐎	🦅	♠	🚆	State	♣	🐎	🦅	♠	🚆
Alabama			3*			North Dakota			17		
Alaska			3*			Oklahoma		3	83		
Arizona			24			Oregon			9		2,044■
California			57	94		Pennsylvania		+			
Colorado	46°		2			Rhode Island		2■			
Connecticut			2			South Dakota	36°		11		1,460
Delaware		3■				Texas			2*		
Florida		+	7*	15ᵇ		Washington			32	146	
Idaho			6			West Virginia		4■			1,742■
Illinois	9					Wisconsin			27		
Indiana	10					Wyoming			1*		
Iowa	13ᶜ	3	4			**Total**	**455**	**29**	**406**	**545**	**10,247**
Kansas			5			Number of states	11	11ᶠ	28	5	6
Louisiana	18ᶜ	3■	3		2,411■						
Maine		1									
Michigan	3		17								
Minnesota			32	1							
Mississippi	29		2								
Missouri	11										
Montana			22	289	390ᵈ						
Nebraska			1*								
Nevada	268ᵉ		4		2,200‡						
New Jersey	12										
New Mexico		5	21								
New York		5■	7								
North Carolina			2								

*Class II games only
°Limited-stakes gaming
+Legalized but not operational
■Video lottery terminals
‡15 slots or fewer
ᵃAs of December 2005
ᵇLocated at the racetracks
ᶜIncludes racetrack casinos
ᵈIncludes only locations with the maximum number of devices (20)
ᵉIncludes only locations with gross gaming revenue of at least $1 million
ᶠRacetrack casinos in Florida and Pennsylvania are legal but not yet operational.

SOURCE: "Casino Locations by Category" and "Casinos per State," in *2006 State of the States: The AGA Survey of Casino Entertainment*, American Gaming Association, 2006, http://www.americangaming.org/assets/files/2006_Survey_for_Web.pdf (accessed September 12, 2006). Data from American Gaming Association, National Indian Gaming Commission, and State Gaming Regulatory Agencies, 2005. Reprinted with permission from the American Gaming Association. All rights reserved.

is a concept often overlooked by gamblers. This is especially true of gamblers who play games of chance such as roulette.

Most roulette wheels have two colors—red and black. On each spin of the wheel, the odds of red or black coming up are equal: fifty-fifty. Many people believe that this means the number of black results will equal the number of red results over the course of time they are playing the game. Thus, when several consecutive spins have come up red, they feel that black is overdue, and bet on that color.

This belief is false, and is known as the Gambler's Fallacy. Each spin of the roulette wheel is independent of the spins that came before, and has the same fifty-fifty chance of being red or black. The fact that four or five results in a row have been red does not change the odds for the next spin. Therefore, while it is true that over the long run the number of red and black results will be roughly equal, during that long run there may be many periods in which large numbers of spins come up red or black.

The same holds true for slot machines. Many gamblers believe that if they have bet on a slot machine many times in a row and lost, this increases the odds of the next bet being a winner. This is not the case. The Colorado Division of Gaming explains slot machines in an undated brochure titled *Understanding How a Slot Machine Works*. The brochure notes that a slot machine with a 97% payout would *theoretically* be expected to pay back 97% of all money taken in over the lifetime of the machine, typically seven years. Therefore, a gambler who gambled on that machine continuously for seven years could expect to attain a 97% payout. But during those seven years there will likely be periods in which he wins frequently, and periods in which he loses frequently, with no way to predict when they will occur.

THE CASINO GAMBLER

In May 2006 the Pew Research Center released *Gambling: As the Take Rises, So Does the Public Concern* by Paul Taylor, Cary Funk, and Peyton Craighill. The report indicated that 29% of poll participants had visited a casino within the previous twelve months. This rate was up substantially from 20% in 1989. (See Figure 2.2 and Figure 2.3 in Chapter 2.)

Demographics

Harrah's Entertainment is one of the major corporations operating commercial casinos in the United States.

FIGURE 3.3

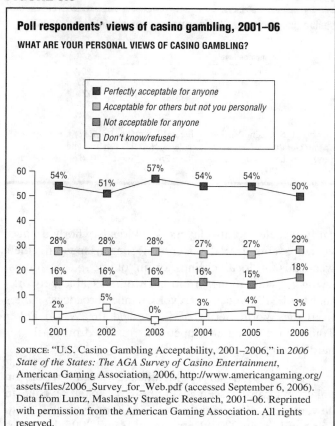

Poll respondents' views of casino gambling, 2001–06

WHAT ARE YOUR PERSONAL VIEWS OF CASINO GAMBLING?

- ■ Perfectly acceptable for anyone
- ■ Acceptable for others but not you personally
- ■ Not acceptable for anyone
- □ Don't know/refused

FIGURE 3.4

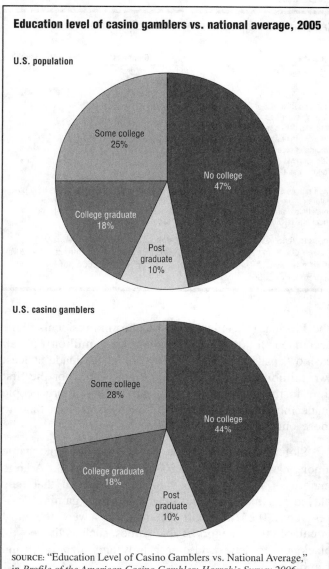

Education level of casino gamblers vs. national average, 2005

SOURCE: "Education Level of Casino Gamblers vs. National Average," in *Profile of the American Casino Gambler: Harrah's Survey 2006*, Harrah's Entertainment, Inc., June 2006, http://www.harrahs.com/images/PDFs/Profile_Survey_2006.pdf (accessed September 12, 2006)

In June 2006 the company presented results of a survey conducted by market researchers Roper ASW and GfK NOP in *Profile of the American Casino Gambler: Harrah's Survey 2006*. The survey included face-to-face interviews with 2,000 American adults and a questionnaire that was mailed to 100,000 adults (57,203 responded). The polling took place between February and December 2005.

The results indicated that 52.8 million people gambled at a casino sometime in the twelve months prior to the survey—about 25% of the American adult population age twenty-one and older. The typical casino gambler is a forty-six-year-old female from a household with an above-average income. About 18% of casino gamblers had college degrees and 10% had education beyond a four-year degree. About 28% had some college credits, and 44% had not attended college. This compares roughly with education levels on a national basis. (See Figure 3.4.)

According to Harrah's survey, Americans made 322 million casino visits in 2005, with the average gambler visiting a casino 6.1 times during the year. Older parents over the age of forty-five, who often have more vacation time and available spending money than younger adults, made up the largest group—23%—of casino gamblers in

2005. (See Table 3.1, which compares the percentages of those who visited a casino during the previous twelve months with those who did not by particular stages of life.)

The survey found that 31% of Americans with annual household incomes in excess of $95,000 were casino gamblers. Participation in casino gambling dropped with decreasing income, with only 20% of Americans with incomes of less than $35,000 per year participating. (See Table 3.2.) Casino gamblers were more likely to be residents of western states (33%) than of the north-central (27%), northeast (28%), or southern (18%) regions of the country. The states whose residents accounted for the largest shares of all casino trips in 2005 were California, New York, Illinois, Nevada,

TABLE 3.1

Gamblers and nongamblers by stage of life, 2005

Lifestage*	Gamblers	Non-gamblers
Young singles (21–35)	3%	2%
Middle singles (35–65)	6%	7%
Older singles (66+)	5%	6%
Young couples (21–44)	10%	8%
Working older couples (45+)	19%	14%
Retired older couples (45+)	9%	7%
Parents of young children (21–44)	12%	15%
Parents of older children (21–44)	11%	14%
Older parents (45+)	23%	26%
Roommates (21+)	2%	1%

*Age ranges are for the head of household. Singles, couples and roommates have no children living at home. Parents of young children have at least one child under 6 in the household. Parents of older children have at least one child in the household, but none under age 6. Older parents have children of any age in the household.

SOURCE: "U.S. Casino Visitation: Lifestage," in *Profile of the American Casino Gambler: Harrah's Survey 2006*, Harrah's Entertainment, June 2006, http://www.harrahs.com/images/PDFs/Profile_Survey_2006.pdf (accessed September 6, 2006)

TABLE 3.2

Casino gambling rates by income level of participants, 2005

Income level	
Under $35,000	20%
$35,001–$55,000	25%
$55,001–$75,000	27%
$75,001–$95,000	29%
Over $95,000	31%

SOURCE: "U.S. Casino Visitation: Income Level," in *Profile of the American Casino Gambler: Harrah's Survey 2006*, Harrah's Entertainment, June 2006, http://www.harrahs.com/images/PDFs/Profile_Survey_2006.pdf (accessed September 6, 2006)

and Florida. (See Figure 3.5.) California residents alone accounted for 16% (more than fifty million) of all casino trips. Residents of thirty-one states made at least two million casino visits. (See Figure 3.6.) For the first time in the survey's thirteen-year history, more people made more trips to their state-licensed casinos than to those out of state.

Slot machines were the most popular casino game among casino gamblers in 2005. (See Table 3.3.) A large majority, 71% of casino gamblers, indicated that they played slot machines and other electronic gaming devices. The $0.25 to $0.50 slot machines were the most popular in this category. Table games, such as live poker, blackjack, roulette, and craps, drew only 14% of casino gamblers.

Female casino gamblers showed a marked preference for electronic gaming, with 79% of those surveyed indicating that it was their favorite type of game, compared with 63% for men. About 41% of women preferred machines in the $0.25- to $0.50-per-play range. Men were more likely to participate in table games (21%) than were women (9%). Game preference also varied by age; more younger gamblers preferred table games than did older gamblers. (See Table 3.4.)

The Popularity of Poker

With the advent of computer-simulated card games and Internet card rooms, poker surged in popularity in the early 2000s. Gamblers were no longer required to play experienced poker players to gain experience themselves. By 2003 a particular type of poker known as Texas Hold 'Em emerged as the game of choice. In Texas Hold 'Em players attempt to make a winning hand from a combination of cards dealt to them face down and community

cards revealed to all players. Individuals who had never visited a commercial poker table began spending their weekends at local casinos or in online poker rooms, trying to wrest money from each other. Cable networks such as ESPN and the Travel Channel broadcast games from the World Series of Poker and the World Poker Tour—once obscure competitions reserved primarily for hard-core poker players.

AGA's 2006 survey included a special report on poker. As can be seen in Figure 3.7, poker revenue in Nevada decreased slightly from $65.6 million in 1995 to $57.5 million in 2003. Between 2003 and 2005, however, poker revenue nearly tripled, totaling $140.2 million. In New Jersey, revenue more than doubled over those three years. The survey revealed that young to middle-aged men visited poker rooms more than any other demographic group. Some 25% of males and 13% of females reported playing poker in 2005, which was up from 15% of males and 10% of females in 2003. Poker playing increased across all age groups. (See Figure 3.8.)

HOW DO CASINOS PERSUADE PEOPLE TO GAMBLE?

Casino gambling is different from other forms of gambling, such as lotteries and Internet gambling, because of its social aspect. Players are either directly interacting with others, as in craps or poker, or surrounded by other people as they play the slot machines. Players often shout out encouragement. Alcoholic drinks are easily accessible and delivered directly to gamblers by waiters circulating throughout the casino. Nonalcoholic drinks and snacks are sometimes provided free of charge. The casino atmosphere is designed around noise, light, and excitement.

According to the AGA's 2002 survey (conducted by Peter D. Hart Research Associates and the Luntz Research Companies), 92% of respondents went to casinos in the company of their spouses, families, and friends or as part of organized groups. Casino gambling was considered "a fun night out" by 82% of those asked.

FIGURE 3.5

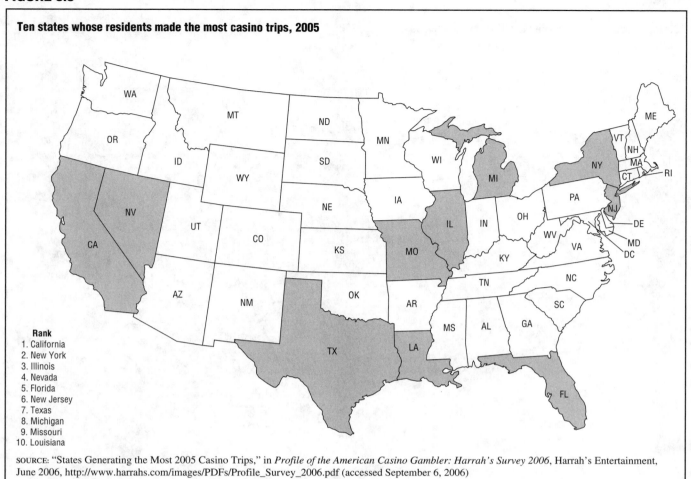

Ten states whose residents made the most casino trips, 2005

Rank
1. California
2. New York
3. Illinois
4. Nevada
5. Florida
6. New Jersey
7. Texas
8. Michigan
9. Missouri
10. Louisiana

SOURCE: "States Generating the Most 2005 Casino Trips," in *Profile of the American Casino Gambler: Harrah's Survey 2006*, Harrah's Entertainment, June 2006, http://www.harrahs.com/images/PDFs/Profile_Survey_2006.pdf (accessed September 6, 2006)

Casinos use sophisticated marketing and design to get gamblers into their facilities and keep them gambling as long and as happily as possible. Most of them invest millions of dollars to determine which colors, sounds, and scents are most appealing to patrons. The legend that oxygen is pumped into casinos to keep customers alert is untrue—it would be an extreme fire hazard. However, casinos do use bright and sometimes gaudy floor and wall coverings that have been shown to have a stimulating and cheering effect. Red is a popular decorating color because it is thought to make people lose track of time. There are no clocks on casino walls, either.

According to *The Tech Of: A Casino* (TechTV, June 2002), casinos use a variety of tricks to attract gamblers. Slot machines and gaming tables are arranged in a maze-like fashion so that wandering patrons are continuously enticed by more gambling options. Slot machines are designed by computers to be appealing to the senses of sight, touch, and sound—the noises of the machines are electronically tuned to the musical key of C to be pleasing to the ear. Bells, lights, whistles, and the clang of dropping coins are constant. Humans are attracted to bright lights, so more than 15,000 miles of neon tubing are used to light the casinos along the Las Vegas Strip.

Casinos also focus on customer service. For example, they provide perks designed to encourage gamblers to spend more and to reward those who do. Most casinos offer "comps," which is short for "complimentaries," or free items. During the 1970s, Las Vegas casinos were famous for their deeply discounted travel packages, cheap buffets, and free show tickets. The strategy at that time was to maximize the volume of people going to Las Vegas. Gambling revenue was driven by filling hotel rooms and the casino floor with as many people as possible.

Today, casinos are choosier. They concentrate their investments on gamblers who spend much more than average—the "high rollers" or "big spenders." Such people often gamble in special rooms, separate from the main casino floor, where the stakes (that is, the amount bet) can be in the thousands of dollars. Casinos make much of their profit from these high-stakes gamblers. Therefore, the high rollers receive comps worth a great deal of money, such as free luxury suites, as well as lavish personal attention.

FIGURE 3.6

States whose residents made more than two million casino trips, 2005

[Shaded in gray]

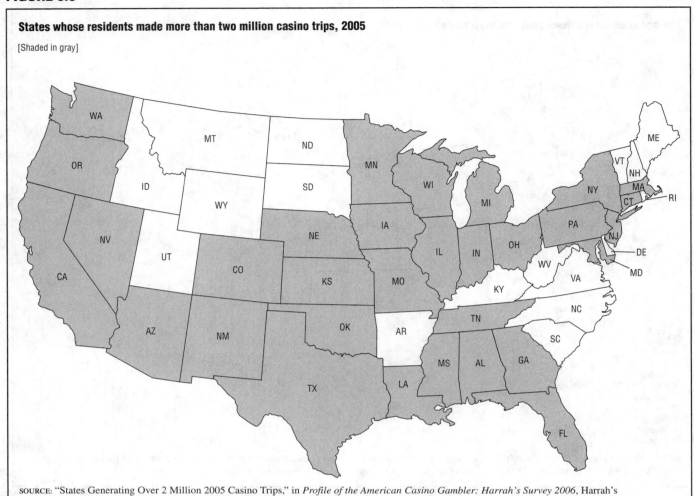

SOURCE: "States Generating Over 2 Million 2005 Casino Trips," in *Profile of the American Casino Gambler: Harrah's Survey 2006*, Harrah's Entertainment, June 2006, http://www.harrahs.com/images/PDFs/Profile_Survey_2006.pdf (accessed September 6, 2006)

TABLE 3.3

Gamblers' favorite games by type, 2005

Casino games played	
Slots/video poker (net)	71%
$.01–.02	7%
$.05–.10	19%
$.25–.50	38%
$1.00–4.00	7%
$5.00+	1%
Table games	14%
Blackjack/21	9%
Roulette	2%
Craps	2%
Live poker	2%
Other	5%
Don't know	9%

SOURCE: "America's Favorite Casino Games," in *Profile of the American Casino Gambler: Harrah's Survey 2006*, Harrah's Entertainment, June 2006, http://www.harrahs.com/images/PDFs/Profile_Survey_2006.pdf (accessed September 6, 2006)

TABLE 3.4

Gamblers' favorite games, by type of game and age of participant, 2005

Age range	21–35	36–50	51–65	66+
Slots/video poker (net)	65%	73%	75%	74%
$.01–.02	6%	6%	7%	7%
$.05–.10	20%	19%	17%	19%
$.25–.50	31%	39%	42%	40%
$1.00–4.00	7%	8%	8%	7%
$5.00+	1%	1%	1%	1%
Table games	21%	14%	10%	9%
Blackjack/21	14%	9%	6%	5%
Roulette	3%	2%	1%	1%
Craps	2%	2%	1%	1%
Live poker	2%	1%	1%	2%
Other	6%	5%	5%	5%
Don't know	8%	8%	9%	12%

SOURCE: "Favorite Games by Age," in *Profile of the American Casino Gambler: Harrah's Survey 2006*, Harrah's Entertainment, June 2006, http://www.harrahs.com/images/PDFs/Profile_Survey2006.pdf (accessed September 6, 2006)

FIGURE 3.7

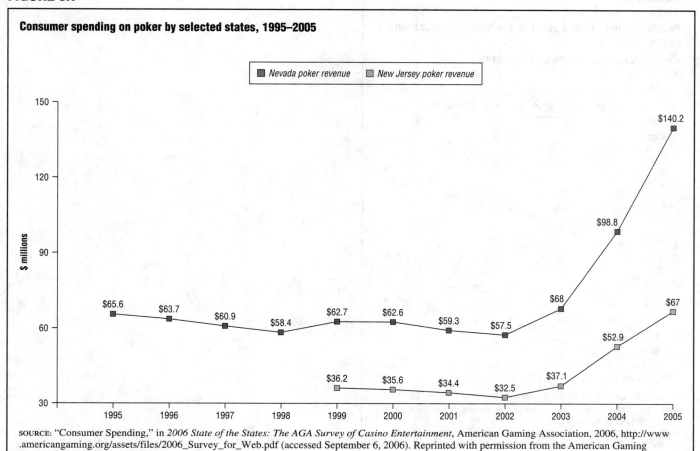

Consumer spending on poker by selected states, 1995–2005

■ Nevada poker revenue   ▦ New Jersey poker revenue

SOURCE: "Consumer Spending," in *2006 State of the States: The AGA Survey of Casino Entertainment*, American Gaming Association, 2006, http://www .americangaming.org/assets/files/2006_Survey_for_Web.pdf (accessed September 6, 2006). Reprinted with permission from the American Gaming Association. All rights reserved.

Less expensive comps are available to smaller spenders. Most casinos offer clubs that are similar to airline frequent-flyer programs. Gamblers who join receive a card that can be swiped electronically before they play a game. Casino computers track their usage and spending habits and tally up points that can be exchanged for coupons for free slot play or for free or discounted meals, drinks, or shows. The comp programs serve as a valuable marketing tool for the casinos, as well: they develop a patron database that can be used for advertising and to track trends in game preference and spending.

FIGURE 3.8

People who have played poker in a selected 12–month period, by age, 2003–05

HAVE YOU PLAYED POKER IN THE LAST 12 MONTHS?

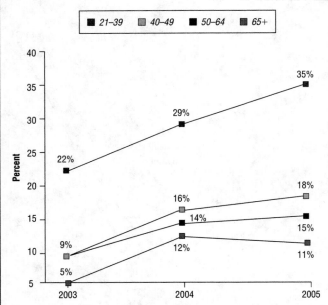

SOURCE: "Poker Players by Age," in *2006 State of the States: The AGA Survey of Casino Entertainment*, American Gaming Association, 2006, http://www.americangaming.org/assets/files/2006_Survey_for_Web.pdf (accessed September 6, 2006). Data from Luntz, Maslansky Strategic Research, 2003–05. Reprinted with permission from the American Gaming Association. All rights reserved.

CHAPTER 4
COMMERCIAL CASINOS

THE MARKET

Commercial casinos are profit-making businesses owned by individuals, private companies, or large public corporations. The term "commercial casino" is used in the United States to indicate a gaming facility that is not owned and operated on Native American lands by a tribal government. (See Chapter 5.) Casinos are closely regulated by state governments. Some states allow land-based casinos, while others restrict casino games to floating gambling halls on barges or riverboats. A handful of states allow casino games such as slot machines at other locations, including horse and dog racetracks or other commercial establishments. Some states allow only limited-stakes gambling, in which a limit is placed on the amount that can be wagered.

In 2005 the commercial casino industry included more than 500 land-based casinos operating in 11 states: Colorado, Illinois, Indiana, Iowa, Louisiana, Michigan, Mississippi, Missouri, Nevada, New Jersey, and South Dakota. In addition, eighty-three riverboat/dockside casinos operated during 2005 in Illinois (nine), Indiana (ten), Iowa (ten), Louisiana (fourteen), Mississippi (twenty-nine), and Missouri (eleven). Major markets for floating casinos included Chicago; Tunica, Mississippi; the Mississippi Gulf Coast; and Bossier City, Shreveport, and Lake Charles, Louisiana. Some of the largest gaming companies, including Harrah's Entertainment, MGM Mirage, and Penn National Gaming, operated floating casinos.

The casino industry measures its revenue by consumer spending, that is, the money gamblers "spend" while gambling. According to the American Gaming Association (*2006 State of the States: The AGA Survey of Casino Entertainment*, http://www.americangaming. org/assets/files/2006_Survey_for_Web.pdf), consumer spending on gambling in 2005 totaled $30.3 billion, which was far less than consumer spending on fast-food meals ($142.4 billion) but greater than spending on other leisure activities, such as amusement and theme parks ($11.2 billion) and

movies ($9 billion). In gambling terminology, the *handle* is the gross amount of money wagered by gamblers. The money that the gamblers win is called the *payout*, and the money that the casinos keep is called the gross gaming revenue, or the *casino win*.

NEVADA

Gambling has a long history in Nevada. It was common in the frontier towns of the Old West but was outlawed around the end of the nineteenth century, a time when conservative values predominated. However, illegal gambling was widely tolerated throughout the state. In 1931 gambling was legalized again in Nevada. The country was in a deep economic depression at the time, and gambling was seen as a source of needed revenue.

Casino development was slow at first. Many businesspeople were not convinced that the desert towns of Nevada could attract sufficient tourists to make the operations profitable. In 1941 El Rancho Vegas opened in Las Vegas. Five years later mobster Benjamin "Bugsy" Siegel opened the Flamingo Hotel, also in Las Vegas. (Siegel was eventually murdered by his business partners because of cost overruns.) Organized crime's relationship with Las Vegas continued for thirty years and tainted casino gambling in many people's minds.

Although the state of Nevada began collecting gaming taxes during the 1940s, regulation of the casinos was lax until the 1970s. Organized crime figures were pushed out of the casino business after Congress passed the Racketeer Influenced and Corrupt Organizations Act in 1970. Corporations moved in to take their place. In 1975 gaming revenues in the state reached $1 billion, according to the Las Vegas Convention and Visitors Authority (http://www.lvcva.com/press/statistics-facts/vegas-history.jsp). By 2005 the gambling industry was the largest employer in Nevada and accounted for more than a third of all taxes paid into the state's general fund.

Many different forms of legal gambling are available in Nevada, including live bingo, keno, and horse racing; card rooms; casino games; and off-track and phone betting on sports events and horse races. Establishments such as bars, restaurants, and stores are restricted to fewer than fifteen slot machines. Casinos are allowed to have more than fifteen machines; many have hundreds of slots.

During 2005 there were 351 nontribal, commercial casinos operating in Nevada—by far the most of any state. According to the state's Gaming Control Board (*Gaming Revenue Report Year Ended December 31, 2005*, 2006), Nevada's commercial casinos generated more than $11.6 billion in revenue from gambling operations during 2005, up from $10.6 billion in 2004, an increase of 10.3%. (See Table 4.1.) Casino revenues have been increasing steadily since 1994, although they leveled off for a brief period at the beginning of this decade after the terrorist attacks of September 11, 2001. (See Figure 4.1.)

Nevada casino revenue, or casino win, for calendar year 2005 is broken down by gambling category in Table 4.2. Slot machines accounted for $7.8 billion (67%) of the casinos' gaming revenue, up from $7.1 billion in 2004, a 9.4% increase. Revenue from games and tables rose by 11.2% from $3.4 billion in 2004 to $3.7 billion in 2005.

Patrons gambled nearly $133 billion playing Nevada's slot machines and nearly $28 billion at games and tables in 2005. Multidenomination slot machines were

TABLE 4.1

Consumer spending on casino gaming, by selected states, 2004 and 2005

State	2004	2005	Change
Colorado	$725.903 million	$755.500 million	+4.1%
Illinois	$1.718 billion	$1.799 billion	+4.7%
Indiana	$2.369 billion	$2.414 billion	+1.9%
Iowa	$1.064 billion	$1.106 billion	+3.9%
Louisiana	$2.163 billion	$2.232 billion	+3.2%
Michigan	$1.189 billion	$1.229 billion	+3.4%
Mississippi	$2.780 billion	$2.467 billion	−11.3%
Missouri	$1.473 billion	$1.532 billion	+4.0%
Nevada	$10.562 billion	$11.649 billion	+10.3%
New Jersey	$4.807 billion	$5.018 billion	+4.4%
South Dakota	$78.019 million	$83.558 million	+7.1%

SOURCE: "State-by-State Consumer Spending on Commercial Casino Gaming, 2004 vs. 2005," in *2006 State of the States: The AGA Survey of Casino Entertainment*, American Gaming Association, 2006, http://www.americangaming.org/assets/files/2006_Survey_for_Web.pdf (accessed September 6, 2006). Reprinted with permission from the American Gaming Association. All rights reserved.

the most popular, accounting for $55 billion, or 41%, of the total wagered at slot machines. Among tables and games, twenty-one had the highest amount wagered ($10.6 billion, or 38% of the total). However, baccarat had the greatest increase in play from the year before: the amount wagered rose from $4.1 billion in 2004 to $5.9 billion in 2005, a 44% increase.

Although casinos are located throughout the state, the major gambling markets in Nevada are in the southern

FIGURE 4.1

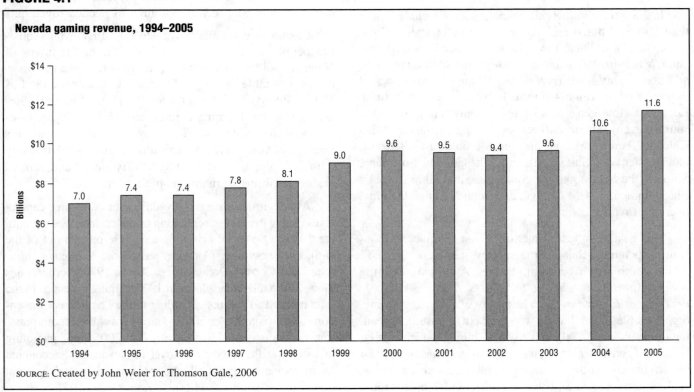

Nevada gaming revenue, 1994–2005

SOURCE: Created by John Weier for Thomson Gale, 2006

TABLE 4.2

Nevada gaming revenue, selected statistics, 2005

Twelve-month summary—01/01/05 to 12/31/05

			# of reporting locations—351		
Unit description	# of locations	# of units	Win amount*	Percent change	Win percent
Games and tables:					
Twenty-one	175	3,273	1,243,859	4.07	11.73
Craps	144	421	471,987	7.34	13.17
Roulette	141	450	322,866	12.36	21.47
3-card poker	123	232	175,938	13.53	25.94
Baccarat	25	118	665,548	33.86	11.24
Mini-baccarat	52	146	214,611	12.89	12.02
Keno	100	183	60,760	−9.69	27.09
Bingo	44	41	9,128	32.74	4.89
Caribbean stud	35	48	30,867	−18.98	28.14
Let it ride	88	135	64,430	−4.82	21.07
Pai gow	40	44	27,100	9.26	17.38
Pai gow poker	93	290	138,637	7.35	22.13
Race book[1]	145	86	99,329	9.14	17.45
Sports pool[2]	178	164	126,176	12.09	5.59
Other games		200	90,052	43.13	20.41
Total games	**186**	**5,831**	**$3,741,287**	**11.18**	**12.92**
Card games	96	701	140,224	42.00	
Slot machines:					
1 cent	246	19,861	950,973	93.36	9.31
5 cent	294	26,827	831,625	−32.04	8.39
25 cent	312	41,153	1,508,921	−15.44	6.25
1 dollar	272	20,259	1,102,475	−6.92	5.01
Megabucks	167	676	88,623	31.63	11.03
5 dollar	121	2,797	251,942	2.44	4.81
25 dollar	69	465	60,957	−6.36	3.86
100 dollar	43	289	50,852	2.41	4.38
Multi denomination	318	62,159	2,747,251	54.53	5.04
Other slot machines		3,399	173,910	−16.68	
Total slot machines	**348**	**177,886**	**$7,767,528**	**9.42**	**5.84**
Total gaming win			**$11,649,040**	**10.29**	
[1]Race pari-mutuel	78	78	94,963	8.88	17.66
[2]Sports pool detail					
Football	167	167	40,366	−13.65	3.84
Basketball	166	166	38,356	25.89	6.62
Baseball	11	11	26,127	187.62	5.63
Sports parlay cards	167	167	15,628	−21.65	24.86
Sports pari-mutuel			−1	0.00	−1.68
Other			5,700	−9.81	5.69

*Win amounts in thousand dollars.

SOURCE: Adapted from "Statewide, All Nonrestricted Locations, Twelve-Month Summary—01/01/05 to 12/31/05," in *State of Nevada Gaming Revenue Report: Year Ended December 31, 2005*, Nevada State Gaming Control Board, 2006, http://gaming.nv.gov/documents/pdf/1g_05dec.pdf (accessed September 6, 2006)

part of the state in Clark County (home of Las Vegas and Laughlin) and along the California border in Washoe County (home of Reno) and the Lake Tahoe resort area.

Las Vegas

Perhaps no other city is more associated with casinos than Las Vegas. According to the Las Vegas Convention and Visitors Authority (LVCVA), the city had 38.6 million visitors in 2005, and they generated $36.7 billion in business (http://www.lvcva.com/getfile/2005Top25Questions.pdf?file ID=106). The city's 133,186 hotel and motel rooms had an occupancy rate of 89.2%. By comparison, the national rate was 63.1%. The LVCVA reported that the average Las Vegas visitor was 47.7 years old and stayed 3.5 nights. During 2005 Las Vegas was the site of more than 22,154 conventions that attracted nearly 6.2 million people.

The casinos on the four-mile stretch of Las Vegas Boulevard known as "the Strip" made up the top commercial casino market in the country in 2005. (See Table 4.3.) More than forty hotel–casinos lined the Strip, a number of which were among the largest hotels in the country. These lavishly decorated mega resorts offer such amenities as spas, pools, top-quality restaurants, and top-notch entertainment. The companies operating these establishments generate a substantial amount of their revenue from nongambling sources, including lodging, dining, and entertainment.

TABLE 4.3

Top 20 casino markets, 2005

	Location	Revenue
1	Las Vegas Strip, NV	$6.031 billion
2	Atlantic City, NJ	$5.018 billion
3	Chicagoland, IN/IL	$2.441 billion
4	Detroit, MI	$1.229 billion
5	Tunica/Lula, MS	$1.187 billion
6	Connecticut	$982.65 million
7	St. Louis, MO/IL	$959.60 million
8	Reno/Sparks, NV	$920.22 million
9	Boulder Strip, NV	$885.99 million
10	Shreveport, LA	$814.23 million
11	Lawrenceburg/Rising Sun/Elizabeth/Vevay, IN	$754.24 million
12	Kansas City, MO (includes St. Joseph)	$718.56 million
13	Downtown Las Vegas, NV	$654.12 million
14	Laughlin, NV	$621.18 million
15	Biloxi, MS	$583.50 million[a]
16	New Orleans, LA	$534.14 million[b]
17	Black Hawk, CO	$531.88 million
18	Lake Charles, LA	$462.07 million[c]
19	Council Bluffs, IA	$433.97 million
20	Charles Town, WV	$414.12 million

[a]Based on 245 days of operation in 2005.
[b]Based on 330 days of operation in 2005, with the exception of Harrah's New Orleans, which did not reopen until 2006 due to damage from Hurricane Katrina.
[c]Based on 348 days of operation in 2005.

SOURCE: "Top 20 U.S. Casino Markets, 2005," in *2006 State of the States: The AGA Survey of Casino Entertainment*, American Gaming Association, 2006, http://www.americangaming.org/assets/files/2006_Survey_for_Web.pdf (accessed September 6,2006). Reprinted with permission from the American Gaming Association. All rights reserved.

In addition to those on the Strip, casinos are located throughout Las Vegas and in other parts of Clark County, including Mesquite, Primm, and Laughlin. In total, the 192 casinos in Clark County, both on the Strip and off, had gaming revenue of $9.7 billion during 2005, according to the Nevada Gaming Control Board. This amounted to 84% of the state's total casino gambling revenues for that year.

Because of the growth of casinos and gambling, Clark County's population increased from 48,289 in 1950 to nearly 1.8 million in 2005. During the 1990s alone the county's population increased by 81%. Traffic congestion had become such a problem on the Strip that the monorail that makes stops at several resorts and the city's convention center was extended in 2004. It carried ten million passengers in 2005.

NEW JERSEY

In June 1976 New Jersey voters legalized casino gambling in Atlantic City, making it the second state to do so. Since then it has become the second-largest gambling market in the country, according to the AGA.

Atlantic City

Atlantic City was an immensely popular resort destination throughout the late 1800s and early 1900s. It was easily accessible by rail, and people visited the beautiful beaches and elegant hotels along the boardwalk, which stretches nearly five miles. During the 1960s the city lost most of its tourist trade to beaches farther south, mainly in Florida and the Caribbean, and the city fell into an economic slump. Casinos were seen as a way to revitalize the city and attract tourists again. The first casino, Resorts International, opened in 1978, followed by Caesars Atlantic and Bally's Park Place in 1979. By 1991 casino gambling was permitted twenty-four hours per day.

The city's twelve casinos had gross revenue of $5 billion in 2005, up from $4.8 billion in 2004, a 4% increase. (See Table 4.4.) All Atlantic City casinos are land-based. According to the *New Jersey Casino Control Commission 2005 Annual Report* (2006), as of December 31, 2005, they offered 1,590 table games, 16 keno windows, and 44,754 slot machines. Atlantic City casinos employed 44,542 people in 2005 and paid wages of $1.1 billion. They paid taxes of $401 million.

Atlantic City differs from Las Vegas in many ways. There are far fewer hotel rooms (only about 15,000) with fewer amenities. Atlantic City is considered a "day-tripper market," attracting people within driving or train distance who visit for the day (many of them from New York City and Philadelphia). Casino development has been sluggish in Atlantic City. No new casinos were built during the 1990s. The Boyd Gaming Corp. and MGM Mirage collaborated to open Borgata, the city's newest casino–hotel, in July 2003.

In Atlantic City each casino is assessed an 8% tax on its gross revenue (that is, casino revenue after all winners are paid but before taxes and other expenses are paid). The tax payments go into a fund that is distributed among various state programs. According to the New Jersey Casino Control Commission, in fiscal year 2005 fund expenditures totaled $499 million. About 70% went to the Department of Health and Senior Services; 24% to the Department of Human Services; 24% to the Department of Transportation; 1% to the Department of Labor and Workforce Development; and 1% to the Department of Law and Public Safety.

The casinos of Atlantic City have not changed the town into a trendy tourist destination as was originally hoped. In fact, Atlantic City has the reputation of being a slum with casinos. Industry experts point to two primary factors for this perception: 1) the town relies on day-trippers rather than long-term vacationers; and 2) casino tax revenues have largely funded physical and mental health programs throughout the state rather than being invested in local infrastructure and economic development.

MISSISSIPPI

In 1989 Mississippi became the first state to permit gambling on cruise ships that were in state waters on their

TABLE 4.4

New Jersey casino revenue, selected statistics, 2004 and 2005

[Dollars in thousands]

Casino hotel	Casino win	Daily average casino win	Recovery of uncollectibles	Gross revenue	Tax	Market share of casino win
AC Hilton						
2005	$289,415	$793	$ —	$289,415	$23,153	5.8%
2004	$295,433	$807	$ —	$295,433	$23,635	6.1%
Bally's Atlantic City						
2005	645,634	1,769	—	645,634	51,651	12.9%
2004	644,728	1,762	—	644,728	51,578	13.4%
Borgata						
2005	704,358	1,930	—	704,358	56,349	14.0%
2004	636,541	1,739	—	636,541	50,923	13.2%
Caesars						
2005	523,544	1,434	—	523,544	41,883	10.4%
2004	495,966	1,355	—	495,966	39,677	10.3%
Harrah's Marina						
2005	476,254	1,305	—	476,254	38,100	9.5%
2004	449,862	1,229	—	449,862	35,989	9.3%
Resorts						
2005	271,984	745	—	271,984	21,759	5.4%
2004	252,785	691	—	252,785	20,223	5.3%
Sands						
2005	176,647	484	—	176,647	14,132	3.5%
2004	190,209	520	—	190,209	15,217	4.0%
Showboat						
2005	414,380	1,135	—	414,380	33,150	8.3%
2004	392,581	1,073	—	392,580	31,406	8.2%
Tropicana						
2005	441,915	1,211	—	441,915	35,353	8.8%
2004*	363,949	994	(116)	364,065	29,125	7.6%
Trump Marina						
2005	250,661	687	—	250,661	20,053	5.0%
2004*	263,030	719	(55)	263,086	21,047	5.5%
Trump Plaza						
2005	303,548	832	—	303,548	24,284	6.0%
2004*	318,435	870	(83)	318,518	25,482	6.6%
Trump Taj Mahal						
2005	519,932	1,424	—	519,932	41,595	10.4%
2004*	503,282	1,375	(287)	503,569	40,285	10.5%
Totals						
2005	$5,018,272	$13,749	$ —	$5,018,272	$401,462	100.0%
2004	$4,806,801	$13,133	$(541)	$4,807,342	$384,587	100.0%

*2004 amount reflects recovery of counter checks previously written off.

SOURCE: "New Jersey Casino Industry Gross Revenue Statistics for the Years Ended December 31, 2005 and 2004 ($ in Thousands)," in *State of New Jersey Casino Control Commission: 2005 Annual Report*, 2006, http://www.state.nj.us/casinos/home/news/pdf/2005_annual_report.pdf (accessed September 6, 2006)

way to or from international waters, but gambling in Mississippi had a long history. Gambling along the Mississippi River and its connecting waterways was widespread during the early 1800s. The rivers were the equivalent of the modern-day interstate highway system, carrying cash-laden farmers, merchants, and tourists to bustling towns along the riverbank. Gambling halls became notorious establishments that attracted professional gamblers, especially cardsharps, who employed various methods of cheating in order to earn a living at cards.

By the 1830s the cardsharps had worn out their welcome. According to Richard Dunstan in *Gambling in California* (California Research Bureau, 1997), five cardsharps were lynched in Mississippi in 1835, and the professional gamblers moved to the riverboats cruising up and down the rivers. Gambling was a popular pastime for riverboat passengers during the 1840s and 1850s. The onset of the Civil War (1861–65) and then the antigambling movement around the turn of the twentieth century dampened, but did not destroy, open gambling in the state.

During and after World War II (1939–45), the Mississippi coast experienced a resurgence in illegal casino gambling, particularly in Harrison County, home of the city of Biloxi and Keesler Air Force Base. The officers' club at the base reportedly operated slot machines. During the 1960s the Alcohol Beverage Control Board began refusing licenses to public facilities that allowed gambling. A few private clubs and lodges continued to offer card games and slot machines, but they were shut down by the mid 1980s.

In 1987 the ship *Europa Star* and several other ships from Biloxi ports began taking gamblers on "cruises to nowhere"—cruises to international waters in the Gulf of Mexico where passengers could gamble legally. Although the cruises were supported by the city of Biloxi, the state initially opposed them until it became apparent that they were reviving tourism in port towns. The state was in desperate economic times—it was proclaimed the poorest state in the country in the 1980 census.

The Mississippi legislature legalized casino gambling in 1990, although each county was allowed to decide whether it would permit gambling within its borders. Fourteen counties along the Gulf Coast and Mississippi River held referenda to allow dockside casinos, and all voted them down. The next year a city-by-city vote was held, and voters in Biloxi, which was nearly bankrupt at the time, approved the referendum. In 1992 nine dockside casinos opened in Biloxi.

Casinos are grouped in three parts of the state: the northern region centered in Tunica; the central region based in Vicksburg and Natchez; and the coastal region centered in Biloxi, Gulfport, and Bay St. Louis. According to the AGA, Tunica was the fifth-largest casino market in 2005; Biloxi ranked fifteenth even though it operated only 245 days that year before Hurricane Katrina devastated the area on August 29, 2005. (See Table 4.3.)

Mississippi has set no limit on the number of casinos that can be built in the state. Instead, it allows competition to determine the market size. Before Katrina, casinos were required to be permanently docked in the water along the Mississippi River and the Mississippi Gulf Coast. The gambling halls of the casinos actually sat on the water, while their associated lodging, dining, and entertainment facilities were on land. After the hurricane partially or completely destroyed all twelve casinos along the Gulf Coast, the legislature passed a law allowing casino operators who had establishments on the coast in Biloxi, Gulfport, and Bay St. Louis to relocate their casinos 800 feet inland so they would be safe from any future storm surges. Along the Mississippi River, the gambling halls sit in slips cut into the riverbank. The Mississippi Band of Choctaw Indians operates the only land-based casinos, which are located mid-state in Neshoba County.

As of June 2006 there were twenty-eight commercial casinos licensed to operate in Mississippi. (See Table 4.5.) Only twenty-two were actually operating (six were closed because of hurricane damage—one of them permanently). In total, they employed 22,289 people and offered nearly one million square feet of gaming space, 25,785 slot machines, 642 table games, and 108 poker games. Games offered include blackjack, craps, roulette, baccarat, keno, poker, and other card games. The state allows round-the-clock gambling with no bet limits. Gross casino revenue for the state was $2.5 billion in calendar year 2005, down from $2.8 billion in 2004. (See Figure 4.2.) Prior to the hurricane, commercial casino revenue had leveled off during the early part of this decade after growing steadily through the 1990s. The casinos received more than 54 million visitors during 2005 and had more than 14,000 hotel rooms before the hurricane hit; the storm cut the number of hotel rooms in half. By the end of 2006, ten casinos had reopened on the Gulf Coast, including the largest, Beau Rivage, which opened on the anniversary of Hurricane Katrina. Several additional properties were under construction in the area, notably the Hard Rock Casino and Hotel, which was scheduled to open in the summer of 2007.

According to statistics released by the Mississippi Gaming Commission, the casino industry produces a substantial percentage of the state's annual budget, generating between $200 million and $300 million in wagering, sales, and income taxes. For fiscal year 2006 (July 2005–June 2006), casinos paid $273 million in taxes. Half went to the state's general fund, a third went to local governments, and the remainder went to retire debt. In total, $3.6 billion was collected in casino taxes in Mississippi between July 1992 and June 2006.

LOUISIANA

Like Mississippi, Louisiana has a long gambling history. In 1823, eleven years after Louisiana became a state, its legislature legalized several forms of gambling and licensed six "temples of chance" in the city of New Orleans. Each was to pay $5,000 per year to fund the Charity Hospital and the College of Orleans. The casinos attracted many patrons, including professional gamblers, swindlers, and thieves. In 1835 the legislature repealed the licensing act and passed laws making gambling hall owners subject to prison terms or large fines.

However, casino-type gambling continued and even prospered throughout the southern part of the state. By 1840 New Orleans had an estimated 500 gambling halls that employed more than 4,000 people but paid no revenue to the city. Riverboat casinos frequented by hundreds of professional gamblers plied the Mississippi River between New Orleans and St. Louis. When the Civil War broke out, the riverboats were pressed into

TABLE 4.5

Mississippi casino statistics, April–June 2006

	Number of employees	Work permitted	Gaming sq. footage	Other sq. footage	Total sq. footage	# slot games	# table games	# poker games	Activities in addition to gaming
Coastal region									
Beau Rivage—Biloxi	725	488	—	2,150,000	2,150,000	—	—	—	12 restaurants, retail promenade, marina, convention center, showroom, marina, spa, and hotel
Boomtown—Biloxi	719	438	33,632	99,368	133,000	1,111	22	—	Motion theater, buffet, restaurant, cabaret, fun center
Hollywood—Bay St. Louis	85	71	—	146,000	146,000	—	—	—	Golf course, hotel, RV park, restaurants, sporting events, Camp Magic, charter boats
Island View Casino—Gulfport	—	—	—	78,452	78,452	—	—	—	Gift shop & restaurants
Grand Casino—Biloxi	735	—	—	218,600	218,600	—	—	—	Restaurants, theatre, hotels, arcade, and Kid's Quest
Grand Casino—Gulfport	4	—	—	—	—	—	—	—	Restaurants, entertainment barge, hotels, Lazy River, arcade, and Kid's Quest
Imperial Palace	2,844	1,053	66,768	127,376	194,144	1,956	54	16	Spa, pool, movie theaters, restaurants, shops, and showroom
Isle of Capri—Biloxi	1,143	674	57,252	618,700	675,952	1,313	29	9	Restaurants & live entertainment
Silver Slipper—Lakeshore	18	16	—	—	—	—	—	—	Live entertainment, restaurants, arcade, and fishing
The New Palace—Biloxi	575	400	22,646	9,500	32,146	841	14	—	Theater, hotel, gift shop, spa, salon, pool, & restaurants
Treasure Bay—Biloxi	219	138	2,165	715	2,880	81	—	—	Arcades, gift shop, restaraunts, tanning bed, and travel agency
Region totals	**7,067**	**3,278**	**182,463**	**3,448,711**	**3,631,174**	**5,302**	**119**	**25**	
North River region									
Bally's—Robinsonville	686	453	46,535	153,543	200,078	1,259	22	—	Restaurants, entertainment
Fitzgerald's—Robinsonville	1,009	656	38,000	525,912	563,912	1,298	34	—	Hotel, restaurant, slot and table game tournaments
Gold Strike—Robinsonville	1,635	908	50,486	1,347,597	1,398,083	1,370	52	16	Restaurants, Millennium Theater, arcade, and hotel
Grand Casino—Tunica	2,337	1,400	136,000	204,000	340,000	2,186	80	14	Restaurants, RV park, arcade, golf course, Kid's Quest, and clay shooting
Resorts—Tunica	641	342	35,000	151,924	186,924	1,162	17	—	Live entertainment, restaurants, and golf
Hollywood—Robinsonville	817	604	54,000	337,613	391,613	1,331	31	6	Restaurants, RV park, arcade, hotel, and pool
Horseshoe—Robinsonville	2,498	1,146	63,000	222,500	285,500	1,806	76	11	Live entertainment, restaurants, health club, and Blues Museum
Isle of Capri—Lula	656	509	63,500	65,000	128,500	1,467	22	5	Movies, concerts, and dining
Sam's Town—Tunica	1,190	746	74,210	21,790	96,000	1,394	39	15	Ent. Center, restaurants & Western Emporium
Sheraton—Robinsonville	744	614	32,800	121,000	153,800	1,121	36	—	Restaurants, ballroom, & spa
Region totals	**12,213**	**7,378**	**593,531**	**3,150,879**	**3,744,410**	**14,394**	**409**	**67**	
South River region									
Ameristar—Vicksburg	939	565	44,503	211,151	255,654	1,481	36	—	Showroom & restaurants
Horizon Casino—Vicksburg	273	285	20,909	4,200	25,109	692	13	8	Restaurants, retail and lodging
Isle of Capri—Vicksburg	549	347	32,000	30,900	62,900	811	20	—	Live entertainment, restaurants, and hotel
Jubilee—Greenville	270	208	28,500	36,937	65,437	822	13	—	Live entertainment & restaurants
Isle of Capri—Natchez	354	254	20,647	3,400	24,047	644	11	8	Live entertainment & restaurants
Lighthouse—Greenville	268	57	22,000	—	22,000	753	9	—	Restaurants & live entertainment
Rainbow—Vicksburg	356	246	25,000	5,000	30,000	886	12	—	Restaurants, gift shop, and hotel
Region totals	**3,009**	**1,962**	**193,559**	**291,588**	**485,147**	**6,089**	**114**	**16**	
State totals	**22,289**	**12,618**	**969,553**	**6,891,178**	**7,860,731**	**25,785**	**642**	**108**	

SOURCE: "Quarterly Survey Information: April 1, 2006–June 31, 2006," in *Mississippi Gaming Commission—Public Information*, Mississippi Gaming Commission, August 2006, http://www.mgc.state.ms.us/ (accessed September 6, 2006)

FIGURE 4.2

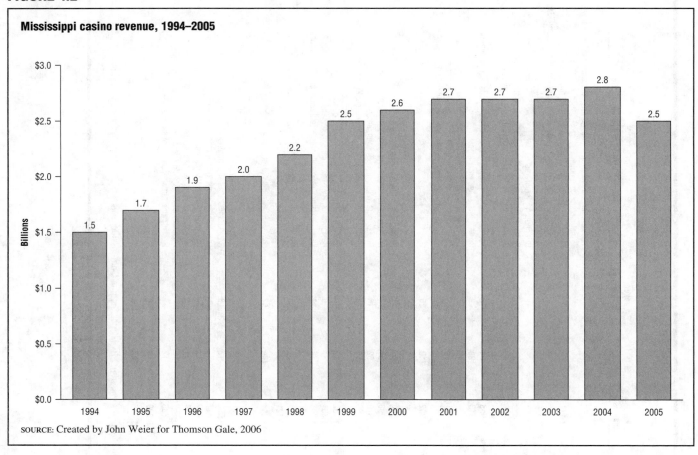

Mississippi casino revenue, 1994–2005

SOURCE: Created by John Weier for Thomson Gale, 2006

military service. In 1869 the legislature legalized casino gambling once again, requiring each casino to pay the state a tax of $5,000.

In *Bad Bet on the Bayou* (2001), author Tyler Bridges credits Louisiana gamblers for popularizing craps and poker in the United States during the nineteenth century. Both were games of chance that had originated in Europe. The Louisiana state lottery began in 1868 but was outlawed in 1892, along with other forms of gambling, after massive fraud was uncovered. Casino gambling went underground and continued to flourish well into the 1960s, thanks to mobsters and political corruption. Two of the state's governors, Earl Long and Edwin Edwards, were well-known gamblers. Edwards reportedly hosted high-stakes gambling games at the governor's mansion; he also went to prison in 2001 for extorting money from people who sought riverboat casino licenses.

During the early 1990s the state legalized gambling again, authorizing a lottery, casinos, and the operation of video poker machines in restaurants, bars, and truck stops. In 1991 the legislature authorized operation of up to fifteen riverboat casinos in the state; all but those along the Red River were required to make regularly scheduled cruises. The riverboat casinos were required to be at least 150 feet long and decorated to look like

nineteenth-century paddleboats. The first riverboat casino, the *Showboat Star*, began operating in 1993.

New Orleans received special permission from the legislature in 1993 to allow a limited number of land-based casinos. In January 1995 Harrah's began construction of one in the heart of the city. By November 1995 the casino had declared bankruptcy. Following years of negotiations with the state and the city, it reopened in 1999 but threatened bankruptcy again in 2001, blaming the state's $100 million minimum tax. The legislature cut the tax to $50 million for 2001 and $60 million for subsequent years to help keep the casino in business.

On April 1, 2001, the legislature ended the so-called phantom cruises of the riverboat casinos, ruling that it would actually be illegal for them to leave the docks. All riverboats were allowed to begin dockside gambling. However, their tax rate was increased from 18.5% to 21.5%.

According to revenue reports published by the Louisiana Gaming Control Board, the state's riverboat casinos admitted almost twenty-seven million people during the fiscal year that ran from July 1, 2005 to June 30, 2006. (See Table 4.6.) The attendance figure, down from twenty-eight million in fiscal year 2005, was likely lower

TABLE 4.6

Louisiana casino activity, selected statistics, July 2005–June 2006

Licensees	Opening date	Admissions	Total adjusted gross revenue	Fee/state tax
Boomtown Bossier	10/4/1996	1,869,424	$100,421,080	$21,590,532
Eldorado Resort	12/20/2000	3,089,452	$125,178,454	$26,913,368
Horseshoe	7/9/1994	2,858,547	$266,521,938	$57,302,217
Isle-Bossier	5/20/1994	1,896,343	$103,275,509	$22,204,234
Sam's Town	5/20/2004	2,091,132	$131,863,589	$28,350,672
Grand Palais	7/12/1996	1,969,257	$134,264,761	$28,866,924
Ilse—Lake Charles	7/29/1995	725,767	$31,375,623	$6,745,759
Harrah's Pride	12/8/1993	364,487	$18,830,078	$4,048,467
Harrah's Star	10/24/1993	224,203	$11,223,348	$2,413,020
L'Auberge du Lac	5/23/2005	4,724,746	$279,730,566	$60,142,072
Bally's	7/7/1995	194,612	$8,198,542	$1,516,730
Boomtown New Orleans	8/6/1994	2,625,198	$209,468,103	$45,035,642
Treasure Chest	9/5/1994	1,257,010	$142,650,412	$30,669,839
Belle of Baton Rouge	9/30/1994	1,358,489	$117,320,237	$25,223,851
Casino Rouge	12/28/1994	1,656,803	$155,606,691	$33,455,439
Riverboat total		**26,905,470**	**$1,835,928,931**	**$394,478,764**
Harrah's New Orleans	**10/26/1999**	**2,749,660**	**$198,146,389**	**$59,999,998**
Delta Downs (slots)	2/13/2002	1,647,856	$142,112,519	$21,558,469
Harrah's LA Downs (slots)	5/21/2003	1,932,550	$100,000,352	$15,170,053
Evangeline Downs (slots)	12/19/2003	2,640,124	$107,465,027	$16,302,445
Racetrack total (slots)		**6,220,530**	**$349,577,898**	**$53,030,967**
Casino total		**35,875,660**	**$2,383,853,218**	**$507,509,729**

SOURCE: Adapted from "Fiscal Year-to-Date Activity Summary—Land-based for the Period of July 1, 2005–June 30, 2006," "Fiscal Year-to-Date Activity Summary—Riverboats for the Period of July 1, 2005–June 30, 2006," and "Fiscal Year-to-Date Activity Summary—Slots at Racetracks for the Period of July 1, 2005–June 30, 2006," in *Louisiana Gaming Control Board Revenue Reports*, Louisiana Gaming Control Board, July 2006, http://www.dps.state.la.us/lgcb/ (accessed September 6, 2006)

because Hurricanes Katrina and Rita severely damaged two riverboat casinos on Lake Charles (*Harrah's Pride* and *Harrah's Star*) and one on Lake Pontchartrain (*Bally's*). Total adjusted gross revenue for the riverboats in fiscal year 2006 was more than $1.8 billion, which was actually up from about $1.6 billion the year before. Analysts believe the increase in revenue was due to an influx of "high rollers" from the Mississippi Gulf Coast region after the hurricanes shut down casinos there.

Louisiana's one land-based casino in New Orleans experienced a dramatic 41% drop in patronage when tourism to that city declined after Hurricane Katrina. In fiscal year 2006, 2.7 million people gambled at the casino, which had gross revenue of $198 million. (See Table 4.6.) During the previous year 6.8 million people were admitted and gross revenue totaled $339 million. Table 4.6 also shows that the state's three racinos, which were not damaged by the hurricanes, grossed nearly $350 million in slot-machine revenue during fiscal year 2006, up from $315 million the year before.

Total gross casino revenue in Louisiana for fiscal year 2006 was $2.4 billion, up from $2.2 billion during fiscal year 2005, despite the hurricanes. Revenues in 2006 were double that from fiscal year 1997 when casinos started operating in Louisiana. (See Figure 4.3.) The state took in approximately $507.5 million in taxes from the casinos and racinos during fiscal year 2006, up from $453 million a year earlier.

The state has four major casino markets: Shreveport–Bossier City, New Orleans, Lake Charles, and Baton Rouge. The Shreveport market was the tenth-largest casino market in the United States in 2005, according to the AGA. (See Table 4.3.) A wide variety of games are allowed at Louisiana casinos, including blackjack, poker, craps, roulette, baccarat, keno, bingo, and slot machines. The state also had 13,571 slot machines in truck stops, bars, restaurants, and other noncasino locations as of June 2006, according to the state's video gaming division. The machines generated $682 million in revenue.

INDIANA

In 1993 the state of Indiana legalized gambling on up to eleven riverboats in specific areas of the state—in the northwest corner along Lake Michigan; at the southern border along the Ohio River; and around Patoka Lake in the southern part of the state. The Patoka Lake site initially received a riverboat license, but it was later vetoed by the U.S. Army Corps of Engineers.

The first riverboat began operation in December 1995 in Evansville. By December 1996, six riverboats were operating. In 2002 new legislation permitted dockside operation of the riverboats in counties that would accept it. Permanent mooring allows patrons to access the casinos anytime during operating hours rather than just during cruise boarding times. The measure was intended to make Indiana casinos more competitive with those in Illinois.

FIGURE 4.3

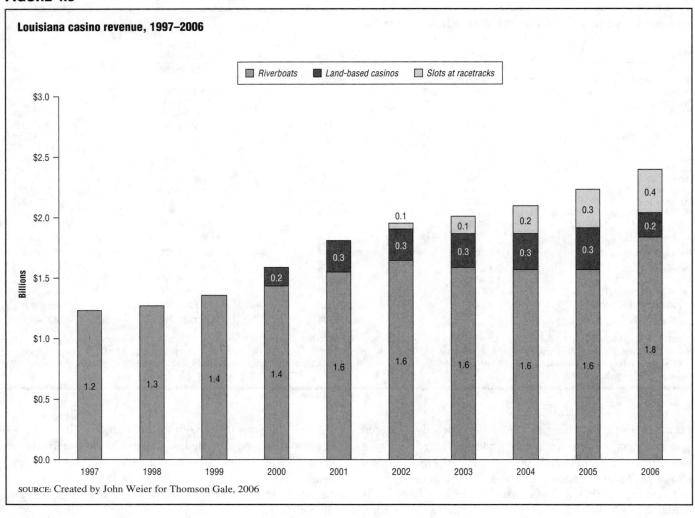

Louisiana casino revenue, 1997–2006

Legend: ■ Riverboats ■ Land-based casinos □ Slots at racetracks

SOURCE: Created by John Weier for Thomson Gale, 2006

The new law also changed the wagering tax structure from a 22.5% flat tax on adjusted gross receipts to a graduated tax rate of 15% to 35%. A portion of the increased tax revenue is distributed to counties that do not have casinos. The admissions tax, which remained at $3 per person, is split among the state, county, and city: each gets one dollar.

In June 2006 there were ten riverboats operating in Indiana. Five of the casinos were along Lake Michigan and five along the Ohio River. Together, the ten riverboats had 17,736 slot machines and 641 table games. Games allowed included blackjack, craps, roulette, baccarat, and poker. Eight of the riverboats were docked at locations with associated land-based hotels, restaurants, and entertainment venues. The other two were docked at pavilions offering only dining and shopping.

Total riverboat admission in Indiana was 27,060, 113 from July 2005 to June 2006, down dramatically from 41,373,160 during 2001 (*Indiana Gaming Commission 2005 Annual Report to the Governor*, 2005). The total win during fiscal year 2005 was $2.4 billion (see Table 4.7), up

from $2.3 billion in the previous fiscal year. In 2005 southeastern Indiana made up the eleventh-largest casino market in the United States in terms of gross revenue, and the combined northwest Indiana/northeast Illinois market was third largest, according to the AGA. (See Table 4.3.) Admission and wagering taxes paid in fiscal year 2006 totaled $803 million. Admission and wagering taxes paid from the inception of riverboat gambling in 1995 through 2006 totaled nearly $4.7 billion.

In November 2003 Orange County voters approved a measure that would allow development of a riverboat casino in their county. As of August 2006, a casino was being constructed in French Lick, although a lawsuit between the two partners building the casino threatened to delay its opening.

ILLINOIS

Illinois legalized riverboat gambling in 1990, the second state to do so. The Illinois Gaming Board was authorized to grant up to ten casino licenses, each of which would allow up to two vessels to be operated at a single specific dock site. Each dock site could have no

TABLE 4.7

Indiana gaming taxes, selected statistics, July 2004–June 2005

	Win	Wagering tax	Admission tax	Total
Argosy	$444,474,777	$140,538,260	$11,381,268	$151,919,528
Belterra	$156,245,649	$39,540,132	$5,980,146	$45,520,278
Blue Chip	$235,999,966	$67,713,809	$8,498,973	$76,212,782
Caesars	$296,806,131	$88,764,239	$10,156,086	$98,920,325
Casino Aztar	$122,114,386	$29,028,350	$4,658,427	$33,686,777
Grand Victoria	$148,843,458	$37,094,477	$5,365,206	$42,459,683
Resorts	$310,089,560	$93,671,769	$10,968,744	$104,640,513
Horseshoe	$409,190,275	$128,234,857	$12,515,067	$140,749,924
Majestic Star	$147,798,378	$36,870,441	$5,283,609	$42,154,050
Trump	$135,816,824	$33,326,711	$5,283,609	$38,610,320
Totals	**$2,407,379,404**	**$694,783,046**	**$80,091,135**	**$774,874,181**

SOURCE: "FY 2005 Tax Overview," in *2005 Annual Report to Governor Mitch Daniels, Indiana Gaming Commission*, Indiana Gaming Commission, 2005, http://www.in.gov/gaming/publications/annual/FY2005-Annual.pdf (accessed September 6, 2006)

TABLE 4.8

Local distribution of Illinois gaming taxes, 2005

Alton	$7,097,896
East Peoria	8,117,498
Rock Island	2,714,536
Joliet	31,721,572
Jo Daviess	0
Metropolis	8,413,434
Aurora	13,606,013
East St. Louis	10,545,446
Elgin	23,066,119
Total	**$105,282,514**

SOURCE: Adapted from "Distribution of Gaming Taxes," in *2005 Illinois Gaming Board Annual Report*, Illinois Gaming Board, 2006, http://www.igb.state.il.us/annualreport/2005igb.pdf (accessed September 6, 2006)

more than twelve hundred gaming positions, and all wagering was to be cashless. Originally, riverboats were required to cruise during gambling, but they were later allowed to operate dockside.

Nine dock sites were in operation in late 2006. The tenth license, issued in 1994, has been dormant since 1997 and the cause of several lawsuits, several of which were still active as of August 2006.

According to the AGA, in 2005 nine riverboat casinos operated within the state: two on the Fox River and two on the Des Plaines River in the northeast part of the state; one on the Illinois River in the central part of the state; one on the Ohio River in the south; and three on the Mississippi River to the west. Illinois riverboat casinos generated $1.8 billion in adjusted gross revenue in 2005, up from $1.7 billion in 2004. The vast majority (87%) of 2005 revenue was from electronic gambling devices; the remainder was from table games. Admissions totaled 15.3 million in 2005, down from 16.6 million in 2003.

Illinois levies an admissions tax and a wagering tax. In 2005 the admissions tax stood at $2 per person for casinos with fewer than one million patrons per year and $3 for all other establishments. Wagering taxes start at 15% for casinos with adjusted gross revenue of less than or equal to $25 million and increase as revenue increases. Casino taxes are shared by the state and communities in which the casinos are located. According to the Illinois Gaming Board's annual report, the casino industry paid $105 million in local taxes in fiscal year 2005 (see Table 4.8) and $644 million in state taxes. The state received 86% of admissions and wagering taxes and the cities and counties received 14%.

MISSOURI

The legalization of riverboat gambling in Missouri started in 1992 with a referendum approved by 64% of the voters. That was followed by a court case, a constitutional amendment (that was defeated by voters), and wrangling over the definition of "games of skill." Eventually, in 1994, the general assembly passed a bill that defined games of skill and authorized riverboats to be located in artificial basins. The first two licenses for riverboat casinos were issued later that year. However, because the casinos could not offer games of chance, such as slot machines, competition from riverboats in Illinois kept customers away, and the casinos were not profitable.

After a petition drive, voters passed an initiative that allowed "only upon the Mississippi River and the Missouri River, lotteries, gift enterprises, and games of chance to be conducted on excursion gambling boats and floating facilities." The result was significant: revenues from casino riverboats during the first quarter of fiscal year 1996 were more than twice what they had been during the first quarter of the previous year. Initially the casinos were only allowed to hold two-hour gambling excursions. In 2000 the law was changed to allow continuous boarding. However, the original $500 loss limit per excursion that had been approved in 1992 still applies. Patrons are allowed to purchase only $500 worth of chips or tokens in any two-hour period, preventing them from losing more than that amount within the "excursion" period.

In 2005, according to the Missouri Gaming Commission, eleven riverboat casinos operated in six markets: St. Louis, Kansas City, Caruthersville, St. Joseph, LaGrange, and Boonville. All of the riverboats remain dockside. Games allowed include blackjack, poker, and other card games, slot machines, craps, roulette, and several wheel games. Gaming revenue topped $1 billion for the first time during fiscal year 2001 and reached $1.5 billion in fiscal year 2005 (July 1, 2004 through June 30, 2005). (See Figure 4.4.) More than twenty-five million people were admitted to the state's casinos during fiscal year 2005. December was the busiest month. (See Figure 4.5.)

FIGURE 4.4

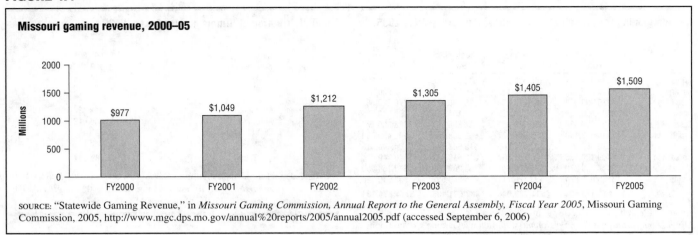

Missouri gaming revenue, 2000–05

SOURCE: "Statewide Gaming Revenue," in *Missouri Gaming Commission, Annual Report to the General Assembly, Fiscal Year 2005*, Missouri Gaming Commission, 2005, http://www.mgc.dps.mo.gov/annual%20reports/2005/annual2005.pdf (accessed September 6, 2006)

FIGURE 4.5

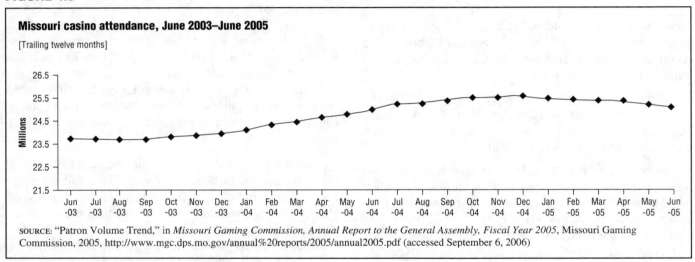

Missouri casino attendance, June 2003–June 2005

SOURCE: "Patron Volume Trend," in *Missouri Gaming Commission, Annual Report to the General Assembly, Fiscal Year 2005*, Missouri Gaming Commission, 2005, http://www.mgc.dps.mo.gov/annual%20reports/2005/annual2005.pdf (accessed September 6, 2006)

Casino operators pay an 18% tax on adjusted gross receipts to the state and a 2% local tax to the home dock city or county. Taxes totaled $302 million in 2005. In addition, a $2 admission fee is paid for each patron per "excursion" that is split evenly between the state and the local jurisdiction. In fiscal 2005 the fees totaled $108 million. The casinos also pay costs associated with Missouri Gaming Commission agents assigned to each casino, which amounted to an average annual cost per casino of $611,000 during 2005.

MICHIGAN

Pari-mutuel horse racing was legalized in Michigan in 1933. During the 1970s, the state lottery was legalized and a concerted effort began to allow casino gambling in Detroit. The casino efforts were unsuccessful until 1994, when the Windsor Casino opened just across the river in Windsor, Ontario. By that time, more than a dozen tribal casinos were operating around the state of Michigan, and

Detroit was in an economic downturn. Attitudes toward casino gambling changed, and in November 1996 Michigan voters narrowly approved ballot Proposal E, which authorized the operation of up to three casinos in any city that had a population of 800,000 people or more and was located within 100 miles of any other state or country in which gaming was permitted. Casino gaming also had to be approved by a majority of voters in the city. Proposal E was subsequently modified and signed into law in 1997. Out of eleven casino proposals submitted, three were accepted: Atwater/Circus Circus Casino (later called MotorCity Casino), owned by Detroit Entertainment; Greektown Casino, owned by the Sault Ste. Marie Tribe of Chippewa Indians; and the MGM Grand, owned by MGM Grand Detroit Casino. The casinos were granted permission to open at temporary locations, with permanent facilities planned for a proposed waterfront casino district.

The first casino, the MGM Grand, opened in July 1999 in a former Internal Revenue Service building. Later that

FIGURE 4.6

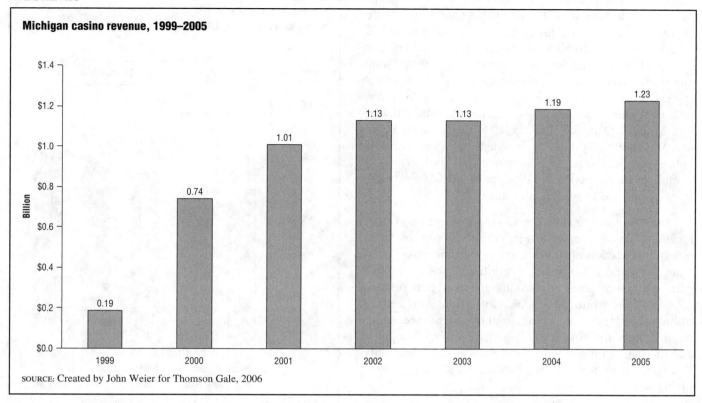

Michigan casino revenue, 1999–2005

SOURCE: Created by John Weier for Thomson Gale, 2006

year the MotorCity Casino started operations in a former bread factory. The Greektown Casino opened in November 2000 in the heart of the city. It was the first tribally owned casino to open off a reservation. Detroit became the largest city in the country to allow casino gambling.

The plan for a downtown casino district was eventually abandoned because of rising real estate prices and local opposition, and the number of hotel rooms initially proposed was cut back after marketing studies showed that many casino customers were regional and did not need overnight lodging. The permanent casinos were also delayed by several lawsuits. However, work began on the permanent MGM Grand Detroit Casino and MotorCity Casino in the summer of 2006. Both casinos were slated to open in late 2007 near their temporary locations. The permanent Greektown Casino, which was awaiting zoning approval in 2006, was expected to be up and running near its temporary location by 2008.

According to the Michigan Gaming and Control Board's 2006 annual report, the Detroit casinos together grossed slightly more than $1.2 billion in calendar year 2005. (See Figure 4.6.) Each casino paid 12.1% of adjusted gross receipts as a state wagering tax. About 8.1%, or more than $99 million, went into a statewide School Aid Fund for K–12, while 3.5% went into the state's general fund and 0.5% went to the Michigan Agriculture Equine Industry Development Fund. The casinos also paid a local wagering tax to the city of Detroit of 11.9% of adjusted gross receipts. The city tax was used for public safety, antigang and youth development programs, taxpayer relief, capital and road improvements, and other programs designed to improve the quality of life in the city.

In addition, each casino paid a yearly licensing fee of $25,000. The three casinos also shared an annual state services fee of about $25 million. The Compulsive Gaming Prevention Fund received $2 million from the state services fee for treatment, prevention, education, training, research, and evaluation of pathological gamblers and their families under the Michigan Department of Community Health. The casinos also shared an annual $4 million municipal services fee.

Unlike casinos in some other states, Detroit's casinos are not permitted under the Michigan Liquor Control Code to provide free alcoholic drinks. Games offered at Detroit casinos include baccarat, blackjack, casino war, craps, keno, poker, roulette, slot machines, and video poker.

IOWA

Gambling was outlawed in the state of Iowa from the time of its statehood in 1846 until 1972, when a provision in the state constitution that prohibited lotteries was repealed. In 1973 the general assembly authorized bingo and raffles by specific parties. A decade later pari-mutuel wagering at dog and horse tracks was legalized, followed by a state lottery in 1985. In 1989 gambling aboard excursion boats was authorized for counties in which voters approved gambling referenda. Between 1989 and 1995 referenda authorizing riverboat gambling were approved in more than a dozen counties. The Iowa Racing and Gaming Commission granted licenses for riverboat gambling in ten counties: Clarke, Clayton, Clinton, Des Moines, Dubuque, Lee, Polk, Pottawattamie, Scott, and Woodbury. By law, the residents of these counties vote every eight years on a referendum to allow riverboat gambling to continue. In 1994 pari-mutuel racetracks gained approval to operate slot machines.

In fiscal year 2006 twelve riverboat casinos and three racetrack casinos operated in Iowa. Games included bingo, blackjack, craps, keno, mini-baccarat, poker, roulette, slots, and video poker. According to the racing and gaming commission, admissions to riverboats totaled 13.4 million, while admissions to racinos totaled 6.9 million. The riverboats are required by law to meet space requirements for nongamblers and to provide shopping and tourism options. Slots are allowed at racetracks only if a specific number of live races are held during each racing season.

As shown in Figure 4.7, during fiscal year 2006 casino revenues totaled $759.2 million, or 66% of adjusted gross gambling revenue in the state. Racino revenues totaled $389.9 million. Nearly $260 million in gaming taxes were collected by cities, counties, and the state in 2005. Iowa's gaming tax rate ranges from 5% to 24%, depending on revenue and the type of venue. According to the Iowa Gaming Association, a trade group that represents the industry, tax revenue in fiscal year 2006 reached $278.8 million (http://www.iowagaming.org/support/media/reinvesting_in_iowa/pdf/2006_Gaming_Revenues.pdf). Distributions included $70 million to the Endowment for Iowa's Health Account, $60 million to the state's general fund, $55.8 million for infrastructure improvements, $35 million for environmental projects, and $11.5 million paid as city and county taxes.

COLORADO

During the 1800s gambling halls and saloons with card games were prevalent throughout the mining towns of Colorado. However, gambling was outlawed in the state around the turn of the twentieth century.

In November 1990 Colorado voters approved a constitutional amendment permitting limited-stakes gaming in the towns of Black Hawk and Central City, near Denver, and Cripple Creek, near Colorado Springs. The first Colorado casinos opened in October 1991 and had gross revenues of nearly $8.4 million during their first month of operation.

FIGURE 4.7

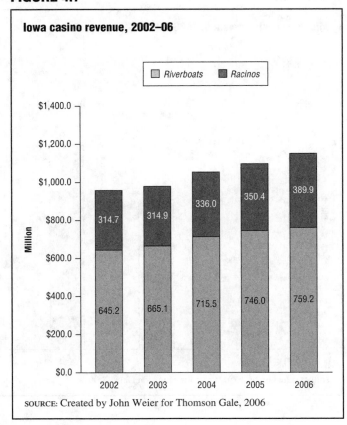

Iowa casino revenue, 2002–06

SOURCE: Created by John Weier for Thomson Gale, 2006

Only blackjack, poker, and slot machines are permitted in Colorado's casinos. The maximum single bet is $5. Any increase in betting limits, additional types of games, or new gambling locations would require a statewide vote authorizing a change in the constitutional amendment. Since 1992 there have been seven votes on whether to expand casino gaming to additional locations; each time expansion has been defeated by at least a two-to-one margin.

According to the Colorado Gaming Commission, forty-seven casinos operated in the state in August 2006. They had gross revenues of $765 million during fiscal year 2006. As shown in Figure 4.8, annual revenue grew steadily from 1992 through 2005, leveling off for a brief period between 2002 and 2004. The Black Hawk casinos have historically been the most successful in the state, accounting for 70% to 75% of casino gaming revenue each year, followed by the Cripple Creek market (20% to 25% of the total) and Central City (5% to 10%).

According to *Gaming in Colorado: Fact Book & 2005 Abstract*, a publication of the Colorado Division of Gaming, from 1992 through 2005 casinos had adjusted gross revenue of more than $7.2 billion and paid more than $940 million in gaming taxes. The tax money has been used to fund historical restoration projects and to offset the costs of casino gaming to state and local governments (including regulatory costs associated with the casino industry).

FIGURE 4.8

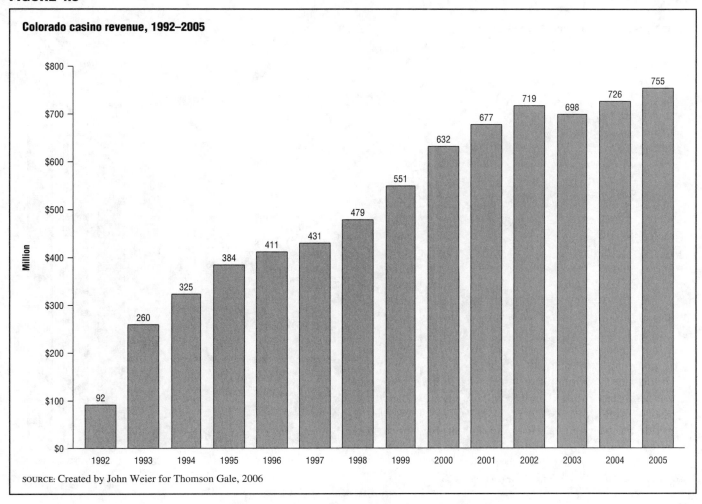

Colorado casino revenue, 1992–2005

SOURCE: Created by John Weier for Thomson Gale, 2006

The gaming tax rate, which is set by the gaming commission annually, is based on each casino's adjusted gross proceeds (the amount of money wagered minus the amount paid out in prizes). In 2005 the tax ranged from less than 1% for casinos with less than $2 million in adjusted gross proceeds to 20% for establishments with adjusted gross proceeds of more than $15 million.

In addition the casinos pay annual device fees: $75 per slot machine and game table to the state and $750 to $1,265 to local jurisdictions. The gaming commission reported in June 2006 that there were 16,885 slot machines and 216 table games operating in the state.

SOUTH DAKOTA

Commercial casino gambling in South Dakota is restricted to the town of Deadwood in Lawrence County. A rustic mountain town about sixty miles from Mount Rushmore, Deadwood was designated a National Historic Landmark and is listed on both the National and South Dakota Registers of Historic Places. It has 112 casinos, more than eighty of them historic. The games allowed are blackjack, poker, and slot machines.

The rocky history of gambling in Deadwood is described in *The Last Gamble: Betting on the Future in Four Rocky Mountain Mining Towns* by Katherine R. Jensen and Audie L. Blevins (1998). The gold rush of 1876 brought large numbers of people into the town, and it soon became packed with saloons and gambling halls. The town became associated with such notorious characters as Wild Bill Hickok, Poker Alice, and Calamity Jane.

Although gambling was outlawed in the Dakota Territory in 1881, it continued quite openly in Deadwood with the apparent complicity of the local sheriff. In 1907 gambling opponents complained that the town's gambling halls "operated as openly as grocery stores, running twenty-four hours a day." On a busy Saturday night in 1947, South Dakota's attorney general sent sixteen raiders into the bars of Deadwood to show the town that the state meant business. The blatant days of gambling were over in Deadwood, although locals say the establishments continued to operate quietly for the next four decades.

In 1984 a group of Deadwood businessmen and community leaders began working to bring legalized

FIGURE 4.9

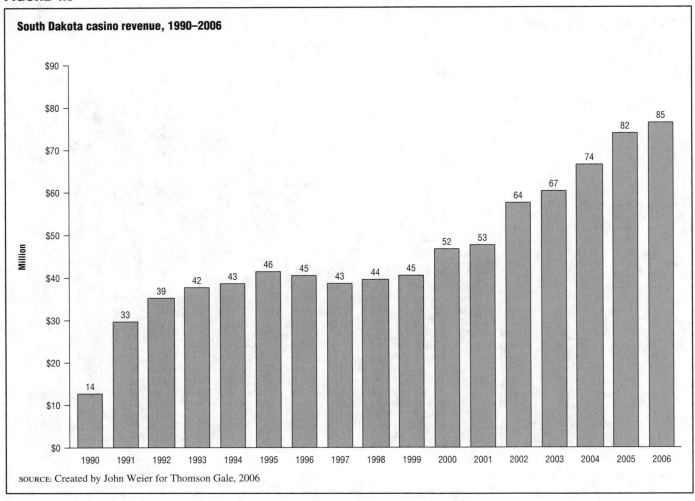

South Dakota casino revenue, 1990–2006

SOURCE: Created by John Weier for Thomson Gale, 2006

gambling back to Deadwood, primarily to raise money to preserve the town's historic buildings. The group developed the slogan "Deadwood You Bet" and had it printed on hundreds of buttons. Despite widespread local support, though, the idea failed at the ballot box in 1984 and was voted down by the legislature in 1988. The measure made it onto the ballot in November 1988 following a massive petition effort. In 1989 South Dakota voters approved limited-stakes casino gambling for Deadwood. Originally, the casinos could only offer a $5 maximum bet. This limit was raised to $100 in 2000.

According to the annual report of the South Dakota Commission on Gaming, Deadwood's casinos had total combined gross revenue of $85.4 million in fiscal 2006, a 4% increase from the previous fiscal year. (See Figure 4.9.) From the reintroduction of legalized casino gambling through June 2006, gross revenue totaled $872 million. The casinos pay an 8% gaming tax on their adjusted gross revenue and an annual fee of $2,000 per card game or slot machine. In fiscal year 2006 nearly $6.7 million in gaming taxes were collected, raising the total taxes paid between fiscal year 1990 and 2006 to nearly $68 million. Of this amount $34 million went to the state's gaming commission fund, $27 million was allocated to promote tourism, and $7 million was turned over to Lawrence County.

CHAPTER 5

NATIVE AMERICAN TRIBAL CASINOS

Casinos operated by Native American tribes made $22.6 billion during 2005, according to the National Indian Gaming Commission (NIGC). That amounted to 43% of the casino market. Commercial casinos, by contrast, made $30.3 billion during the same year, as reported by the American Gaming Association (*2006 State of the States: The AGA Survey of Casino Entertainment*). The Native American percentage of the casino market is expected to grow throughout the decade.

According to 2005 estimates by the U.S Census Bureau, 4.5 million people in the United States (approximately 1.5% of the total population) identified themselves as Native Americans or Alaskan Natives and belonged to 561 federally recognized tribes. In 2006 more than 220 tribes engaged in gaming enterprises. The National Indian Gaming Association (NIGA) reported in *An Analysis of the Economic Impact of Indian Gaming in 2004* that more than nineteen million Americans visited tribal gaming facilities in 2003. According to *Harrah's Survey 2003: Profile of the American Casino Gambler,* Native American casinos were the top casino destination for residents of Arizona, California, Connecticut, Florida, Massachusetts, Minnesota, New Hampshire, New Mexico, North Carolina, North Dakota, Oklahoma, Oregon, Rhode Island, South Carolina, South Dakota, Washington, and Wisconsin.

HISTORY

The growth of tribal casinos can be traced to the late 1970s, when Native American tribes began to operate bingo halls to raise funds for tribal purposes. Tribes in Florida and Wisconsin tried to open high-stakes bingo games on their reservations. Bingo games were legal in those states but subject to restrictions on the size of the jackpot and how often games could be held. The Oneida Tribe of Wisconsin and the Seminole Tribe of Florida took their respective states to court, arguing that the tribes were sovereign nations and not subject to state limitations on gambling.

In 1981 the U.S. Fifth Circuit Court of Appeals ruled in *Seminole Tribe of Florida v. Butterworth*, 658 F.2d 310, that the tribe could operate a high-stakes bingo parlor because the state of Florida did not have regulatory power over the tribe, a sovereign governing entity. A similar ruling was issued in *Oneida Tribe of Indians v. Wisconsin*, 518 F.Supp. 712. Both cases concluded that the states' gambling laws were regulatory, or civil, in nature rather than criminal, because the states already allowed bingo games to take place.

Other tribes also sued, and the issue eventually reached the U.S. Supreme Court. In *California v. Cabazon Band of Mission Indians*, 480 U.S. 202 (1987), the court ruled that California could not prohibit a tribe from conducting activities (in this case, high-stakes bingo and poker games) that were legal elsewhere in the state. In 1989 the Bay Mills Indian Community opened the King's Club in Brimley, Michigan, the first Native American gambling hall to offer slot machines and blackjack.

GAMBLING CLASSES

In 1988 the U.S. Congress passed the Indian Gaming Regulatory Act, which allows federally recognized tribes to open gambling establishments on their reservations if the state in which they are located already permits legalized gambling. It set up a regulatory system and three classes of gambling activities:

- Class I—social gaming for minimal prizes and traditional gaming (for example, in tribal ceremonies or celebrations)

- Class II—bingo and bingolike games, lotto, pull tabs (paper tickets that have tabs concealing symbols or numbers), tip jars (lotterylike games played with preprinted tickets), punch boards (thick cardboard with symbols or numbers concealed behind foil), and nonbanking card games (such as the type of poker that is played against other players instead of the house)

- Class III—banking card games (card games in which the player bets against the house), casino games, slot machines, pari-mutuel betting on horse and dog racing and jai alai, electronic facsimiles of any game of chance, and any other forms of gaming not included in Class I or II

Class I gaming is regulated exclusively by the tribes and requires no financial reporting to other authorities. Class II and Class III games are allowed only if such games are already permitted in the state where the tribe is located. According to the U.S. Government Accountability Office (GAO), the investigatory branch of Congress, court rulings have maintained that tribes can operate casinos in states that only offer state-run lotteries and charitable casino nights.

Both Class II and Class III operations require that the tribe adopt a gaming ordinance that is approved by the NIGC. In addition, Class III gaming requires that the tribe and state have an agreement, called a tribal-state compact (or treaty), that is approved by the U.S. Secretary of the Interior. A compact is supposed to balance the interests of the state and the tribe in regard to standards for operation and maintenance, the applicability of state and tribal laws and regulations, and the amount needed by the state to defray its regulatory costs. Tribes may have compacts with more than one state and may have different compacts for different types of gambling operations.

REGULATION

Native American casinos are regulated at three levels of government: federal, state, and tribal. Federal regulation is performed by the NIGC, which oversees the licensing of gaming employees and management and reviews tribal gaming ordinances. The NIGC also has enforcement powers. For example, in June 2004 the commission temporarily closed a casino operated by the Coyote Valley Band of Pomo Indians in Redwood Valley, California, for allegedly operating Class III gambling devices without a compact with the state. However, most violations do not result in closure, but in notification followed by fines. In 2006, for instance, the Santa Rosa Rancheria Tachi-Yokut Tribe was found in violation for failing to conduct proper background checks on casino employees. The tribe had ninety days to check the background of the employees in question or face fines of up to $25,000 per day.

The federal government also has criminal jurisdiction over cases involving embezzlement, cheating, and fraud at tribal gaming operations, because such crimes are federal offenses.

State regulation is spelled out in the tribal-state compacts. They cover such matters as the number of slot machines that may be operated; limits on types and quantities of card games that can be offered; minimum gambling ages in the casinos; authorization for casino workers to unionize; public health and safety issues; compulsive gambling issues; the effects of tribal gaming on other state enterprises; and how much revenue should be paid to the state and how often.

The tribes themselves are the primary regulators of tribal gaming. The NIGA, a trade organization for Native American casinos, reported in 2005 that more than 2,800 regulatory and enforcement personnel are employed by tribes and that more than $212 million was spent by the tribes on regulation of their industry.

FEDERAL RECOGNITION

Native American casinos must be a tribal endeavor, not an individual endeavor—a random group of Native Americans cannot start a tribal casino. Only a tribe's status as a sovereign entity, granted by the federal government, allows it to conduct gaming.

The list of federally recognized tribes is maintained by the Bureau of Indian Affairs (BIA), an agency of the U.S. Department of the Interior. The most current list, which includes the names of 561 tribes, was published in the *Federal Register* (November 25, 2005; http://www.loc.gov/catdir/cpso/biaind.pdf).

Throughout history, tribes have received federal recognition through treaties with the U.S. government, via congressional actions, or through BIA decisions. Most tribes were officially recognized during the eighteenth and nineteenth centuries. Today recognition can be achieved either through an act of Congress or through a series of actions, known as the "federal acknowledgment process," that can take many years. Under federal regulation 25 CFR Part 83, a group of Native Americans must meet seven criteria to be federally recognized as a tribe:

- They must have been identified as an American Indian entity on a substantially continuous basis since 1900.

- A predominant portion of the group must comprise a distinct community and have existed as a community from historical times to the present.

- They must have maintained political influence or authority over their members as an autonomous entity from historical times until the present.

- They must submit a copy of the group's current governing documents, including membership criteria.

- The group's membership must consist of individuals who descended from a historical Indian tribe or from historical Indian tribes that combined and functioned as a single autonomous political entity.

TABLE 5.1

Tribal gaming revenue by region, 2004 and 2005

[Dollar amounts in thousands]

	Fiscal year 2005		Fiscal year 2004		Increase (decrease)		
	Number of operations	Gaming revenues	Number of operations	Gaming revenues	Number of operations	Gaming revenues	Revenue percentage
Region I	47	$1,829,195	45	$1,601,710	2	$227,485	14.2%
Region II	57	$7,042,686	54	$5,822,114	3	$1,220,572	21.0%
Region III	48	$2,529,128	45	$2,159,872	3	$369,256	17.1%
Region IV	118	$3,984,449	117	$3,815,857	1	$168,592	4.4%
Region V	93	$1,729,981	87	$1,258,717	6	$471,264	37.4%
Region VI	28	$5,514,136	27	$4,820,864	1	$693,272	14.4%
Totals	**391**	**$22,629,575**	**375**	**$19,479,134**	**16**	**$3,150,441**	**16.2%**

Notes: Compiled from gaming operation audited financial statements received by the National Indian Gaming Commission through June 29, 2006; 12 operations' revenue figures compiled from fee worksheets, as audited financial statements of those operations were not received.
Region I   Alaska, Idaho, Oregon, and Washington
Region II   California and northern Nevada
Region III   Arizona, Colorado, New Mexico, and southern Nevada
Region IV   Iowa, Michigan, Minnesota, Montana, North Dakota, Nebraska, South Dakota, Wisconsin, and Wyoming
Region V   Kansas, Oklahoma, and Texas
Region VI   Alabama, Connecticut, Florida, Louisiana, Mississippi, North Carolina, and New York

SOURCE: "National Indian Gaming Commission Tribal Gaming Revenues (in Thousands) by Region, Fiscal Year 2005 and 2004," in *Tribal Data*, National Indian Gaming Commission, 2005, http://www.nigc.gov/Portals/0/NIGC%20Uploads/Tribal%20Data/2005vs2004gmgrevbyregn.pdf (accessed September 6, 2006)

- The membership of the group must be composed primarily of people who are not members of an existing acknowledged North American Indian tribe.

- The tribe must not be the subject of congressional legislation that has terminated or forbidden a federal relationship.

Federal recognition is important to Native American tribes if they are to be eligible for billions of dollars in federal assistance. By the end of 2005 the federal government held about fifty-six million acres of land in trust for federally recognized Indian tribes and their members. If a tribe does not have a land base, the federal government can take land in trust for the tribe once it receives recognition. That land is no longer subject to local jurisdiction, including property taxes and zoning ordinances.

Most tribes require that a person have a particular degree of Native American heritage (usually 25%) to be an enrolled member. Some tribes require proof of lineage. According to the GAO, federally recognized tribes had approximately 1.8 million members as of February 2005.

One of the most contentious issues related to tribal casinos is the authenticity of the tribes themselves. Critics charge that some Native American groups want federal recognition only as a means to enter the lucrative gambling business. The GAO examined this issue in a report titled *Improvements Needed in Tribal Recognition Process* (November 2001). According to the GAO there were 193 tribes with gambling facilities at that time. The report noted that 170 of the tribes (88%) could trace their federal recognition at least back to the time of the Indian

Reorganization Act (IRA) of 1934 or similar legislation from the 1930s. About 59% of those tribes were engaged in gambling operations in 2001. By contrast, 45% of the tribes recognized since 1960 were engaged in gambling operations.

The GAO report indicated that the procedures established by the BIA in 1978 to ensure that recognition of tribes be uniform and objective had become too lengthy and inconsistent. Backlogs have been constant since the number of petitions for recognition began to climb during the 1990s. However, in testimony before the U.S. House of Representatives in February 2005 Robin M. Nazzaro of the GAO noted that the backlog of cases had been steadily reduced and was expected to be completed by 2008 (http://www.gao.gov/new.items/d05347t.pdf).

REVENUES

Because tribes are sovereign governments, they are not required by law to make public statements of their revenues, so financial information on individual tribal casinos is not publicly released. Each year the NIGC announces total gaming revenue for the previous year for all tribal gaming facilities combined. It also breaks down the revenue by U.S. region and revenue class. On June 29, 2006, the NIGC released financial information showing that tribal casinos made $22.6 billion during 2005, up from $19.5 billion in 2004. This revenue is broken down by region in Table 5.1 and by revenue class in Table 5.2.

As shown in Table 5.1 tribal casinos in Region II (California and northern Nevada) were the most profitable

TABLE 5.2

Tribal gaming revenue, 2000–05

Gaming revenue range	Number of operations	Revenues (in thousands)	Percentage of Operations	Revenues	Mean (in thousands)	Median (in thousands)
Gaming operations with fiscal years ending in 2005						
$250 million and over	21	9,738,744	5.4%	43.0%	463,750	379,129
$100 million to $250 million	39	6,209,904	10.0%	27.4%	159,228	145,771
$50 million to $100 million	43	2,897,277	11.0%	12.8%	67,379	63,518
$25 million to $50 million	58	2,019,555	14.8%	8.9%	34,820	33,116
$10 million to $25 million	75	1,268,546	19.2%	5.6%	16,914	16,383
$3 million to $10 million	68	411,773	17.4%	1.8%	6,055	5,474
Under $3 million	87	83,776	22.3%	0.4%	963	483
Total	**391**	**22,629,575**				
Gaming operations with fiscal years ending in 2004						
$250 million and over	15	7,200,911	4.0%	37.0%	480,061	376,449
$100 million to $250 million	40	6,277,698	10.7%	32.2%	156,942	155,160
$50 million to $100 million	33	2,240,010	8.8%	11.5%	67,879	67,233
$25 million to $50 million	60	2,144,496	16.0%	11.0%	35,742	33,391
$10 million to $25 million	71	1,180,438	18.9%	6.1%	16,626	16,035
$3 million to $10 million	58	354,050	15.5%	1.8%	6,104	6,040
Under $3 million	98	81,531	26.1%	0.4%	832	530
Total	**375**	**19,479,134**				
Gaming operations with fiscal years ending in 2003						
$250 million and over	11	5,381,204	3.1%	32.0%	489,200	343,230
$100 million to $250 million	32	5,333,377	8.9%	31.7%	166,668	163,916
$50 million to $100 million	35	2,459,698	9.7%	14.6%	70,277	65,416
$25 million to $50 million	57	2,040,711	15.9%	12.1%	35,802	35,219
$10 million to $25 million	69	1,170,169	19.2%	7.0%	16,959	16,741
$3 million to $10 million	57	350,398	15.9%	2.1%	6,147	5,819
Under $3 million	98	90,825	27.3%	0.5%	927	522
Total	**359**	**16,826,382**				
Gaming operations with fiscal years ending in 2002						
$250 million and over	10	4,640,064	2.9%	31.5%	464,006	302,298
$100 million and over	31	4,870,596	8.9%	33.1%	157,116	150,174
$50 million to $100 million	24	1,694,606	6.9%	11.5%	70,609	68,225
$25 million to $50 million	55	1,978,519	15.8%	13.4%	35,973	38,984
$10 million to $25 million	65	1,067,513	18.6%	7.3%	16,423	16,570
$3 million to $10 million	63	386,399	18.1%	2.6%	6,133	5,373
Under $3 million	101	79,965	28.9%	0.5%	800	469
Total	**349**	**14,717,662**				
Gaming operations with fiscal years ending in 2001						
$100 million and over	39	8,398,523	11.8%	65.5%	215,347	158,836
$50 million to $100 million	19	1,415,755	5.8%	11.0%	74,513	79,083
$25 million to $50 million	43	1,528,611	13.0%	11.9%	35,549	34,264
$10 million to $25 million	58	997,546	17.6%	7.8%	17,199	16,328
$3 million to $10 million	57	385,654	17.3%	3.0%	6,766	7,292
Under $3 million	114	96,257	34.5%	0.8%	844	575
Total	**330**	**12,822,346**				
Gaming operations with fiscal years ending in 2000						
$100 million and over	31	6,606,284	10.0%	60.3%	213,106	141,684
$50 million to $100 million	24	1,693,510	7.7%	15.5%	70,563	73,314
$25 million to $50 million	41	1,360,777	13.2%	12.4%	33,190	29,944
$10 million to $25 million	50	856,464	16.1%	7.8%	17,129	17,335
$3 million to $10 million	55	350,110	17.7%	3.2%	6,366	6,250
Under $3 million	110	91,545	35.4%	0.8%	832	365
Total	**311**	**10,958,690**				

SOURCE: "National Indian Gaming Commission Tribal Gaming Revenues," in *Tribal Data*, National Indian Gaming Commission, 2005, http://www.nigc.gov/Portals/0/NIGC%20Uploads/Tribal%20Data/tribalgamingrevenues05.pdf (accessed September 6, 2006)

in 2005, earning $7 billion. Because there are no tribal casinos in northern Nevada, all of this revenue was actually from California tribal casinos. California tribes with gaming facilities earned 31% of all tribal casino revenue. Their market share was $1 billion more than that reported for commercial casinos on the Las Vegas Strip during 2005.

The second most profitable region for tribes with gaming operations during 2005 included the states of Alabama, Connecticut, Florida, Louisiana, Mississippi, New York, and North Carolina. The region was responsible for $5.5 billion in casino revenues, or 24% of total tribal revenue. Casinos operating in Connecticut are thought to be the largest source of that region's revenue.

FIGURE 5.1

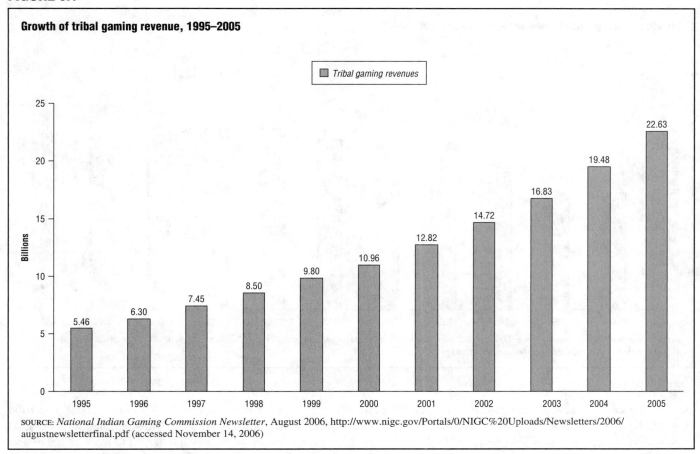

Growth of tribal gaming revenue, 1995–2005

SOURCE: *National Indian Gaming Commission Newsletter*, August 2006, http://www.nigc.gov/Portals/0/NIGC%20Uploads/Newsletters/2006/augustnewsletterfinal.pdf (accessed November 14, 2006)

According to the GAO, tribal gambling revenues grew from $171 million in 1988 (when the Indian Gaming Regulatory Act was passed) to $3.8 billion in 1994. Revenues reported by the NIGC for 1995 through 2005 are shown in Figure 5.1. Over this period tribal casino revenues grew from $5.5 billion to $22.6 billion, an increase of more than 300%. By contrast, revenues at commercial casinos grew from $16 billion in 1995 to $30.3 billion in 2005, an increase of 89%. Between 1995 and 2005, the number of tribal gaming operations also grew at an impressive rate. In 1995 only 215 tribal gaming operations existed; by 2005 this number had increased to 391 operations, an 82% jump. (See Figure 5.2.)

Tribal gaming revenues reported by the NIGC for 2005 are broken down by revenue class in Table 5.2. About 22.3% of tribal gambling operations reported revenues of less than $3 million each. Sixty operations (15.4% of the total number) earned $100 million or more. Those sixty facilities accounted for 70.4% of all tribal casino revenue.

The Indian Gaming Regulatory Act requires that net revenues from tribal gaming be used:

- to fund tribal government operations or programs
- to provide for the general welfare of the tribe and its members

- to promote tribal economic development
- to donate to charitable organizations
- to help fund operations of local government agencies

Tribes with gaming operations may distribute gaming revenues to individual tribe members through per capita payments but are not required to do so. Such payments must be approved by the U.S. Secretary of the Interior as part of the tribe's Revenue Allocation Plan (RAP) and are subject to federal income tax.

The NIGA reported in *An Analysis of the Economic Impact of Indian Gaming in 2004* that tribal casinos are increasingly making money from their nongambling enterprises, such as lodging, restaurants, and entertainment. These enterprises brought in $2.5 billion in revenue during 2004.

TRIBAL-COMMERCIAL CASINO VENTURES

Building casinos can be expensive. Tribes that have built them have had to borrow large sums of money and/or obtain investors to do so. In general, the law requires that tribes partner with companies for no more than five years at a time and limits the companies' take to 30% of the total revenue. Under some circumstances, the

FIGURE 5.2

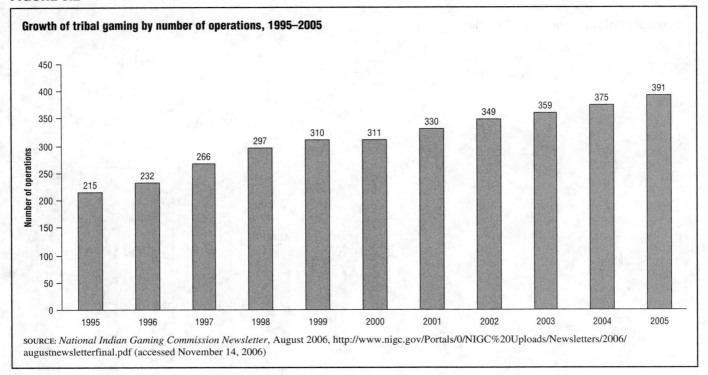

Growth of tribal gaming by number of operations, 1995–2005

SOURCE: *National Indian Gaming Commission Newsletter*, August 2006, http://www.nigc.gov/Portals/0/NIGC%20Uploads/Newsletters/2006/augustnewsletterfinal.pdf (accessed November 14, 2006)

partnership can last seven years and the companies' portion can be as much as 40% of total revenue. These five-to seven-year contracts can also be renewed if both parties and the state government agree to the renewal.

As of 2006 the NIGC reported that fifty tribes had management contracts in place with commercial companies (http://www.nigc.gov/ReadingRoom/ManagementContracts/ApprovedManagementContracts/tabid/491/Default.aspx). More than a quarter of the contracts were with gaming companies based in Las Vegas and Reno, Nevada. Harrah's Entertainment was a partner in six of these contracts.

Native American casinos have often faced fierce opposition from commercial casino operators hoping to thwart competition. Tribal casinos in California, for example, could cut deeply into the Nevada casino business because California residents, who have long provided a large share of Nevada's gambling revenue, could gamble closer to home. However, some commercial casino operators have seen expanded opportunities for revenue through partnerships with Native American tribes, and some tribes—especially small tribes—have welcomed the investment capital and management experience offered by commercial partners.

For example, Thunder Valley Casino is a $215 million venture about thirty miles northeast of Sacramento, California. The casino, which opened in June 2004, was owned by the United Auburn Indian Community, which had around 250 adult members. The casino was financially backed and managed by Station Casinos of Las Vegas, a commercial company with revenue of $1.1 billion in 2005. The tribe selected the company because it was willing to put up $200 million to build the casino and agreed to manage the casino for the tribe; in return Station receives 24% of the casino's net revenues. Before the casino opened, tribe members lived in poverty on a three-acre reservation.

Casino ventures between companies and very small tribes are particularly controversial. Critics say that small tribes are being manipulated by outside investors who only want to cash in on tribal casinos. The California Nations Indian Gaming Association insists that small tribes should not be denied the tremendous economic opportunities offered by casinos. "The reason some of these tribes have only one or two people left is because Indians were exterminated," said Susan Jensen, a spokesperson for the group ("Lawsuit in California Asks, Whose Tribe Is It, Anyway?" http://www.nytimes.com, April 10, 2002).

Tribal Casinos Off the Reservation

Another hot topic is the construction of tribal casinos on land outside reservations. According to Brad Knickerbocker in "Tribal Casinos Push Beyond Reservations" (*Christian Science Monitor*, October 14, 2005), three dozen tribes had applied to the U.S. Bureau of Indian Affairs to build casinos outside of their reservations by 2005. Many of these tribes had casinos on their reservations and were looking to expand into different markets, many closer to major cities. To build a new casino on nonreservation land, tribes must convince the BIA that they have claim to a parcel of land where they would like to build the new casino. The BIA can then put the land into a trust for the tribe.

Some of these deals involve several tribes. The Cowlitz Tribe of Washington, for instance, planned to build a casino in Ridgefield, Washington, about twenty miles north of Portland, Oregon. The tribe bought a parcel of land and petitioned the BIA to designate the land as "restored tribal land" and put it into a trust for the tribe. The casino, at 160,000 square feet, would have been the fifth-largest casino complex in the country, and the Mohegan tribe in Connecticut agreed to finance the construction and then manage the operation. Though the Cowlitz Tribe had been in southern Washington for centuries, the tribe had no reservation of its own prior to 2006. Construction of the casino was expected to commence after the BIA completed an environmental impact study on the land in 2007. In September 2006, however, the U.S. House Committee on Resources overwhelmingly approved a bill that would ban the construction of casinos off existing reservations. If the bill were to become law, the Cowlitz project would be terminated.

THE STORY OF NATIVE AMERICAN CASINOS IN TWO STATES

Connecticut

Tribal casinos are not required by law to make their financial records public. Although exact figures are not known, various reports indicate that the tribal casinos operating in Connecticut are extremely profitable. For example, in the *2006-07 Indian Gaming Industry Report* (2006), economist Alan Meister estimated the annual revenue of Connecticut's tribal casinos to be $2.3 billion.

Only two tribal casinos were operating in Connecticut as of mid 2006. The Foxwoods Casino and Resort is operated by the Mashantucket Pequot in Ledyard, and the Mohegan Sun is operated by the Mohegan in nearby Uncasville. Both are located in a rural area of eastern Connecticut.

Foxwoods is often described as the world's largest casino complex. In August 2006 it had six casinos, 1,400 hotel rooms, a spa, 25 large conference rooms, a golf and country club, a shopping mall, dozens of restaurants, and a theater that seats an audience of 1,400. Foxwoods has more than 7,000 slot machines, 400 gaming tables, and the world's largest bingo hall. It also offers keno and sports gambling. The resort receives about 40,000 visitors every day. The Mohegan Sun has almost 1,200 hotel rooms, 30 restaurants, and 300,000 square feet of casino floor. It also includes an arena that seats 10,000, a showroom, an extensive retail complex, and its own gas station.

The Foxwoods Casino in particular has an interesting history. According to Kim Isaac Eisler in *Revenge of the Pequots: How a Small Native American Tribe Created the World's Most Profitable Casino* (2001), a law passed in Connecticut in the 1980s allowed the wagering of "play money" on casino games such as blackjack, roulette, craps, and poker. The law was championed by the Mothers Against Drunk Driving organization to encourage high schools to hold casino-type events following proms to reduce drunk driving by teenagers. Under this law, the Mashantucket Pequot Tribe was able to get a license for a "charity" gambling casino. They also procured $60 million from resort developer Sol Kerzner to begin construction.

Foxwoods opened in 1992. At that time, slot machines were not permitted. In 1993 the tribe negotiated a deal with Connecticut's governor that provided the tribe with exclusive rights to operate slot machines within the state. In return, the tribe agreed to make yearly payments to the state of $100 million or 25% of the revenue from their slot machines, whichever was greater. By 1997, Foxwoods was considered the largest and most profitable casino in America.

The next year the Mohegan tribe signed its own compact with the governor to operate a casino. The Mashantucket Pequots granted the Mohegan tribe permission to include slot machines in its new casino. In return, the state set the annual payment required from each tribe at $80 million or 25% of their slot revenue, whichever was greater. The Mohegan Sun opened in 1996 after receiving financing from Sol Kerzner.

The Mashantucket Pequot's standing as a tribe is not without controversy. In *Without Reservation: The Making of America's Most Powerful Indian Tribe and Foxwoods, the World's Largest Casino* (2001), Jeff Benedict claimed that the Pequots never should have been legally recognized as a tribe by the federal government because some members were not actually descendants of the historic Pequot tribe. The tribe achieved its recognition by an act of Congress. Benedict made his allegations a major part of his unsuccessful run for Congress during the summer of 2002. He later helped found the Connecticut Alliance against Casino Expansion (CAACE), a nonprofit coalition that lobbied against additional casinos in Connecticut and successfully led the drive to repeal the state's "Las Vegas Night" law that provided the legal opening for the original casinos. CAACE also seeks federal legislation to reform the tribal recognition process.

In Connecticut, legalized gambling is regulated by the Division of Special Revenue, which conducts licensing, permitting, monitoring, and education. It also ensures that the correct revenues are transferred to the state's general fund and to each municipality that hosts a gaming facility or charitable game. Table 5.3 shows the annual and cumulative revenues paid into the general fund by the Foxwoods and Mohegan Sun casinos. Connecticut collected nearly $2.3 billion from Foxwoods between 1993 and June 2006 and $1.5 billion from Mohegan Sun between 1998 and June 2006—about 37% of all

TABLE 5.3

Connecticut tribal gaming payments to state general fund, 1993–2006

FYE 6/30	Casinos		
	Foxwoods	Mohegan Sun	Subtotal
1993	$30,000,000		30,000,000
1994	113,000,000		113,000,000
1995	135,724,017		135,724,017
1996	148,702,765		148,702,765
1997	145,957,933	$57,643,836	203,601,769
1998	165,067,994	91,007,858	256,075,852
1999	173,581,104	113,450,294	287,031,398
2000	189,235,039	129,750,030	318,985,069
2001	190,683,773	141,734,541	332,418,314
2002	199,038,210	169,915,956	368,954,166
2003	196,300,528	190,953,944	387,254,472
2004	196,883,096	205,850,884	402,733,980
2005	204,953,050	212,884,444	417,837,494
2006	204,505,785	223,020,826	427,526,611
	$2,293,633,294	**$1,536,212,613**	**3,829,845,907**

Notes:
Revenue transferred on cash basis per fiscal year.
The above transfers represent:
   a) actual lottery transfers through July 31, 2006 as reported by the Connecticut Lottery Corporation.
   b) collection of parimutuel taxes, net of payments to municipalities, for performances conducted through July 31, 2006 for the jai alai and greyhound facilities.
   c) collection of parimutuel taxes, net of payments to municipalities, for races conducted through July 31, 2006 for off-track betting.
   d) estimated sealed ticket and bingo revenue through July 31, 2006.
   e) actual casino contributions through Aug 15, 2006, based on reported video facsimile/slot machine revenue through July 31, 2006.
3. From its inception in 1976 through June 30, 1993, the off-track betting (OTB) system was state operated. For that period, transfers represented the fund balance in excess of division needs. The OTB system was sold to a private operator effective July 1, 1993 and since then transfers are based on a statutory parimutuel tax rate.

SOURCE: Adapted from "Transfers to General Fund," in *Connecticut Division of Special Revenue Transfers to General Fund*, State of Connecticut, Division of Special Revenue, August 16, 2006, http://www.ct.gov/dosr/lib/dosr/stmt2007.pdf (accessed September 6, 2006)

FIGURE 5.3

Connecticut gaming payments to state general fund, 1972–2006

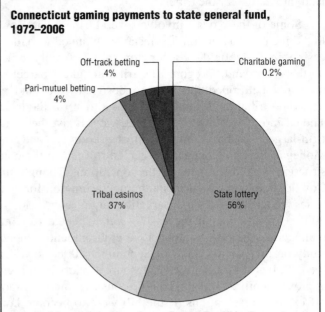

SOURCE: Adapted from "Transfers to General Fund," in *Connecticut Division of Special Revenue Transfers to General Fund*, State of Connecticut, Division of Special Revenue, August 16, 2006, http://www.ct.gov/dosr/lib/dosr/stmt2007.pdf (accessed September 6, 2006)

gambling revenue collected for the state's general fund since 1972. (See Figure 5.3.)

California

In 2006 fifty-four tribes in California had gaming operations, by far the most of any state. According to the NIGC, the state's tribal casinos earned more than $7 billion in 2005, approximately one-third of the nationwide tribal total and more than the casinos on the Las Vegas Strip. Industry analysts predict that this percentage will continue to grow as the California market matures. The state includes 106 federally recognized tribes, nearly one-fifth of the national total. Most are described as small extended family groups living on a few acres of federal trust property called *rancherias*. Some tribes have only a handful of members.

Prior to 2000 California tribes were largely limited to bingo halls because state law prohibited the operation of slot machines and other gambling devices, certain card games, banked games, and games where the house collects a share of the amount wagered. In 2000 California voters passed Proposition 1A, which amended the state constitution to permit Native American tribes to operate

lottery games, slot machines, and banking and percentage card games on tribal lands. The constitutionality of the measure was immediately challenged in court.

In January 2002 California Governor Gray Davis signed sixty-two gambling compacts with California tribes. The compacts allowed each tribe to have a maximum of 2,000 slot machines. The governor also announced plans to cap the number of slot machines in the state at 45,000. At the time, there were already 40,000 slot machines in operation and dozens of tribal casinos in the planning stages. The governor put a moratorium on new compacts while Proposition 1A made its way through the courts. In August 2002 a U.S. district court ruled that tribal casinos were entitled to operate under the provisions of the state gaming compacts and Proposition 1A.

In 2003 the State of California suffered a severe budget crisis. Davis was ultimately forced out of office through a special recall election in which Arnold Schwarzenegger became the governor. In televised campaign ads Schwarzenegger promised voters to make tribal casinos "pay their fair share," arguing that "their casinos make billions, yet pay no taxes and virtually nothing to the state." The California Nations Indian Gaming Association (CNIGA) was outraged, calling the remarks "hurtful" and accusing Schwarzenegger of having "a complete and almost frightening lack of understanding of the legal status of Indians and tribal governments." CNIGA also reminded voters that the gaming tribes paid more than $100 million per year into a special fund designated to pay for the effects of tribal gaming on local communities ("Schwarzenegger Far off the Mark on Tribal Governments,"

California Nations Indian Gaming Association press release, September 23, 2003).

In June 2004 Schwarzenegger signed new compacts that preserved the exclusive gaming rights of five California tribes: the Pala Band of Mission Indians; the Pauma Band of Mission Indians; the Rumsey Band of Wintun Indians: the United Auburn Indian Community; and the Viejas Band of Kumeyaay Indians. The slot machine cap was also raised above 2,000 machines per tribe. In exchange the tribes agreed to pay the state $1 billion up front and a licensing fee for each new slot machine added above the current limit. Payments were expected to total $150 million to $275 million per year through the compacts' expiration date in 2030.

The governor also announced plans to negotiate similar deals with other tribes in the state. However, several tribes decided to fight the new compacts. The Rincon Indian Tribe sued the state, arguing that the new compacts showed favoritism to some tribes and put others at an economic disadvantage. A federal judge, however, ruled against the Rincon. The judge reasoned that all tribes are sovereign entities, so different gambling deals could be structured by different tribes.

The state continued to form tribal compacts that permitted casino expansion in exchange for higher taxes. One of the more notable deals was made with the Agua Caliente Band of Cahuilla Indians. The tribe owned two casinos in Palm Springs. In August 2006 the state agreed to let them open a third casino with 5,000 slot machines if the tribe paid an estimated $1.9 billion in taxes over the following 23 years. Many Californians were concerned that if such deal-making were allowed to continue, casinos could be as prevalent as shopping malls and lead to higher instances of gambling addiction.

CHAPTER 6

THE ECONOMIC AND SOCIAL EFFECTS OF CASINOS

Assessing the effects of casinos on society is complicated because many factors have to be considered. Most relate to economics, but some address quality of life and moral issues. Proponents of casino gambling consider it part of the leisure and entertainment sector—like amusement parks or movie theaters. In a casino, participants exchange their money for a good time. Those who support casino gambling generally do not see it as a moral issue.

Opponents are less unified in their opinions. Some disapprove of gambling on religious grounds because it contradicts moral principles of thrift, hard work, and sober living. Others are wary of an industry that was associated with mobsters, swindlers, and corrupt politicians throughout much of its history in this country. Still others point out that casinos provide a place for those who are prone to problem gambling to act on those urges. Easy accessibility to casinos, they say, encourages some people to gamble who otherwise would not and should not. Outlawing casinos is one way to protect people from their own bad judgment.

There is also the so-called NIMBY factor: "not in my backyard." Some people support casinos in theory and may even visit them on vacation, but they do not want them in their hometowns, for whatever reason. According to an annual survey by the American Gaming Association (AGA), four out of ten Americans did not want a casino in their own neighborhoods, although just over five out of ten thought casino gambling was perfectly acceptable for anyone (*2004 State of the States: The AGA Survey of Casino Entertainment*). Local residents and politicians are often opposed to casinos because they fear increased traffic and crime and may want to protect their communities' image. Also, many state governments are running lotteries and do not want competition from casinos for their residents' gambling dollars.

NATIONAL PUBLIC OPINION

According to *Gambling: As the Take Rises So Does Public Concern* by Paul Taylor, Cary Funk, and Peyton Craighill (Pew Research Center, May 2006), 42% of the people surveyed said casinos are detrimental to their communities, while 34% said casinos have a positive impact. The rest did not have an opinion or could not decide. However, a smaller percentage of people who lived near a casino (38%) had negative views of casinos' influence on their communities than those who did not live near a casino (42%). (See Table 6.1.) The 2004 AGA poll, conducted by Peter D. Hart Research Associates and Luntz, Maslansky Strategic Research, showed that about two-thirds of those surveyed believed that casinos brought widespread economic benefits to other industries and businesses in their region.

It is perhaps not surprising that elected officials and civic leaders had a much more positive view of casinos in their communities. A 2005 poll taken for the AGA asked 201 elected officials and civic leaders about the effects of casinos in their communities: 79% said casinos had had a positive impact, while only 13% saw a negative impact (*2005 State of the States: The AGA Survey of Casino Entertainment*). Some 63% praised casinos as helping other businesses, and 79% touted casinos as being responsible corporate citizens.

THE EFFECTS OF NATIVE AMERICAN CASINOS

Native American tribes that encounter opposition to their casino plans attribute opposition to the same issues faced by corporate casinos, although some also see racism as a factor.

The Pros

In 2005 the National Indian Gaming Association (NIGA) published *An Analysis of the Economic Impact*

TABLE 6.1

Public opinion on the impact of casinos on local communities, 2006

OVERALL, WOULD YOU SAY CASINOS HAVE A POSITIVE OR NEGATIVE IMPACT ON THE LOCAL COMMUNITY?

	All adults	Casino nearby	Casino not nearby	Been to casino?	
				Yes	No
	%	%	%	%	%
Positive	34	40	30	52	26
Negative	42	38	45	27	49
Both/neither (volunteered)	10	12	8	10	9
Don't know	14	10	17	11	16
	100	100	100	100	100

SOURCE: Paul Taylor, Cary Funk, and Peyton Craighill, "Are Casinos Good for the Local Community," in *Gambling: As the Take Rises, So Does Public Concern*, Pew Research Center, May 23, 2006, http://pewresearch.org/assets/social/pdf/Gambling.pdf (accessed September 6, 2006)

of Indian Gaming in 2004. The report notes that tribal gaming and associated businesses had:

- generated revenues of nearly $18.5 billion in 2004

- created nearly 553,000 jobs

- paid wages of approximately $6 billion to employees of tribal governments and economic development enterprises

- provided millions of dollars to nongaming tribes through special trust funds

- provided a means for trade and commerce between gaming and nongaming tribes—for example, through the purchase of goods and services

- contributed more than $100 million to charities and nonprofit organizations in 2004

- funded essential tribal programs, such as schools; hospitals; water and sewer systems; roads; police and firefighting programs; and cultural and social projects

The report concludes that "gaming has given Tribal leaders the opportunity to acquire the knowledge, skills and self-confidence needed to build strong Tribal governments and, for the first time in generations, provide for the health, education, and welfare of their people."

A study by Jonathan B. Taylor and Joseph P. Kalt (*The American Indians on Reservations: A Databook of Socioeconomic Change between the 1990 and 2000 Censuses*, Harvard University, 2005) found that income increased by 35% between 1990 and 2000 on non–Navajo gaming reservations, while income only grew by 14% on nongaming, non-Navajo reservations. (Navajo do not have casinos, and the Navajo reservation has more than ten times the membership of any other Native American tribe.)

Most tribal lands are located in areas of the country that have limited natural resources and industry, so tribal casinos often bring much needed wealth to the tribes and their neighbors. The NIGA report pointed to specific instances in which gaming helped to revitalize impoverished communities in and around Native American lands. For example, in 1995 Del Norte was one of the more indigent counties in California: the biggest economic development in the works was a new maximum-security prison in Crescent City. Then the Tolowan Tribe opened Elk Valley Rancheria and Casino, also in Crescent City. It quickly became the county's largest employer, providing more than 5,000 new jobs for tribal and nontribal members of the community by 2004. Using money from the casino, the tribe helped finance a $35 million wastewater-treatment plant in the county.

Another example is Avoyelles Parish in central Louisiana, which was one of the poorest counties in the state until the Tunica-Biloxi Tribe built the Paragon Casino and Resort in 1994. NIGA reported that the casino contributed greatly to the local economy, purchasing more than $20 million in goods yearly from area vendors. As of 2006 the casino and resort employed 1,780 people, and an expansion was under way that included a new hotel, performance center, movie theatre, retail shops, spa, cocktail lounge, and coffee shop (http://www.paragoncasinoresort.com/about/coming.asp). According to the Bureau of Labor Statistics (BLS), the unemployment rate for Avoyelles Parish averaged 8.4% in 1996; by 2006 it had declined significantly, averaging 4.7% during the first nine months of the year ("Local Area Unemployment Statistics," November 2006).

The Cons

Critics contend that tribal casinos:

- unfairly compete against local hotels, restaurants, and pari-mutuel operators

- hurt state lottery sales

- place an increased burden on states to address problems resulting from pathological gambling

- introduce opportunities for money laundering and organized crime

Some critics say casinos encourage and perpetuate a cycle of dependence: tribe members who were formerly dependent on the federal government are now dependent on their tribal governments. They believe that, ultimately, casinos will hurt the culture and political stability of the tribes.

A report by Charlene W. Simmons (*Gambling in the Golden State, 1998 Forward*, California State Library, May 2006) cataloged all the known positive and negative effects that Native American casinos had had on California communities. According to the report, Indian casinos led to slightly higher incidences of bankruptcy and crime, particularly violent crimes such as aggravated assault. The casinos also strained the local infrastructure. Most of the casinos brought many people into rural areas with narrow two-lane roads and limited sewage systems. While casinos helped the economies of their immediate communities, they often siphoned money away from adjacent communities: people spent their money at casinos rather than at stores and eating establishments in their own neighborhoods.

THE LACK OF BALANCED DATA

In 1996 Congress created the National Gambling Impact Study Commission (NGISC) to examine the economic and social impacts of legalized gambling. After conducting hearings in Las Vegas, Atlantic City, Chicago, San Diego, and Biloxi, Mississippi, the commission made these assessments:

- Casinos are associated with increased per capita income in the construction, hotel, lodging, recreation, and amusement industries but decreased per capita income for those working in local restaurants and bars.

- The financial benefits of casinos are particularly impressive in economically depressed communities.

- Casinos create full-time entry-level jobs that are badly needed in areas suffering from chronic unemployment and underemployment.

- Unemployment rates, welfare payments, and unemployment insurance declined by approximately one-seventh in communities close to newly opened casinos.

- In terms of income, health insurance, and pensions, casino jobs in the destination resorts of Las Vegas and Atlantic City are better than comparable jobs in the service industries.

- Small business owners located near casinos often suffer from loss of business.

- Tribal casino workers have complained about lack of job security, an absence of federal and state antidiscrimination laws, and the lack of workers' compensation benefits.

- Elected officials from casino towns expressed support for casinos because they improved the quality of life in their towns and funded community improvements.

- Problems with pathological gambling increased in seven of nine communities surveyed.

- The American Gaming Association is the largest source of funding for research on pathological gambling.

- Many casinos train management and staff to identify problem gamblers among customers or employees.

- Many tribal casinos contribute money to nonprofit groups dealing with problem gambling.

The report concluded that lack of objective research data on gambling issues was a major hurdle in determining the extent of its effects on society.

PURE ECONOMICS

Altogether, American casinos took in nearly $52.6 billion during 2005, making the casino industry a very big business. Most casinos have been huge successes for their investors, who range from middle-class stockholders in major corporations to billionaires like Donald Trump and Steve Wynn. Most tribal casinos have been economically successful as well, bringing unimagined wealth to Native Americans, many of whom were at the very bottom of the U.S. economic ladder only a decade ago. Casinos are also labor-intensive businesses that employ hundreds of thousands of people, who support their families, pay taxes, and buy goods and services—factors that contribute to the economic health of their communities.

The economic effects of casinos on local and state governments are also significant. Commercial casinos pay billions of dollars every year to government agencies in the form of application fees, regulatory fees, wagering taxes, and admission taxes. While governments incur increased costs for more police, roads, and sewers, casino taxes and fees help fund programs that improve the quality of life in the immediate vicinity or state. Tribal casinos, though exempt from state and local taxation, pay billions of dollars each year to compensate states and municipalities for regulatory and public-service expenses.

Economic factors alone do not justify or vilify an industry. Benefits and harms must be weighed against one another. In addition to crime, bankruptcy, and suicide rates, important issues that are affected by the presence of casinos include employment, tourism, compulsive and underage gambling, and politics.

DIRECT GOVERNMENT REVENUE

From Commercial Casinos

In its *2006 State of the States* survey, the AGA reported that commercial casinos generated tax revenues of $4.9 billion in 2005, up from $4.7 billion in 2004 (http://www.american gaming.org/assets/files/2006_Survey _for_Web.pdf). Nevada generated the most gambling tax revenue in 2005 ($952.6 million), followed by Indiana ($777.8 million) and Illinois ($749.7 million). (See Figure 6.1.) Racetrack casinos paid taxes of $1.3 billion to local and state governments in 2005, up from $1.1 billion in 2004.

The AGA reported in its *2003 State of the States* survey that 70% of respondents said legalized casino gambling was a good way to generate local and state revenues without having a general tax increase. However, respondents seemed uncertain as to how those gaming tax

FIGURE 6.1

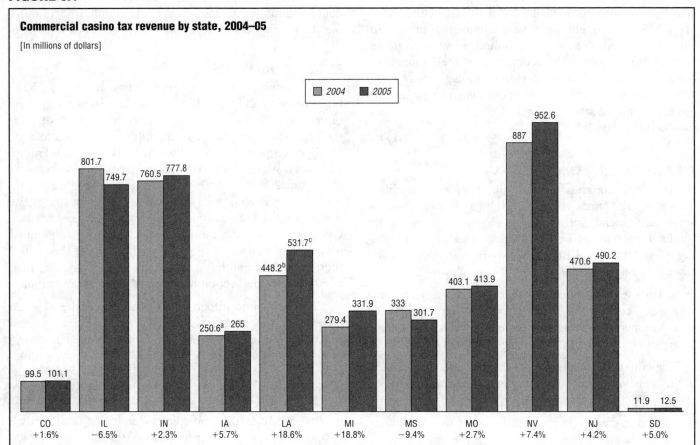

Commercial casino tax revenue by state, 2004–05

[In millions of dollars]

Legend: 2004, 2005

State	2004	2005
CO +1.6%	99.5	101.1
IL −6.5%	801.7	749.7
IN +2.3%	760.5	777.8
IA +5.7%	250.6[a]	265
LA +18.6%	448.2[b]	531.7[c]
MI +18.8%	279.4	331.9
MS −9.4%	333	301.7
MO +2.7%	403.1	413.9
NV +7.4%	887	952.6
NJ +4.2%	470.6	490.2
SD +5.0%	11.9	12.5

[a]Iowa revised its tax contribution figures after the release date of the 2005 state of the states report. This year's report has been amended to reflect the more accurate data.
[b]The 2005 state of the states incorrectly excluded local parish taxes in its 2004 tax revenue figure. This year's report has been amended to correct this error.
[c]Figure does not include taxes paid by two gaming properties that were unable to access record stop articipate in the American Gaming Association's (AGA) data-gathering efforts.

SOURCE: "Commercial Casino Tax Revenue by State, 2004 vs. 2005," in *2006 State of the States: The AGA Survey of Casino Entertainment*, American Gaming Association, 2006, http://www.americangaming.org/assets/files/2006_Survey_for_Web.pdf (accessed September 6, 2006). Data from State Gaming Regulatory Agencies. Reprinted with permission from the American Gaming Association. All rights reserved.

revenues were used. Only 58% of those polled agreed that such revenues have helped pay for local roads, schools, hospitals, and other projects.

When polled by the AGA in 2004, some 67% of elected officials and civic leaders with casinos in their communities said that the casinos had increased the tax revenue in their communities (http://www. americangaming. org/assets/files/uploads/2005_State_of_the_States.pdf). More important, 73% of those community leaders agreed that such tax revenue and casino-development agreements allowed their communities to complete projects that would not have been feasible without the additional revenue.

Gaming taxes can be a substantial portion of a state's revenue. Nevada's budget in 2005 was $5.7 billion. According to the Nevada Gaming Commission, casino taxes amounted to roughly 18% of state revenues that year. This amount was six times higher than the revenue generated by property taxes.

Total taxes collected in Mississippi in 2005 amounted to $5.4 billion, as reported by the U.S. Census (http://www.census.gov/govs/statetax/0525msstax.html). Gaming taxes amounted to approximately 6% of those taxes, with $335 million collected during the fiscal year ending June 30, 2005, according to the Mississippi Gaming Commission (http://www.mstc.state.ms.us/taxareas/misc/gaming/stats/gamtax.pdf). This meant that casino taxes contributed more to the state budget in 2005 than the combined corporate income taxes paid by all other corporations in the state ($283 million).

From Native American Casinos

The Indian Gaming Regulatory Act requires that net revenues from tribal gaming be used to fund tribal government operations and programs; to promote tribal economic development; to donate to charitable organizations; and to help fund operations of local government agencies. (See Chapter 5.)

The revenues earned by tribal casinos are not taxable because the casinos are operated by tribal governments: just as the U.S. government does not tax the states for revenue earned from lottery tickets, it does not tax tribal governments for revenue earned from casinos. Therefore, tribal casinos generate less tax revenue than commercial casinos. Tribe members who live on reservations and are employed at tribal enterprises, such as casinos, are not subject to state income taxes. On the other hand, tribe members do pay federal income tax, FICA, and Social Security taxes on their wages, even if those wages are earned at tribal enterprises. Wages paid to tribe members living off reservations and to nontribe employees are subject to state income taxes.

In *An Analysis of the Economic Impact of Indian Gaming in 2004* the NIGA revealed that tribal casinos and associated business generated $5.5 billion in federal taxes during 2004. That amount included employer and employee Social Security taxes, personal and corporate income taxes, and excise taxes.

According to the report, tribal governments spent more than $290 million on regulatory costs in 2004, including $228 million on tribal regulatory entities, $58 million paid to state agencies, and $11 million paid to the NIGC for oversight expenses. The NIGA also noted that tribal casinos and associated businesses generated approximately $1.8 billion in state revenues during 2004 through revenue-sharing plans and taxes on gaming and related businesses; it estimated that tribal gaming generated $100 million in revenue for local governments. Furthermore, according to the NIGA, jobs created by tribal casinos reduced federal unemployment and welfare payments by $1.4 billion during 2004.

EMPLOYMENT AND CAREERS

As of May 2005 about 423,000 people were directly employed by casino hotels or other gambling establishments, with many thousands more employed indirectly through related businesses or on a contract basis, according to the Bureau of Labor Statistics (BLS; *Occupational Employment Statistics*, 2006). Because they are employed in an entertainment and hospitality industry, gaming workers need excellent communication and customer-service skills, but the financial aspect of casino activities also requires personal integrity and the ability to maintain composure when dealing with angry or emotional patrons. A high school diploma or the equivalent is usually preferred for all entry-level jobs. Table 6.2 describes the duties, qualifications, training requirements, and earnings of several categories of casino workers.

All casino employees—from managers to dealers to slot repair technicians—must be at least twenty-one years old and have licenses from the appropriate regulatory agency. Obtaining a license requires a background investigation—applicants can be disqualified from casino employment for a variety of reasons, including links to organized crime, a felony record, and gambling-related offenses. Requirements for education, training, and experience are up to individual casinos. The BLS considers the overall employment outlook for the industry to be good, as increasing competition should result in more jobs for gaming workers. Gaming dealers and gaming managers, in particular, are predicted to be among the fastest growing U.S. occupations between 2004 and 2014, with an increase between 18% and 26% during that period (*2006–07 Occupational Outlook Handbook*, http://www.bls.gov/oco/ocos275.htm).

The growth of the casino employment market has spurred a related increase in vocational and professional training for casino workers. The University of Nevada at Las Vegas, only one-and-a-half miles from the Strip, offers a major in gaming management that includes instruction in gaming operations, marketing, hospitality, security, and regulations. At Tulane University's School of Continuing Studies in New Orleans, students can choose from several programs lasting between one and four years, including a bachelor's degree in casino resort management. Students pursuing a degree in hospitality and tourism management at the University of Massachusetts can specialize in casino management. Central Michigan University, which is located near the Soaring Eagle Casino and Resort operated by the Saginaw Chippewa Tribe, offers a business degree in gaming and entertainment management, including coursework in the protection of casino table games, gaming regulations and control, the mathematics of casino games, and the sociology of gambling. The Casino Career Institute, which includes a large mock casino, is a division of Atlantic Cape Community College in downtown Atlantic City, New Jersey. When it opened in 1978 it was the first gaming school in the country affiliated with a community college.

Employment at Commercial Casinos

According to the AGA's 2006 survey, commercial casinos employed nearly 355,000 people in 2005, up slightly from 2004. Nevada accounted for 57% of the total. (See Figure 6.2.) In addition, racetrack casinos in Delaware, Iowa, Louisiana, Maine, New Mexico, New York, Rhode Island, and West Virginia employed about 17,200 people during 2005, up 20% from 2004 and up 215% from 2001.

Employment at commercial casinos grew rapidly during the 1990s, then stagnated overall between 2000 and 2005. In 2000 the AGA reported 356,860 casino employees nationwide, which was more than the 2005 figure of 354,921. In Mississippi casino employment decreased 21% from 36,306 in 2000 to 28,820 in 2005, based on figures submitted for the last quarter of operations

TABLE 6.2

Casino occupations, 2006

Title	Responsibilities	Education/training	Salary
Gaming supervisors	Oversee gaming operations and personnel in an assigned area. Circulate among the tables to ensure that all stations and games are attended to each shift. Interpret the casino's operating rules for patrons. Plan and organize activities for guests staying at casino hotels. Address service complaints.	Associates or Bachelor's degree. Hands-on experience may be substituted for formal education. Most supervisors gain experience in other gaming jobs before moving into supervisory positions.	Median $40,840/year
Slot key persons (also called slot attendants or slot technicians)	Coordinate and supervise the slot department and its workers. Verify and handle payoff winnings to patrons, reset slot machines after payoffs, refill slot machines with money, make minor repairs and adjustment to the machines, enforce safety rules and report hazards.	No formal education requirements, but completion of technical training helpful. Most positions are entry-level and provide on-the-job training.	Median $23,010/year
Gaming change persons and booth cashiers	Exchange coins and tokens for patrons' money. Issue payoffs or obtain a patron's signature on a receipt when the winnings exceed the amount held in the slot machine. Count and audit money in cash drawers.	Usually trained in-house. Should have experience handling cash or using calculators or adding machines. May have to pass a math test.	Median $9.87/hour
Gaming and sports book writers and runners	Assist in the operation of games such as bingo. Scan tickets presented by patrons and calculate and distribute winnings. May operate equipment that randomly selects the numbers, announce numbers selected, pick up tickets from patrons, collect bets, or receive, verify, and record patrons' cash wagers.	High school diploma or GED. Usually trained on the job.	Median $18,390/year
Gaming dealers	Operate casino table games such as craps, baccarat, blackjack, or roulette. Determine winners of game, calculate and pay winning bets, and collect losing bets. May be required to monitor patrons to determine if they are following the rules of a particular game.	Completion of a training program at a vocational or technical school. An in-depth knowledge of casino games may be substituted for formal education. Most casinos require employees to audition for such jobs.	Median $14,320/year

SOURCE: Adapted from "Gaming Service Occupations," in *2006–07 Occupational Outlook Handbook*, U.S. Department of Labor, Bureau of Labor Statistics, August 2006, http://www.bls.gov/oco/ocos275.htm (accessed September 6, 2006)

before Hurricane Katrina interrupted business along the Mississippi Gulf Coast in August. Illinois casino employment was down 15% from 10,566 to 8,987, and New Jersey casino employment declined 6% from 47,366 in 2000 to 44,542 in 2005. Missouri and Iowa each experienced a loss of about 900 casino jobs over the period.

Not all areas of the country suffered a decline, however. In Michigan, employment was up 47% from 4,895 in 2000 to 7,187 in 2005, and in Colorado casino employment reached 8,029 in 2005 from 5,923 in 2000, a 36% increase. Nevada, the country's largest commercial casino market, which lost 13,000 casino jobs in the economic downturn that followed the terrorist attacks of September 11, 2001, experienced a 2% increase overall during the period, from 198,992 in 2000 to 202,209 in 2005, according to the AGA.

While employment numbers fell and then rose again during the period 2000 to 2005, commercial casino wages rose steadily. In 2000, according to the AGA's *2001 State of the States*, commercial casino wages totaled $10.9 billion; as of 2005 wages reached $12.6 billion (*2006 State of the States*), an increase of nearly 16%.

Employment at Native American Casinos

In its analysis of Indian gaming in 2004, the NIGA reported that tribal gambling directly employed 220,000

people during 2004. (See Figure 6.3.) About 158,000 of those jobs were at tribal casinos; the other jobs were at indirectly associated businesses and tribal government enterprises. Seventy-nine thousand other jobs were attributed to the indirect effects of tribal casinos—for example, businesses at which casino workers spent their wages. The NIGA estimated that tribal casinos were indirectly responsible for 214,000 other jobs by purchasing goods and services from businesses around the country. Capital construction projects—for example, casino building—were associated with the creation of 40,000 other jobs. In total the NIGA credited tribal gaming for the employment of 553,000 people during 2004.

The NIGA estimated that in 2004 roughly 25% of tribal casino employees were Native Americans and 75% were non–Native Americans. In some cases the percentages reflected the fact that several tribes had fewer members than employees.

Historically, employees at tribal casinos have not been covered by the federal labor laws that protect workers at commercial casinos. As sovereign entities tribes were considered excluded from Title VII of the Civil Rights Act of 1964 and Title I of the Americans with Disabilities Act of 1990, which prohibit discrimination in employment on the basis of race, sex, physical impair-

FIGURE 6.2

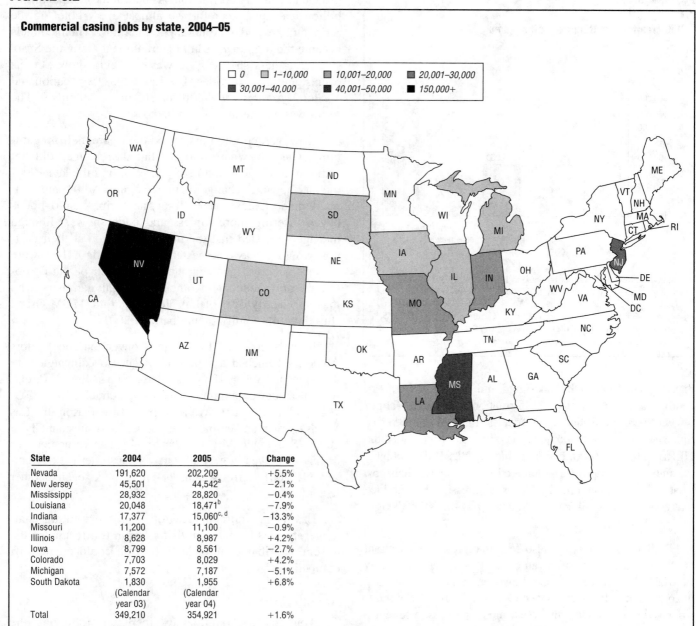

Commercial casino jobs by state, 2004–05

Legend			
☐ 0	▨ 1–10,000	▨ 10,001–20,000	▨ 20,001–30,000
▨ 30,001–40,000	▨ 40,001–50,000	■ 150,000+	

State	2004	2005	Change
Nevada	191,620	202,209	+5.5%
New Jersey	45,501	44,542[a]	−2.1%
Mississippi	28,932	28,820	−0.4%
Louisiana	20,048	18,471[b]	−7.9%
Indiana	17,377	15,060[c, d]	−13.3%
Missouri	11,200	11,100	−0.9%
Illinois	8,628	8,987	+4.2%
Iowa	8,799	8,561	−2.7%
Colorado	7,703	8,029	+4.2%
Michigan	7,572	7,187	−5.1%
South Dakota	1,830	1,955	+6.8%
	(Calendar year 03)	(Calendar year 04)	
Total	349,210	354,921	+1.6%

[a]Figure for locations with gross gaming revenue in excess of $1 million for fiscal year 2005.
[b]For Mississippi properties affected by hurricane Katrina, figures represent totals as of the end of second quarter 2005.
[c]Louisiana properties affected by hurricanes Katrina and Rita submitted pre-storm employment data for this report.
[d]Figure does not include employees from two gaming properties that were unable to access records to participate in the American Gaming Association's (AGA) data-gathering efforts.

SOURCE: "Commercial Casino Jobs by State, 2004 vs. 2005," in *2006 State of the States: The AGA Survey of Casino Entertainment*, American Gaming Association, 2006, http://www.americangaming.org/assets/files/2006_Survey_for_Web.pdf (accessed September 6, 2006). Data from State Gaming Regulatory Agencies, State Gaming Associations, and Individual Properties. Reprinted with permission from the American Gaming Association. All rights reserved.

ment, and other criteria. In addition the National Labor Relations Act exempts government entities from the requirement that they allow employees to form unions. Tribes, having been ruled to be sovereign governments by both the National Labor Relations Board (NLRB) and a federal court, operated under their own laws and blocked unions if they chose to do so.

However, some court cases have held that Occupational Safety and Health Administration (OSHA) requirements, the Fair Labor Standards Act, and the Employee Retirement Income Security Act do apply to tribal businesses conducted on reservations. And the NLRB, after a challenge by UNITE HERE, a union that represents hotel and restaurant employees, in 2004 overturned thirty years of precedent and ruled

FIGURE 6.3

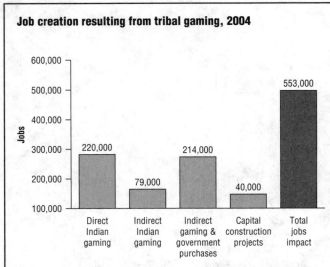

Job creation resulting from tribal gaming, 2004

SOURCE: "Direct and Indirect Increase in Employment, 2004 Gains, Due to Class II and III Indian Gaming," in *Tribal Government Gaming: The Native American Success Story—An Analysis of the Economic Impact of Indian Gaming in 2004*, National Indian Gaming Association, 2005, http://www.indiangaming.org/NIGA_econ_impact_2004.pdf (accessed September 14, 2006)

that the San Manuel Indian Bingo and Casino in Southern California could not stop the formation of a union (http://www.nlrb.gov/nlrb/shared_files/decisions/341/341-138.pdf). Since then the tribe, in conjunction with other tribes, sued the NLRB in federal court, claiming that the NLRB did not have the authority to impose labor-protection laws on tribal casinos. That case is still pending. In 2006 a congressional committee was considering a bill that would take away the NLRB's right to regulate the tribes' activities.

Tribal sovereignty has also been interpreted to mean that employees at Native American casinos were not covered by state labor laws. In recent years, however, tribal-state compacts negotiated in California, Connecticut, New York, and Wisconsin have recognized the right of casino employees to be represented by unions as their collective-bargaining agents.

TOURISM

According to the AGA in *2006 State of the States*, 72% of those polled in 2005 said casinos can play an important role in a community's entertainment and tourism options.

Las Vegas

No destination better represents the marriage between gambling and tourism than Las Vegas. It has had its ups and downs, however. In the early 1990s the city experienced a steep decline in revenues because of competition from legal gambling on riverboats and tribal casinos in other states (http://gaming.nv.gov/gaming_revenue_rpt.htm). To counteract this development, the city began a drive to shift its focus from an adult play-

ground to a family destination. As part of the campaign $12 billion was spent to refurbish almost every hotel on the Strip and to add entertainment facilities. Theme hotels became the big draw. Adult entertainment along the Strip, such as topless shows, gave way to magic shows, circus events, and carnival rides. The Las Vegas Convention and Visitors' Authority focused advertising on families. The result was a huge increase in visitors.

However, children distracted their parents from gambling. Casino owners noticed that the changes did not bring in more gambling revenue, so during the late 1990s the city began to change its image again. Adult entertainment made a comeback along the Strip: casino–hotels began offering more topless and nude shows, although managers insisted that the nudity presented at their casinos would always be tasteful and artistic. They were anxious not to offend shareholders of their parent corporations or to alienate women, potential gamblers who make up nearly 60% of Las Vegas visitors. MGM Grand shut down its family theme park in 2001.

In early 2003 the Las Vegas Convention and Visitors Authority launched a somewhat risqué ad campaign with the slogan "What Happens Here, Stays Here" (http://www.usatoday.com/money/advertising/adtrack/2003-08-03-vegas_x.htm). It may have been part of the reason that Las Vegas tourism and casino revenue increased substantially in 2005. (See Figure 4.1 in Chapter 4.) The resurgence of travel—it slowed in general for two years after the September 11, 2001, terrorist attacks—may have been another factor.

Las Vegas tourism faces one particular future challenge: it relies heavily on visitors from California, so the advent of tribal gaming in California could create stiff competition.

Atlantic City

Tourism in Atlantic City increased following the introduction of casino gambling, but not as fast or as much as many had hoped. From the 1880s to the 1940s, Atlantic City was a major tourist destination, particularly for people living in the Northeast. Visitors went for the beaches and to walk along the town's boardwalk and piers, which featured carnival-like entertainment. During the 1950s and 1960s, the town fell into economic depression as tourists ventured farther south to beaches in Florida and the Caribbean.

Casino gambling was legalized in 1976 in the hopes that the city would recapture its former glory and rival Las Vegas as a tourist destination. Progress was slow through the 1980s and early 1990s: although visitors began to go to Atlantic City, they mostly arrived by bus or car and stayed only for a day or two. In 1984 the state established the Casino Reinvestment Development

Authority (CRDA) to revitalize the city using the funds from a 1.25% tax on casino revenues.

The economic troubles that had ravaged the town's businesses before gambling was legalized were not easily overcome. Vacant lots, buildings in disrepair, and housing projects surrounded the casinos. The overall atmosphere was not particularly appealing to vacationers or convention-goers. Mike Kelly, a reporter for a West Paterson, New Jersey, newspaper, described the city in 1993 as "trapped in a web of poverty and blight" ("Gambling with Our Future: City Poised to Hit Jackpot, or Lose Everything," *The Record*, July 1, 1993). At that time, the typical visitor was a retiree who arrived by bus and stayed only for the day. According to Kelly, Atlantic City's thirty million annual visitors actually represented about five million people making multiple trips.

In the late 1990s initiatives by CRDA and other groups began to pay off. Hundreds of new homes were built, and commercial businesses were established. One of the largest convention centers in the country—it has thirty-one acres of space—opened in May 1997. The city's image began to improve, and tourism showed a moderate surge. City and casino officials still see three factors that limit tourism growth in Atlantic City, however: lack of a major airport; lack of usable land; and cold winters.

CRIME

Officials must realize that legal gambling will attract an unsavory element that can jeopardize the safety and well-being of the city's residents and the many visitors who come to gamble.

—*FBI Law Enforcement Bulletin*, Federal Bureau of Investigation, January 2001

When gambling was legalized in Nevada in 1931, the law kept corporations out of the casino business by requiring that every shareholder obtain a gaming license. This law, which was designed to safeguard the integrity of the casinos, unintentionally gave organized crime a huge advantage. The nation was in the midst of the Great Depression, and building a flashy casino–hotel was expensive. Few legitimate businessmen had the cash, and banks were reluctant to loan money for what they saw as a poor investment. Organized crime groups had made fortunes selling bootleg liquor during Prohibition, so they were able to make the capital investments needed to build and operate lavish casino–hotels that attracted visitors.

The marriage between casinos and organized crime in Nevada lasted for decades but was eventually ended by gaming officials and law enforcement. Today there is no strong evidence of organized crime activity in the casino industry. Regulatory agencies keep a watchful eye on casinos to make sure mobsters and their associates do not gain a new foothold.

TABLE 6.3

Arrests made by Missouri Gaming Division troopers, by charges filed, July 2004–June 2005

Type of charge	Number
Arson	1
Assault	44
Burglary	2
Damaged property	16
Dangerous drugs	73
Family offense	8
Flight/escape	13
Forgery	53
Fraud	44
Violation of gambling laws	230
Invasion of privacy	2
Violation of liquor laws	7
Miscellaneous federal charges	6
Motor vehicle	81
Obstruction of judicial process	598
Obstructing police	18
Peace disturbance	7
Public order	1
Robbery	v
Sex offenses	3
Sexual assault	1
Stealing	158
Stolen property	5
Weapons	5
Total charges	***1,380**

Notes: These totals reflect the number of charges filed by agents of the commission. The number of individuals arrested will be lower as some individuals may have multiple charges filed as a result of an individual incident. These totals also include arrests made attendant to outstanding warrants for criminal activity that did not occur on property of excursion gambling boats.

SOURCE: "Charges Filed as a Result of Arrests Made by Troopers Assigned to the Gaming Division from July 1, 2004 through June 30, 2005," in *Missouri Gaming Commission, Annual Report to the General Assembly, Fiscal Year 2005*, Missouri Gaming Commission, 2005, http://www.mgc.dps.mo.gov/annual%20reports/2005/annual2005.pdf (accessed September 6, 2006)

Casinos keep an equally watchful eye on their patrons and employees. The casino floor is constantly monitored by a host of security guards and cameras. Observers watch dealers and patrons at the gaming tables and all money-counting areas. Some casinos use high-tech facial recognition programs to scan incoming patrons and quickly identify any known felons or other undesirables. Although the industry does not release data on crimes committed by casino employees, analysts say employee theft and embezzlement account for millions of dollars in losses each year.

Vice crimes, particularly prostitution, and weapons crimes also occur. Details of the type of crimes found around casinos are illustrated by the *Missouri Gaming Commission Annual Report to the General Assembly: Fiscal Year 2005*. Commission agents filed 1,380 charges between July 1, 2004, and June 30, 2005, as shown in Table 6.3. The total includes charges for acts committed at the casinos as well as arrests made for criminal activities that did not occur on casino property. Roughly half of the charges (598) were made against people who obstructed the judicial process in cases involving gambling. Two hundred thirty people were charged with violating gambling laws, and 158 people were charged with stealing.

The amount of crime in a community with a casino has a direct relationship to the maturity of the casino, according to a study by Earl L. Grinols of Baylor University and David B. Mustard of the University of Georgia ("Casinos, Crime, and Community Costs," *Review of Economics and Statistics*, April 2006). They collected crime data from all 3,165 counties in the United States with and without casinos between 1977 and 1996. Their analysis showed that when a casino first opened in a county, crime changed very little, but slowly rose and then grew steadily in subsequent years. While increased employment and expanded law enforcement might reduce crime initially, over time these effects were overtaken by factors related to casinos. "Specifically, problem and pathological gamblers commit crime as they deplete their resources, nonresidents who visit casinos may both commit and be victims of crime, and casino-induced changes in the population start small but grow," the researchers said. Overall, according to their analysis, 8.6% of property crimes and 12.6% of violent crimes (which include robberies) in counties with casinos were due to the presence of the casinos. They found "mixed evidence" about whether casino openings increase crime rates in neighboring counties.

SUICIDE

The possible link between casino gambling and suicide rates has been the subject of much investigation. For example, a 1997 study in *Suicide & Life-Threatening Behavior* concluded that "visitors to and residents of major gaming communities experience significantly elevated suicide levels" (David P. Phillips et al., "Elevated Suicide Levels Associated with Legalized Gambling," December 1997). They found that in Atlantic City "abnormally high suicide levels" for visitors and residents appeared only after casinos opened. However, five years later another study in the same journal found little to no correlation between suicide rates and the presence of casino gambling in U.S. communities (Richard McCleary et al., "Does Legalized Gambling Elevate the Risk of Suicide?" July 2002). After comparing the 1990 suicide rates of 148 metropolitan areas in different regions of the country, the researchers found that the presence of casinos could account for only 1% of the regional differences in suicide rates. They also compared "before and after" suicide rates for cities in which gambling had been legalized. Although increased suicide rates were noted in Atlantic County, New Jersey, and Harrison County, Mississippi, after the advent of gambling, the increases were not considered statistically significant. The study notes that suicide rates dropped significantly in Lawrence County, South Dakota, after casino gambling was introduced in the town of Deadwood.

TABLE 6.4

Suicide rates by state, 2003

[By number and rate per 100,000 population]

State	Deaths	Rate
Wyoming	109	21.8
Montana	180	19.6
Nevada	434	19.4
Alaska	124	19.1
New Mexico	343	18.3
Oregon	592	16.6
Colorado	728	16.0
Idaho	217	15.9
Arizona	840	15.1
West Virginia	266	14.7
Utah	336	14.2
Kentucky	567	13.8
Arkansas	374	13.7
Oklahoma	476	13.6
Florida	2,297	13.5
Vermont	83	13.4
South Dakota	102	13.3
Washington	803	13.1
Tennessee	762	13.0
North Dakota	102	12.8
United States	31,484	10.8

SOURCE: Created by John Weier for Thomson Gale, 2006

Nevada, a state in which gambling is widely practiced, has the third-highest suicide rate in the nation. According to the Centers for Disease Control and Prevention, the suicide rate in Nevada in 2003 was 19.4 suicides per 100,000 population. (See Table 6.4.) This was nearly twice the national average of 10.8 per 100,000 population. However, many mental health experts attribute Nevada's high suicide rate to the huge inflow of new residents who lack a support system of family and friends. Loneliness and despair are more likely to overwhelm such people than those who have an emotional safety net in place. In general, suicide rates are higher in the western states than in any other region. Even Utah, which allows no legal gambling, was among the fifteen states with the highest suicide rates in 2003, with a rate of 14.2 suicides per 100,000 population.

BANKRUPTCY

Establishing a definitive link between gambling habits and bankruptcy is difficult. A study published in 2001 by SMR Research Corporation of Hackettstown, New Jersey, attributed 14.2% of U.S. bankruptcy filings to gambling problems. The researchers compared bankruptcy-filing rates during 2000 for more than 3,000 counties. They found that the 244 counties in which casinos operated had a bankruptcy rate that was 13.5% higher than counties without a casino. The president of the AGA disputed the report's findings, pointing out that other factors had not been considered, such as liberal bankruptcy laws and the ease with which credit cards can be obtained.

In 2005 Ernest Goss and Edward A. Morse, researchers at Creighton University School of Law in Omaha, Nebraska, released a study examining bankruptcy rates in more than 250 counties with casinos between the years of 1990 and 2002. According to their analysis, those counties actually saw a drop in bankruptcies when the casinos first opened their doors. They reasoned that the insurgence of revenue and jobs brought in by the casino likely helped the residents' financial situation. After a casino was open for nine years, however, bankruptcies trended the other way. Eventually the bankruptcy rate in a county with a casino was 2.3% higher on average than a county without a casino.

COMPULSIVE GAMBLING

For the AGA's 2003 survey about casino gambling, participants were asked to indicate who they thought bore the most responsibility for addressing compulsive gambling in the United States. The majority of respondents (63%) said that gamblers themselves should be held most responsible, while 15% thought society at large should take the most responsibility, and 10% put the burden on the owners of gambling facilities.

Self-Exclusion Programs

Many casinos operate self-exclusion programs in which people can voluntarily ban themselves from casinos. A number of states also offer self-exclusion programs for all casinos within their borders. For example, Missouri's voluntary exclusion program was created in 1996 after a citizen requested that he be banned from the riverboats because he was unable to control his gambling. As of spring 2006 more than 9,000 people were on the exclusion list. The Missouri Gaming Commission requires that the casinos remove self-excluded persons from their direct marketing lists; deny them check-cashing privileges and membership in players' clubs; and cross-check for their names on the list before paying out any jackpots of $1,200 or more. The casinos are not responsible for barring listed people from the casinos, but anyone listed is to be arrested for trespassing if he or she violates the ban and is discovered in a casino. Excluded people can enter the casino for employment purposes, however.

Programs in other states are similar. A self-excluded person discovered in an Illinois casino is to have any chips and tokens in his or her possession taken away and their value donated to charity. The Illinois self-exclusion program runs for a minimum of five years. After that time, people can be removed from the program if they provide written documentation from a licensed mental health professional that they are no longer problem gamblers. Self-exclusion in Michigan is permanent; a person who chooses to be on the Disassociated Persons List is banned for life from Detroit casinos. In New Jersey the Casino Control Commission allows people to voluntarily suspend their credit privileges at all Atlantic City casinos. The commission

maintains a list of those who have joined the program and shares the list with the casinos.

In addition to casinos and states, companies that provide the ATMs and cash-advance services for casinos have put self-exclusion programs into place. Global Payments, for example, provides self-exclusion and even self-limit services for people with gambling problems. Those who put their names on the self-exclusion list are denied money or cash advances, while the self-limit program puts a limit on how much money patrons can withdraw in a specified period of time.

Hotlines and Treatment

All of the states operate gambling hotlines that either refer callers to other groups for help or provide counselors over the phone. According to the Mississippi Council on Problem and Compulsive Gambling, 54% of the callers to their hotline obtained the number through a casino in 2005. Missouri operates a gambling hotline that received an average of 216 calls per month during 2005, down substantially from 2004. Between its inception and the end of 2005 the hotline had received more than 10,000 calls.

Missouri also offers free treatment to residents suffering from problem gambling and to their families. The program is administered by the Department of Mental Health through a network of private mental health providers that have been certified as compulsive-gambling counselors. Until July 2001 the program was funded by communities that hosted gambling activities. Since then legislation allowed the state to allocate to the program up to one cent of each $1 paid to the state for admissions to casinos. Three hundred sixty people received free treatment for gambling addiction through this program in 2005.

Iowa's Department of Public Health tracks statistics on clients admitted to its gambling treatment program. Table 6.5 shows the primary types of gambling that clients had engaged in for the six months prior to their admittance to the program. Data for fiscal years 1998 through 2005 show that slot machines were the game of choice for a majority of those who sought treatment.

AGA Educational Efforts

The AGA publishes the *American Gaming Association Code of Conduct for Responsible Gaming*, which describes the actions that AGA members pledge to take to ensure that responsible gambling is conducted and encouraged at casinos. Those actions include proper training of employees and promotion of responsible gambling on company Web sites and through brochures and signs posted at the casinos. AGA members also agree to provide opportunities for patrons to self-exclude themselves from casino play.

TABLE 6.5

Clients admitted to the Iowa Gambling Treatment Program, by primary type of wager made in the six months prior to admission, 1998–2005

Fiscal year	1998	1999	2000	2001	2002	2003	2004	2005
Slots	59%	62%	63%	59%	64%	69%	61%	62%
Table games	16%	12%	14%	11%	12%	9%	12%	14%
Video	10%	9%	11%	12%	11%	6%	8%	5%
Lottery/scratch tickets	4%	4%	4%	4%	3%	3%	4%	5%
Sports	2%	2%	2%	4%	4%	4%	5%	4%
Other	9%	11%	6%	10%	6%	6%	10%	10%

SOURCE: "Iowa Gambling Treatment Program: A Profile of Gamblers Admitted to Treatment in Fiscal Years 1998 through 2005," in *Iowa Gambling Treatment Program: A Profile of Gamblers Admitted to Treatment in Fiscal Years 1998 through 2005*, Iowa Department of Public Health, Iowa Gambling Treatment Program, 2005, http://www.1800betsoff.org/ (accessed September 6, 2006)

UNDERAGE GAMBLING

The legal gambling age in all commercial casinos in the United States is twenty-one; in tribal casinos it varies from eighteen to twenty-one.

AGA's 2003 casino survey asked participants who they thought bore the most responsibility for addressing the problem of underage gambling in the United States. Respondents said owners of gambling facilities should be held most responsible (39%), followed by gamblers themselves (24%) and society at large (22%). When asked to rate the job that the casino gaming industry was doing in preventing underage gambling, a majority (65%) rated the casino industry as doing a fairly good or very good job. The reputation of the casino industry for doing a good job in preventing "underage use of their product" was considered superior to that of the tobacco (30%), alcohol (38%), and gun (42%) industries.

In 2000 the Nevada Gaming Commission banned slot machines with themes that were "derived from or based on a product currently and primarily intended or marketed for use by persons under twenty-one years of age" (http://www.gaming.nv.gov/stats_regs/all_regs.pdf). The so-called slots-for-tots regulation is supposed to prevent the introduction of slot machines displaying cartoon characters that might appeal to children. The issue receives particular attention in Nevada because the state's casinos allow escorted children to walk through the casino. Most states prohibit the passage of minors through the gambling area.

The AGA's code of conduct guidebook lists a number of rules that member casinos should follow to ensure that minors do not gamble in casinos. For example, they should not display cartoon figures, pictures of underage people, or pictures of collegiate sports athletes on the casino floor. They are also supposed to stop any minor from loitering on the casino floor, and casino employees

TABLE 6.6

Minors and casinos in Detroit, Michigan, by selected statistics, 2005

	MGM Grand 1/1/05–12/31/05	MotorCity 1/1/05–12/31/05	Greektown 1/1/05–12/31/05
1. The number of minors who were denied entry into the casino.	543	4,431	800
2. The number of minors who were physically escorted from the casino premises.	2	3	4
3. The number of minors who were detected participating in gambling games other than slot machines.	0	1	0
4. The number of minors who were detected using slot machines.	1	0	1
5. The number of minors who were taken into custody by a law enforcement agency on the casino premises.	2	3	1
6. The number of minors who were detected illegally consuming alcohol on the casino premises.	0	0	0

SOURCE: "Casino Licensees' Reported Contacts with Minors on Licensed Casino Premises during Calendar Year 2005," in *Michigan Gaming Control Board Annual Report to the Governor, Calendar Year 2005*, Michigan Gaming Control Board, 2006, http://www.michigan.gov/documents/annrep05_161485_7.pdf (accessed September 6, 2006)

are to be trained to deal with minors who attempt to buy alcohol or gamble.

Casinos seem to be successful in following the guidelines. For example, data compiled by the Michigan Gaming Control Board are shown in Table 6.6. A total of 5,774 minors tried to enter the three Detroit casinos in 2005, but were denied entry. Nine minors were caught on casino premises and escorted out by casino personnel. Six other minors were taken into custody by law enforcement agencies.

POLITICS

Gambling and politics have always been linked, largely because casinos and other gaming establishments are so heavily regulated; the number of licenses available is often limited; and so much money can be made by people who get those licenses. Lobbying—a common factor in the political system—can easily turn into influence peddling and bribery at all levels of government.

Some jurisdictions have become so concerned about the confluence of political pressure and money that they prohibit casino license applicants from making contributions to political candidates. Mississippi decided to limit the temptation by setting no limit on the number of casinos that can be built. State officials claimed their policy would prevent the bribery, extortion, and favoritism that had plagued neighboring Louisiana, where the number of licenses available for riverboat casinos was set at fifteen. Those licenses were so highly prized that Governor Edwin Edwards sought $3 million from people who wanted them. In May 2000 he was convicted of racketeering, extortion, and fraud and sentenced to ten years in prison.

On the federal level, politics and gambling intersect on issues that affect more than one state or Native American tribe. At that intersection, some people see opportunities to make a lot of money.

One such operator was Jack Abramoff, a prominent lobbyist in Washington, D.C., who pleaded guilty to fraud, tax evasion, and conspiracy to bribe public officials in January 2006. He was sentenced to five years and ten months in prison and ordered to pay $21 million in restitution.

Many credit Abramoff and his colleagues with securing the defeat of the Internet Gambling Prohibition Act of 1999. The bill was one of the first anti–Internet gambling bills proposed in Congress. It was passed in the Senate in 1999 and was put forth in the House of Representatives the following year. At the time Abramoff was working for eLottery, an Internet site that intended to sell state lottery tickets online. Their business was threatened by the legislation, so Abramoff sent money to conservative special interest groups to get them to pressure conservative House members to drop the bill because it contained exceptions for horse racing and jai alai. Through procedural maneuvering a two-thirds majority was needed to pass the bill; it failed. When the bill's original supporters demanded that it be revived, Abramoff targeted ten Republican House members in vulnerable districts with media and direct-mail campaigns that accused them of being "soft on gambling" if they voted for the bill. The congressmen got so much pressure from their constituents that the House Republican leadership, fearing the party might lose four seats in the 2000 election, decided not to bring the bill up for another vote.

Later in his career, Abramoff and his team defrauded Indian tribes out of millions of dollars. Typically, he promised that, as their lobbyist, he could secure funding from the government for special projects, such as wider roads or new schools, and that he could keep the government from interfering in their operations, including casinos. In return the tribes paid his lobbying firm and a public relations company more than $85 million.

In some instances, Abramoff worked against a tribe behind the scenes and then offered to help it out for huge sums of money. In 2002, for instance, he and his colleagues were instrumental in shutting down the Speaking Rock Casino in El Paso, Texas. He then went to the Tigua Tribe, which operated the casino, and claimed that he and his colleagues could get Congress to reopen the casino. The tribe paid $4.2 million in lobbying fees, but the casino never reopened.

CHAPTER 7

LOTTERIES

A lottery is a game of chance in which people pay for the opportunity to win prizes. Part of the money taken in by a lottery is used to award the winners and to pay the costs of administering the lottery. The money left over is profit. Lotteries are extremely popular and legal in more than a hundred countries.

In the United States all lotteries are operated by state governments, which have granted themselves the sole right to do so. In other words, they are monopolies that do not allow any commercial lotteries to compete against them. The profits from U.S. lotteries are used solely to fund government programs. As of August 2006, lotteries operated in forty-two states and the District of Columbia, so 95% of the U.S. population lived in a state with an operating lottery. (See Figure 7.1.) In addition, lottery tickets could be legally purchased by any adult physically present in a lottery state, even if that adult did not reside in the state.

As shown in Figure 7.2, Americans wagered $52.6 billion in lotteries during fiscal year 2005 (July 2005 to June 2006), according to the North American Association of State and Provincial Lotteries (NASPL). U.S. lottery sales were up from $48.8 million in fiscal year 2004, an increase of 8%.

LOTTERY HISTORY

Early History

The drawing of lots to determine ownership or other rights is recorded in many ancient documents, including the Bible. The practice became common in Europe in the late fifteenth and the sixteenth centuries. Lotteries were first tied directly to the United States in 1612 when King James I of England created a lottery to provide funds to Jamestown, Virginia, the first permanent British settlement in America. Lotteries were used by public and private organizations after that time to raise money for towns, wars, colleges, and public-works projects.

An early American lottery, conducted by George Washington in the 1760s, was designed to finance construction of the Mountain Road in Virginia. Benjamin Franklin supported lotteries to pay for cannons during the Revolutionary War. John Hancock ran a lottery to finance the rebuilding of Faneuil Hall in Boston. Lotteries fell into disfavor in the 1820s because of concerns that they were harmful to the public. New York was the first state to pass a constitutional prohibition against them.

The Rise and Fall of Lotteries

The southern states relied on lotteries after the Civil War to finance Reconstruction. The Louisiana lottery, in particular, became widely popular. In 1868 the Louisiana Lottery Company was granted permission by the state legislature to operate as the state's only lottery provider. In exchange, the company agreed to pay $40,000 per year for twenty-five years to the Charity Hospital of New Orleans. The company was allowed to keep all other lottery revenues and to pay no taxes on those revenues. The Louisiana lottery was very popular nationwide—more than 90% of its revenue came from out of state. It was also extremely profitable, returning a 48% profit to its operators.

In 1890 the U.S. Congress banned the mailing of lottery materials. The Louisiana lottery was abolished in 1895 after Congress passed a law against the transport of lottery tickets across state lines. Following its closure, the public learned that the lottery had been operated by a northern crime syndicate that regularly bribed legislators and committed widespread deception and fraud. The resulting scandal was huge and widely publicized. Public opinion turned against lotteries, and by the end of the nineteenth century, they were outlawed across the country.

Negative attitudes about gambling began to soften during the early twentieth century, particularly after the failure of Prohibition. The state of Nevada legalized casino gambling in the 1930s, and gambling for charitable

FIGURE 7.1

States with lotteries, 2006

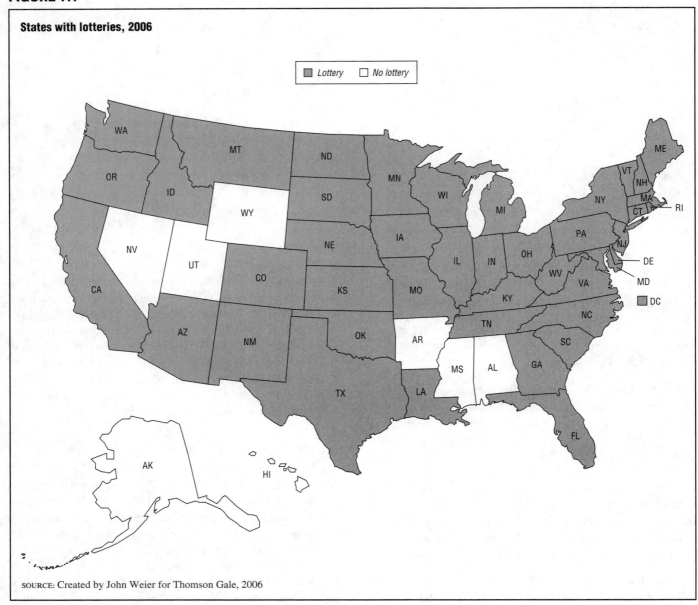

☐ Lottery   ☐ No lottery

SOURCE: Created by John Weier for Thomson Gale, 2006

purposes became more commonplace across the country. Still, lingering fears about fraud kept public sentiment against lotteries for two more decades.

Rebirth in the 1960s

In 1964 the New Hampshire legislature authorized a sweepstakes to raise revenue. The state had no sales or state income tax at that time and desperately needed money for education programs. Patterned after the popular Irish Sweepstakes, the game was much different from the lotteries of today. Drawings were held infrequently, and the largest prize was $100,000. Tickets sold for $3. The biggest prizes were tied to the outcomes of particular horse races at the Rockingham Park racetrack in Salem, New Hampshire. Nearly $5.7 million was wagered during the lottery's first year.

New York introduced a lottery in 1967. It was particularly successful, grossing $53.6 million during its first year. It also enticed residents from neighboring states to cross state lines and buy tickets. Twelve other states established lotteries during the 1970s (Connecticut, Delaware, Illinois, Maine, Maryland, Massachusetts, Michigan, New Jersey, Ohio, Pennsylvania, Rhode Island, and Vermont). Analysts have suggested that the lottery became so firmly entrenched throughout the Northeast for three reasons: 1) each state needed to raise money for public projects without increasing taxes; 2) each state had a large Catholic population that was generally tolerant of gambling; and 3) history has shown that states are most likely to start a lottery if one is already offered in a nearby state.

During the 1980s lottery fever spread south and west. Seventeen states (Arizona, California, Colorado, Florida,

FIGURE 7.2

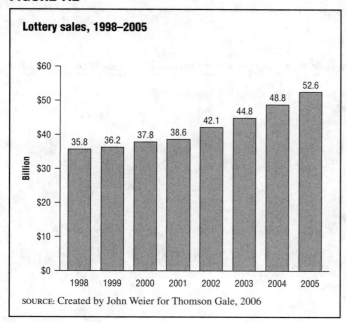

Lottery sales, 1998–2005

Year	Billion
1998	35.8
1999	36.2
2000	37.8
2001	38.6
2002	42.1
2003	44.8
2004	48.8
2005	52.6

SOURCE: Created by John Weier for Thomson Gale, 2006

Idaho, Indiana, Iowa, Kansas, Kentucky, Missouri, Montana, Oregon, South Dakota, Virginia, Washington, West Virginia, and Wisconsin) plus the District of Columbia started lotteries. Six more states started lotteries during the 1990s (Georgia, Louisiana, Minnesota, Nebraska, New Mexico, and Texas). They were joined in the first decade of the twenty-first century by North Carolina, North Dakota, Oklahoma, South Carolina, and Tennessee.

LOTTERY GAMES

Early lottery games were simple raffles in which a person purchased a ticket preprinted with a number. The player might have had to wait for weeks for a drawing to determine if the ticket was a winner. These types of games, called "passive drawing games," were the dominant lottery games in 1973. By 1997 they had ceased to exist, as consumers demanded more exciting games that provided quicker payoffs and more betting options. Table 7.1 describes lotto and the other types of lottery games available today. Table 7.2 lists the games available in each state.

TABLE 7.1

Modern lottery games

Type	Description	Administration
Lotto	A game where players select a group of numbers from a large set and are awarded prizes based on how many match a second set chosen by a random drawing. In a typical lotto game, a player might be asked to select six numbers from a set of 49. At a predetermined time six numbers are randomly selected by the lottery. The player wins a major prize if all six of their numbers match those chosen in the random drawing. The player wins smaller prizes for matching three, four, or five of the drawn numbers.	Drawings are held anywhere from once a day to once a week. Requires computers and communication networks.
Cash lotto	Cash lotto is a lotto where the prize is awarded as a lump-sum cash payment. Unwon jackpots do not roll over. Cash lotto games typically have a smaller top prize than large jackpot games, more favorable odds of winning that top prize, and require players to select fewer numbers out of a smaller field.	
Spiel	An add-on feature to a lotto game. For an additional fee an extra set of numbers (typically four to six numbers) is printed on the bottom of a ticket. Players win by matching one or more of these numbers to those selected in a random drawing.	
Scratch-off instant games	Players purchase preprinted paper tickets on which spaces have been coated with a latex substance that can be scratched off to reveal numbers or text underneath. They must match posted sequences to win.	Do not require computerized terminals. Can be sold out of vending machines.
Pull tabs (also called breakopens)	Players purchase two-ply laminated paper tickets that have perforated tear-away tabs that can be pulled back to reveal symbols or numbers underneath. A winning ticket must match the posted symbol combinations either across, down, or diagonally (similar to tic-tac-toe).	
Daily numbers games	Players select three or four digits (0 to 9) and match them with a similar set selected at random by the lottery. The player can select several different types of wagers with payoffs varying accordingly. For example, players making a "straight" bet win if their three digits match the three digits selected by the lottery in the same order.	Requires computers and communication networks.
Keno	A lotto game in which a set of numbers (typically 20) is selected from a large field of numbers (typically 80). Players select a smaller set of numbers (up to 10) and are awarded prizes based on how many of their numbers match those in the drawn set. Players have discretion over how many numbers to select, and can choose to play for a small prize with good odds (by selecting a small set of numbers such as three), a large prize with much greater odds (by selecting a large set of numbers such as 10) or combinations in between. In "fast keno" drawings may be held every few minutes. Fast keno is typically hosted by bars, lounges, and other establishments.	Requires computers and communication networks.
Video lottery terminals (VLTs)	Electronic games of chance played on a video screen. They often simulate popular casino games such as blackjack, poker, or spinning-reel slot machines. Unlike slot machines, video lottery terminals do not dispense money. Rather, a winning player is provided a ticket that is redeemed by the retailer for prizes.	Limited to only a few states.
Sports lottery	Games where outcomes are determined by the results of sports events. Sports lotteries are the most popular lottery games in much of the world (where they are frequently called "toto" or "football pools").	Available only in Oregon.

SOURCE: Adapted from "Modern Lottery Games," in *Glossary of Lottery Terms*, North American Association of State & Provincial Lotteries, 2001, http://www.naspl.org/terms.html (accessed September 14, 2004)

TABLE 7.2

State lottery games, 2006

State	State lottery	Powerball	Mega Millions[a]	Hot Lotto[b]	Wild Card 2[c]	Tri-State Megabucks[d]	Win for Life[e]	2 By 2
Alabama	None							
Alaska	None							
Arizona	X	X						
Arkansas	None							
California	X		X					
Colorado	X	X						
Connecticut	X	X						
Delaware	X	X						
D.C.	X	X		X				
Florida	X							
Georgia	X		X				X	
Hawaii	None							
Idaho	X	X			X			
Illinois	X		X					
Indiana	X	X						
Iowa	X	X		X				
Kansas	X	X		X				X
Kentucky	X	X					X	
Louisiana	X	X						
Maine	X	X				X		
Maryland	X		X					
Massachusetts	X		X					
Michigan	X		X					
Minnesota	X	X		X				
Mississippi	None							
Missouri	X	X						
Montana	X	X		X	X			
Nebraska	X	X						X
Nevada	None							
New Hampshire	X	X		X		X		
New Jersey	X		X					
New Mexico	X	X						
New York	X		X					
North Carolina	X	X						
North Dakota	X	X		X	X			
Ohio	X		X					
Oklahoma	X	X						
Oregon	X	X						
Pennsylvania	X	X						
Rhode Island	X	X						
South Carolina	X	X						
South Dakota	X	X		X	X			
Tennessee	X	X						
Texas	X		X					
Utah	None							
Vermont	X	X				X		
Virginia	X		X				X	
Washington	X		X					
West Virginia	X	X		X				
Wisconsin	X	X						
Wyoming	None							

[a]Formerly called "The Big Game."
[b]Formerly called "The Multi-State Rolldown."
[c]Formerly called "Wild Card."
[d]Formerly called "Megabucks."
[e]Formerly called "Lotto South."

SOURCE: Created by John Weier for Thomson Gale, 2006

Nearly all states that operate lotteries offer cash lotto and instant games. Most offer other numbers games, such as three-digit and four-digit games. Pull tabs, spiel, keno, and video lottery games are much less common. Keno and video lottery games are considered by many to be casino-type games, which makes them more controversial and generally less acceptable than more traditional lottery games.

Most lotto tickets sell for $1. Each dollar buys a chance to choose a small set of numbers out of a larger set of numbers. Drawings are held once or twice per week to determine the winning numbers.

Today many lottery games are conducted using computer networks. Retail outlets have computer terminals that are linked by phone lines to a central computer at the lottery commission, which records wagers as they are made. The computer network is a private, dedicated network that can be accessed only by lottery officials and retailers. Players can either choose their numbers themselves or allow the computer to select numbers randomly, an option known as "Quick Pick." The computer link allows retailers to validate winning tickets.

Most lotto drawings are televised live. Some states also air lottery game shows in which contestants compete for money and prizes. For instance, the California lottery's thirty-minute game show, *The Big Spin*, has been broadcast since 1985. Contestants, who are chosen through lottery drawings or special promotions, spin a big wheel to win cash prizes in front of a cheering audience.

Lottery winners generally have six months to one year to collect their prizes, depending on state rules. If the top prize, usually called "the jackpot," is not won, the amount of the jackpot rolls over to the next drawing, increasing the jackpot. Lotteries are often most popular when the jackpot has rolled over several times and grown to an unusually large amount.

Most states allow players to choose in advance how a jackpot will be paid to them—either all at once (the "cash lump-sum prize") or in installments (an annuity, usually paid out over twenty or twenty-five years). Either way, taxes are subtracted from the prize.

Scratch Games

In 1974 Massachusetts became the first state to offer an instant lottery game using scratch-off tickets. Today games involving scratch tickets (or "scratchers," as they are called in some states) are extremely popular. Lottery organizations offer many different scratch games with various themes.

Scratch games run for a specified period of time, usually for several months to a year. Many scratch tickets allow a player to win multiple times on each ticket. The top prize amounts are often hundreds of thousands of dollars. However, some of the games offer prizes besides money, including merchandise, trips, vehicles, and tickets to sporting events and concerts. For instance, in 2006 a Missouri scratch game gave away a seat at a table at the World Poker Tour tournament. The total winnings for such prizes often include payment by the lottery commission of federal and state income taxes on the value of the prizes.

Many lotteries have teamed with sports franchises and other companies to provide popular products as prizes. For example, in 2006 lotteries in several states offered scratch games in which Harley-Davidson motorcycles were the top prizes. Many brand-name promotions feature famous celebrities, sports figures and teams, or cartoon characters. These merchandising deals benefit the companies through product exposure and advertising; the lotteries benefit because the companies share advertising costs.

In 2006 most states offered "high profit point tickets," scratch tickets priced as high as $30 which are often part of a holiday or themed promotion. (Traditional scratch tickets sell for $1 to $5.) The higher-priced tickets appeal to many scratch players because they offer more valuable prizes and payouts than regular-priced tickets.

Most lotteries operate toll-free numbers or Web sites that provide information on scratch-game prizes. Patrons can find out which prizes have been awarded and which remain to be claimed.

Second-Chance Games

Sometimes even nonwinning lottery tickets have value. Most state lotteries run occasional second-chance drawings—and even third-chance drawings—in which holders of nonwinning tickets for particular games can still win cash or prizes. The New York lottery, for instance, held a second-chance drawing during the summer of 2006 in which holders of nonwinning Subway Series scratch tickets could win Mets and New York Yankees tickets and merchandise. Other state lotteries have offered new vehicles, concert tickets, and a variety of other prizes.

Video Lottery Games

Video lottery games are computer games played on video lottery terminals (VLTs). They are monitored and controlled by a central computer system overseen by a state's lottery agency. They are highly profitable. VLTs were operated in eight states in 2006—Delaware, Louisiana, Montana, New York, Oregon, Rhode Island, South Dakota, and West Virginia. Three of these states, Rhode Island, Delaware, and West Virginia, launched the first multistate, progressive video lottery game in 2006 (a "progressive" jackpot is one that increases with each game played.) Known as Ca$hola, the game begins with a $250,000 jackpot.

VLTs in Louisiana, Montana, and South Dakota are owned by private entities. Those in Rhode Island are leased by the state to private operators. VLTs in the other states are owned by state lottery commissions. In Delaware, New Mexico, New York, and Rhode Island, VLTs are only allowed at racetracks. Except in New York, profits from the VLTs are split between the racetracks and the state lotteries. VLTs in New York were challenged in court because the state's constitution requires that lottery proceeds benefit education programs. Some VLT revenue was going to racetracks, so the courts declared the diversion of lottery revenue unconstitutional. In 2005 the state legislature amended the law. Under the new legislation, the money for the racetrack owners comes out of the state's general fund and all the money gathered from the VLTs goes to education.

In Iowa, VLTs were introduced in 2003, and eventually nearly six thousand VLTs were bringing in $1.14

billion in revenue. However, according to the Cedar Rapids *Gazette Online* (July 15, 2006), calls to the state's hotline for gambling problems rose 17% in 2005, largely because of VLTs, and the state legislature shut down the VLT program in May 2006.

Video lottery games have become controversial because many people consider them "hard-core" gambling. They allow continuous gambling for large sums of money, as opposed to lotto play, which features drawings only once or twice a week. Opponents of video lottery games contend that they are much more addictive than traditional lottery games because of their availability and instant payoffs. They also contend that the games have a special appeal to young people, who are accustomed to playing video games.

Multistate Games

POWERBALL. During the 1980s lottery officials realized that multistate lotteries could offer higher payoffs than single-state lotteries because the costs of running one game could be shared. The Multi-State Lottery Association (MUSL) was formed in 1987 as a nonprofit association of states offering lotteries. It administers a variety of games, the best known of which is Powerball. In this lotto game each ticket has six numbers: five numbers are selected out of fifty-five numbers, and then a separate number, the "Powerball," is selected out of forty-two numbers. The odds of winning the jackpot are about 146 million to one. Drawings have been held twice weekly since the first drawing on April 22, 1992. The largest jackpot ever paid out, in February 2006, was $365 million. It was split evenly among eight coworkers in Lincoln, Nebraska.

As of August 2006 MUSL had thirty-one members. Each member state offered at least one MUSL game, and twenty-nine member states and the District of Columbia offered the Powerball. (See Table 7.2.) Each member keeps 50% of its own Powerball ticket sales; the rest is paid out in prizes.

MEGA MILLIONS. This popular multistate game is offered in twelve states. (See Table 7.2.) Players choose six numbers from two separate number pools: five numbers from 1 to 56, and one number from 1 to 46. All six numbers must be chosen in the drawing to win the jackpot. Odds of winning the jackpot are about 175 million to one. Drawings are held twice weekly.

Mega Millions was originally known as the Big Game. The first Big Game drawing took place on September 6, 1996. It became very popular and soon offered jackpots in excess of $50 million. Its largest jackpot was won in May 2000—two winners, one in Michigan and one in Illinois, split $363 million.

But Big Game sales lagged during fiscal year 2001, so game operators renamed it Mega Millions and increased the initial jackpot to $10 million, twice what it had been for the Big Game. Ticket sales increased dramatically. In 2005 the minimum jackpot was raised to $12 million when California joined the lottery. The biggest jackpot ever won on a Mega Millions ticket was $315 million, which was claimed by seven coworkers in Anaheim, California, in November 2005.

LOTTERY GAMES OUTSIDE NORTH AMERICA

Lotteries operate in more than one hundred countries around the world. According to *La Fleur's 2006 World Lottery Almanac*, worldwide lottery sales in 2005 totaled $180 billion. NASPL reports on its Web site that U.S. lotteries accounted for $52.6 billion (or 29% of this total) in fiscal year 2005. Canadian lotteries had sales of Can$8.4 billion, meaning that the two countries together accounted for about one-third of worldwide lottery sales during 2005.

More than seventy-five government and private lotteries operated in Europe during 2004. The European market generally accounts for 40% to 45% of world lottery sales. According to Scientific Games Corporation, a company that manufactures lottery tickets, VLTs, and other gaming equipment, the top five lotteries in terms of sales during 2003 were in Spain, Japan, France, Italy, and the United Kingdom (http://www.scigames.com/sgcorp/industryinfoLottery.asp#L1). In 2004 Spain, France, and the United Kingdom teamed together to start the Euro Millions lottery.

One of the most popular lotteries in the world is the Spanish lotto, El Gordo ("The Fat One"), which has been played since 1812. Drawings are held six times a year, and the December drawing, called the Navidad (Christmas) Lottery, is the largest single gambling event in the world. In 2006 only eighty thousand tickets were printed, of which roughly thirteen thousand were winning tickets, meaning that the odds of winning a prize were about one in six. Prize money for El Gordo totaled $2.6 billion; the jackpot was $648 million. Winnings were paid out in lump sums and were not taxed by the Spanish government.

HOW LOTTERIES OPERATE

In 2006 the vast majority of lotteries were administered directly by state lottery boards or commissions. The lotteries in Connecticut, Georgia, Kentucky, Louisiana, and Tennessee were operated by quasi-governmental or privatized lottery corporations. In most states enforcement authority regarding fraud and abuse rested with the attorney general's office, state police, or the lottery commission. The amount of oversight and control that each legislature has over its lottery agency differs from state to state.

Although lotteries are a multimillion-dollar business, lottery commissions employ only a few thousand people nationwide. Lottery commissions set up, monitor, and run the games offered in their states, but the vast majority of lottery sales are by retail outlets that contract to sell their games.

Retailers

According to the NASPL Web site, about one hundred ninety thousand retailers sold lottery tickets in the country in 2005. California had the most retailers (19,000), followed by Texas (16,281), and New York (15,900). Half of all lottery retailers were convenience stores. Other outlets included various kinds of stores, nonprofit organizations (churches and fraternal organizations), service stations, restaurants and bars, bowling alleys, and newsstands.

Retailers get commissions on lottery sales and bonuses when they sell winning tickets. They also get increased store traffic and media attention, especially if they become known as "lucky" places to purchase lottery tickets. Some state lottery Web sites list the stores where winners purchased their tickets. One retailer in Port Hueneme, California, sold six winning million-dollar-plus tickets between 1987 and 1994 (http://www.calottery.com/SecondaryNav/Retail Locations/Lucky Retailers/).

Lottery tickets are often impulse purchases, so retailers sell them near the checkout. This also allows store operators to keep an eye on ticket vending machines to prevent play by underage customers. Because convenience stores increasingly offer pay-at-the-pump gasoline sales—transactions that are likely to decrease in-store traffic—lottery officials in Minnesota and several other states are contemplating ways to sell and print tickets at the gas pumps. Lottery officials in South Dakota have expressed interest in selling lottery tickets in mass-merchandise stores, such as Wal-Mart.

According to the National Association of Convenience Stores, the average convenience store in 2005 made $12,899 in gross profits from the lottery (*State of the Industry*, 2006). However, NACS noted that the average cost of handling a lottery transaction is higher than that of a nonlottery transaction. Lottery tickets actually have a lower profit margin than most other convenience store items, particularly those pushed at the front counter, such as batteries and candy.

LOTTERY PLAYER DEMOGRAPHICS

A national poll conducted by the Pew Research Center in 2006 (Paul Taylor, et. al, *Gambling: As the Take Rises, So Does Public Concern*, pewresearch.org/assets/

FIGURE 7.3

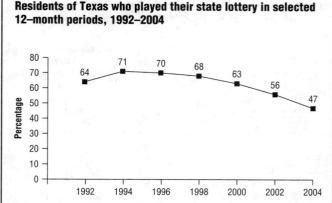

Residents of Texas who played their state lottery in selected 12–month periods, 1992–2004

SOURCE: "Figure 7. Percentages of Texans Playing the Texas Lottery," in *Demographic Study of Texas Lottery Players*, Texas Lottery, March 2005, http://www.txlottery.org/info/demographicreport2004.pdf (accessed September 6, 2006). Data from Lottery Demographic Studies, 1995–2003, and ESRL Data, 2004.

social/pdf/Gambling.pdf) found that 52% of adults had purchased a lottery ticket within the previous year. (See Figure 2.2 in Chapter 2.) Many state lottery commissions conduct demographic studies to get a better picture of lottery players, largely because they want to better target them in marketing campaigns. Findings in two states provide some insight into lottery players.

Texas

In 2005 the Texas Lottery released the *Demographic Study of Texas Lottery Players* (www.txlottery.org/info/demographicreport2004.pdf), which was conducted by Texas Tech University's Earl Survey Research Laboratory. Researchers interviewed 1,255 Texans. As Figure 7.3 shows, 47% played the lottery in 2004, which was the lowest level since the lottery began in 1992. The percentages were in line with Pew's findings. Overall, there were few demographic differences among those who played the lottery and those who did not, although employed people were more likely to play than unemployed people (67.4% of employed people vs. 32.6% of unemployed people), and Hispanics were more likely to play than other racial and ethnic groups (54.8% of Hispanics vs. 46.9% of whites and 37.7% of African-Americans).

The amount of money various demographic groups spent on the lottery differed greatly, however. As Table 7.3 reveals, young people, African-Americans, males, and individuals with less education and lower incomes were likely to spend the most on the lottery. (Note that Table 7.3 excludes "outliers"—people who hardly play at all or people who play to excess.) The most popular game was Lotto Texas, which was played by more than a third of all Texans polled. Individuals spent the most

TABLE 7.3

Amount of money people spend on the Texas lottery per month, by demographic characteristics, 2004

Demographic variables	Average spent per month on lottery among lottery players
Income	
Less than $20,000	$48.74
$20,000 to $29,000	$60.33
$30,000 to $39,000	$64.33
$40,000 to $49,000	$57.95
$50,000 to $59,000	$39.24
$60,000 to $75,000	$34.37
$76,000 to $100,000	$28.96
More than $100,000	$30.58
Education	
Less than HS diploma	$62.55
HS degree	$67.19
Some college	$42.28
College degree	$26.82
Ethnic group	
White	$30.76
Black	$88.98
Hispanic	$64.83
Other	$72.73
Age	
18–24	$71.22
25–34	$50.91
35–44	$40.15
45–54	$47.73
55–64	$38.73
65+	$33.67
Gender	
Male	$48.65
Female	$41.66
Overall	$44.55

Notes: Outliers (people who represent the most extreme cases of monthly lottery spending) have been excluded.

SOURCE: "Table 1b. Expenditures of Lottery Players, Outliers Excluded," in *Demographic Study of Texas Lottery Players*, Texas Lottery, March 2005, http://www.txlottery.org/info/demographicreport2004.pdf (accessed September 6, 2006)

money on scratch games, with the average player spending nearly $30 per month on such games.

South Carolina

The South Carolina Education Lottery regularly publishes a detailed report on lottery demographics. Market-Search Corporation, which compiled the *Player Profile Study 2005*, interviewed 1,252 people. Roughly 51% of those polled had played the South Carolina lottery. About 54% of males surveyed had played the lottery, as opposed to 48% of females. A higher percentage of African-Americans (61%) had played the lottery than whites (46%). Of all age groups, a higher percentage of people between thirty-five and fifty-four had played the lottery (55%) than any other age group. The age category with the fewest players was fifty-five and older (42%).

About 13% of players said they played the lottery more than once a week ("frequent players"); 12% said they played about once a week ("regular players"); and the rest said they played one to three times a month ("occasional players") or less ("infrequent players"). In South Carolina, high-school educated, middle-aged, Caucasian men in the middle of the economic spectrum were more likely to be "frequent players" than any other demographic group.

The South Carolina survey also reported where and when South Carolinians purchased their tickets. In 2005 people usually purchased tickets at a gas station or convenience store that sells gas (93%), as opposed to a grocery store (9%), a convenience store without gas (6%), or somewhere else (3%). Most players purchased their tickets on the weekdays (43%), versus the weekend (31%), or both (21%). More than half (54%) claimed to purchase their tickets after four in the afternoon. The most popular game was Powerball, which was played by 38% of those polled. Scratch tickets came in a close second (35%).

GROUP PLAY

Groups of people frequently pool their money and buy lottery tickets, particularly for very large jackpots. Group wins are beneficial to the lotteries because they generate more media coverage than solo wins and expose a wider group of friends, relatives, and coworkers to the idea that lotteries are winnable. However, pooling arrangements, even those between only two people, can lead to headaches if a group actually wins a jackpot. Several such groups have ended up in court, but given the number of winners every year, such cases are relatively rare.

The California lottery started the Jackpot Captain program in 2001 to help so-called group leaders manage lotto pools. Lotto captains have access to a special Web site that gives them tips on organizing and running group play. They can download and print forms that help them track players, games, dates, and jackpots. As an incentive, lotto captains can participate in special drawings for cash and prizes. According to state lottery officials, far more people enrolled to be captains than was expected. The lottery described them as hard-core players who promote lottery games, recruit new players, and provide valuable feedback about lottery promotions. In January 2004 the Missouri Lottery started a Lottery Captain program for group-play organizers.

WHY DO PEOPLE PLAY LOTTERIES?

A lottery is a unique gambling event because it costs only a small amount of money for a chance to win a very large jackpot. While the odds are extremely long, the huge jackpot is the main selling feature. Rollover jackpots spur ticket sales. As more people buy tickets, the jackpot grows, while the odds of winning *decrease*. However, this does not deter people from buying tickets—sales actually increase under these circumstances.

A study performed on behalf of European lotteries by Mark D. Griffiths and Richard T. A. Wood (*Lottery Gambling and Addiction: An Overview of European Research*, 1999, https://www.european-lotteries.org/data/info_130/Wood.pdf) looked at why people continue to play the lottery despite the long odds. Among the most common reasons were:

- the lure of a very large jackpot in exchange for a very small investment

- successful advertising

- publicity about jackpot winners

- ignorance of probability theory

- televised drawings

- overestimating the positive outcomes and underestimating the negative ones

- the credibility of government backing

- players' belief in their own luck

Perhaps the study's most important finding, however, concerns the role of "entrapment." According to the researchers, many people select the same numbers week after week. As time goes by and their numbers are not selected, they do not become discouraged. Instead, they think their chances of winning are getting better. Often players experience near misses, in which two or more of their numbers come up in the jackpot drawing. This only convinces them that they are getting closer to the big win. They become increasingly entrapped in playing their numbers and fear skipping even one drawing. This mind-set, according to Wood and Griffiths, has its roots in a common myth that the probability of winning increases the longer a losing streak lasts.

THE EFFECTS OF LOTTERIES

Economic Effects

Proponents of lotteries usually use economic arguments to justify their positions. They point out that lotteries provide state governments with a relatively easy way to increase their revenues without imposing more taxes. The games are financially beneficial to the many small businesses that sell lottery tickets and to larger companies that participate in merchandising campaigns or provide advertising or computer services. In addition, lottery advocates say, the games provide cheap entertainment to people who want to play, while raising money for the betterment of all.

Lottery opponents also have economic arguments. They contend that lotteries contribute only a small percentage of total state revenues and, therefore, have a limited effect on state programs. Lotteries cost money to operate and lure people into parting with their money under false hopes. In addition, opponents contend that those targeted by lotteries come particularly from lower income brackets and may not be able to afford to gamble.

THE DIVISION OF LOTTERY MONEY. Lottery money can be categorized as sales, prizes, administrative costs, retailer commissions, and state profits. The sales amount is the total amount taken in by the lottery. In general 50% to 60% of U.S. lottery sales are paid out as prizes to winners. Administrative costs for advertising, employee salaries, and other operating expenses usually account for 1% to 10% of sales. On average retailers collect 5% to 8% of sales in the form of commissions and approximately 2% as bonuses for selling winning tickets. The remaining 30% to 40% is profit turned over to the state.

U.S. state lotteries had approximately $52.6 billion in sales for fiscal year 2005. (A fiscal year is defined differently from state to state, but in most states it runs from July 1 to June 30.) According to NASPL ("Lottery Sales and Profits", 2006, http://www.naspl.org/index.cfm?fuseaction=content&PageID=3&PageCategory=3), national sales were up 7.8% in fiscal year 2005 from the previous fiscal year's sales of $48.8 billion. Puerto Rico, the District of Columbia, and nine states—Kansas, Kentucky, Louisiana, Missouri, Montana, New Hampshire, New Mexico, Washington, and Wisconsin—reported declining sales for 2005 compared with 2004. (See Table 7.4.) Louisiana had the sharpest decline—9.7%—as sales dropped from $340 million in 2004 to $307 million in 2005. By contrast three jurisdictions had sales increases: North Dakota (up 228%), Tennessee (up 97.4%), and Texas (up 26.1%).

NASPL's data show that during fiscal year 2005 New York had the highest lottery sales ($6.3 billion), followed by Massachusetts ($5.8 billion), and Texas ($3.7 billion). Those three states accounted for 30% of national lottery sales. Fifteen states had lottery sales in excess of $1 billion during 2005.

The states allocate their lottery profits in different ways. Table 7.5 describes each state's cumulative allocation of profits from each lottery's inception to June 2005. A total of $222 billion was given to various beneficiaries. New York topped the list with $27 billion in profits allocated to education over the years. California followed with $17 billion to education, and Florida, $15 billion.

RETAILER PAYMENTS. According to *La Fleur's 2004 World Lottery Almanac*, the average prize payout from each state lottery from inception to fiscal year 2003 was 53% of cumulative sales. The average state profit was 34%. Administrative costs and retailer payments made up about 13% of cumulative lottery sales.

The primary means of retailer compensation is a commission on each ticket sold. In other words, a lottery retailer keeps a certain percentage of the money taken in from lottery

TABLE 7.4

Sales and profit of lotteries by state, 2004–05

Lottery jurisdiction	Population (in millions)	Fiscal year 04 sales	Fiscal year 04 profit	Fiscal year 05 sales	Fiscal year 05 profit
Arizona	5.58	$366.58	$107.76	$397.56	$116.80
California	35.48	$2,945.89	$1,044.06	$3,333.60	$1,795.30
Colorado	4.55	$401.25	$104.07	$416.97	$103.74
Connecticut	3.48	$907.66	$280.76	$932.93	$268.52
Delaware[d]	0.82	$640.92	$222.00	$689.29	$234.00
District of Columbia[c]	0.56	$245.04	$75.77	$233.43	$71.05
Florida	17.02	$3,070.96	$1,050.00	$3,470.73	$1,103.63
Georgia	8.68	$2,710.46	$782.69	$2,922.33	$802.24
Idaho	1.37	$109.32	$23.00	$113.50	$26.00
Illinois	12.65	$1,709.19	$570.10	$1,842.88	$614.00
Indiana	6.2	$734.87	$199.44	$739.63	$189.04
Iowa	2.94	$209.92	$55.10	$210.67	$51.09
Kansas	2.72	$224.20	$73.00	$206.72	$62.28
Kentucky	4.12	$725.25	$193.48	$707.26	$158.19
Louisiana	4.5	$340.09	$121.20	$307.01	$108.92
Maine	1.31	$185.88	$42.53	$209.29	$50.33
Maryland	5.51	$1,395.41	$458.37	$1,485.73	$477.10
Massachusetts	6.43	$4,381.25	N/A	$4,484.72	$936.13
Michigan[c]	10.08	$1,967.80	$645.00	$2,069.49	$667.58
Minnesota	5.06	$386.90	$100.00	$408.57	$106.18
Missouri	5.7	$791.52	$230.32	$785.00	$218.60
Montana	0.92	$36.74	$8.12	$33.81	$6.22
Nebraska	1.74	$92.64	$19.72	$100.66	$23.86
New Hampshire	1.29	$237.12	$71.50	$227.90	$69.30
New Jersey	8.64	$2,188.50	$793.00	$2,273.80	$804.42
New Mexico	1.87	$148.70	$35.94	$139.27	$32.23
New York[a]	19.19	$5,847.50	$1,907.40	$6,270.49	$2,062.70
North Dakota	0.63	$5.84	N/A	$19.15	$6.46
Ohio	11.44	$2,154.71	$648.10	$2,159.10	$645.10
Oregon[d]	3.56	$893.26	$387.12	$943.11	$415.48
Pennsylvania	12.37	$2,352.07	$818.67	$2,644.86	$852.56
Puerto Rico	3.88	$344.00	$128.80	$317.90	$79.00
Rhode Island[e]	1.08	$1,480.63	$281.03	$1,636.84	$313.47
South Carolina	4.15	$950.00	$290.10	$956.95	$277.50
South Dakota[e]	0.76	$664.42	$114.77	$675.58	$119.32
Tennessee	5.84	$427.70	$123.70	$844.32	$227.42
Texas[b]	22.12	$2,904.86	$839.26	$3,662.46	$1,076.82
Vermont	0.62	$92.33	$19.50	$92.59	$20.35
Virginia	7.39	$1,262.36	$408.10	$1,333.94	$423.52
Washington	6.13	$481.44	$117.30	$457.62	$115.60
West Virginia[d]	1.81	$1,303.49	$512.14	$1,399.07	$588.26
Wisconsin	5.47	$482.93	N/A	$451.87	$128.54
Total U.S. ($US)	**265.66**	**$48,801.60**	**$13,902.92**	**$52,608.60**	**$16,478.72**

Note: Results are unofficial and unaudited.

[a]FY ends 3/31.

[b]FY end 8/31.

[c]FY end 9/30.

[d]Includes net video lottery terminal (VLT) sales (cash in less cash out).

[e]Include gross video lottery terminal (VLT) sales (cash in).

SOURCE: "Sales and Profits," in *NASPL: Where the Money Goes*, North American Association of State and Provincial Lotteries, 2006, http://www.naspl.org/sales&profits05.html (accessed September 6, 2006). Data from North American Association of State & Provincial Lotteries.

sales. Most states also have incentive-based programs for retailers that meet particular sales criteria. For example, the Wisconsin lottery pays retailers a bonus for increasing ticket sales by particular amounts. Lottery officials believe that the incentive program, which encourages retailers to ask customers if they would like to buy lottery tickets, is more effective than an increase in commission. Retailers that sell a winning ticket of $600 or more in Wisconsin receive 2% of the value of the ticket (up to $100,000).

UNCLAIMED LOTTERY WINNINGS. Unclaimed lottery winnings add up to hundreds of millions of dollars each year, and each state handles them differently. Some states, such as New York, require that unclaimed winnings be returned to the prize pool. Other states allocate such funds to lottery administrative costs or to specific state programs. For example, in Texas unclaimed prizes go to funds that benefit hospital research and payment of indigent health care. The California lottery turns the money over to educational programs—more than $27 million in fiscal 2005 (more than $550 million since 1985).

STATE BUDGETS. Lottery revenues make up a very small portion of state budgets. One study (Charles T. Clotfelter et al., *State Lotteries at the Turn of the Century: Report to the National Gambling Impact Study*

TABLE 7.5

Cumulative distribution of state lottery proceeds as of June 30, 2005

[From startup to 6/30/05, dollars in millions]

Arizona (1982)

Local transportation assistance fund	$535.00
County assistance fund	$144.98
Heritage fund	$278.52
Economic development fund	$46.15
Mass transit	$44.35
Healthy Arizona	$20.67
General fund (by category)	
Education	$419.47
Health and welfare	$166.34
Protection and safety	$77.56
General government	$44.34
Inspection and regulation	$7.55
Natural resources	$6.45
Court appointed special advocate fund (unclaimed prizes)	$25.88
Clean air fund (unclaimed prizes)	$0.50
State general fund (unclaimed prizes)	$1.50
	$1,819.26

California (1985)

Education	**$17,166.46**

Colorado (1983)

Capital construction fund	$439.80
Division of parks and outdoor recreation	$148.90
Conservation trust fund	$596.10
Great Outdoors Colorado trust fund	$411.40
General fund	$1.30
School fund	$16.30
	$1,613.80

Connecticut (1972)

General fund (to benefit education, roads, health and hospitals, public safety, etc.)	**$5,562.82**

D.C. (1982)

General fund	**$1,340.00**

Delaware (1975)

General fund	**$2,072.70**

Florida (1987)

Education enhancement trust fund	**$15,203.00**

Georgia (1993)

HOPE scholarships	$3,058.88
Pre-kindergarten program	$2,405.78
Capital outlay and technology for primary and secondary schools	$1,800.00
	$7,264.66

Idaho (1989)

Public schools (K-12)	$150.50
Public buildings	$150.50
	$301.00

Illinois (1974)

Illinois Common School Fund (K-12)	**$12,896.00**

Indiana (1989)

Build Indiana fund	$1,920.40
Teachers retirement fund	$462.60
Police & fire pension relief fund	$276.30
Help America Vote Act	$1.80
	$2,661.10

Iowa (1985)

Iowa Plan (economic development)	$170.32
CLEAN fund (environment and agriculture)	$35.89
Gambler's treatment program	$10.37
Special appropriations	$20.83
Sales tax	$135.98
General fund	$561.46
	$934.85

Kansas (1987)

Economic development initiatives fund	$604.56
Correctional institutions building fund	$71.28
County reappraisal project (fiscal years 88–90)	$17.20
Juvenile detention facilities fund	$22.69
State general fund (fiscal years 1995–2004)	$105.99
Problem gambling grant fund	$0.40
	$822.12

Kentucky (1989)

Education	$214.00
Vietnam Veterans	$32.00
General fund	$1,387.60
Post-secondary & college scholarships	$609.60
Affordable housing trust fund	$20.80
Literacy programs & early childhood reading	$18.00
	$2,282.00

Louisiana (1991)

Various state agencies	$147.30
State general fund	$69.20
Minimum foundation program—funding elementary & secondary education in public schools	$1,283.45
Problem gambling	$4.50
	$1,504.45

Maine (1974)

General fund	$732.00
Outdoor Heritage fund	$11.91
	$743.91

Maryland (1973)

General fund	$8,790.40
Subdivisions (for one year only fiscal years 84–85)	$31.25
Stadium authority	$422.13
	$9,243.78

Massachusetts (1972)

Cities and towns	$12,028.14
Arts council	$189.90
General fund	$2,991.44
Compulsive gamblers	$10.46
	$15,219.94

Michigan (1972)

Education (K-12)	**$12,800.00**

Minnesota (1989)

General fund	$800.59
Environmental and natural resources trust fund	$349.00
Game & fish fund	$50.87
Natural resources fund	$50.87
Other state programs	$36.70
Compulsive gambling	$18.70
	$1,306.73

Missouri (1986)

Public education	$1,915.34
General revenue fund (1986–1993)	$542.54
	$2,457.88

TABLE 7.5

[From startup to 6/30/05, dollars in millions]

Montana (1987)

Property tax relief	$15.34
Elementary and secondary schools	$34.09
Juvenile detention	$2.53
General fund	$69.10
Study of socioeconomic impact on gambling	$0.10
	$121.16

Nebraska (1993)

Compulsive gamblers assistance fund	$5.29
Education innovation fund	$101.49
Environmental trust fund	$94.05
Solid waste landfill closure assistance fund	$18.46
General fund	$5.00
State fair support & improvement fund	$1.59
Nebraska scholarship fund	$11.02
	$236.90

New Hampshire (1964)

Education	**$999.90**

New Jersey (1970)

Education and institutions	**$14,725.80**

New Mexico (1996)

Public school capital outlay	$66.55
Lottery tuition fund	$182.65
	$249.20

New York (1967)

Education	**$27,000.00**

North Dakota (2004)

Compulsive gambling fund	$0.40
State general fund	$7.27
	$7.67

Ohio (1974)

Education	**$13,670.00**

Oklahoma (2005)

	No FY' 05 sales

Oregon (1985)

Economic development	$1,500.00
Public education	$2,400.00
Natural resource programs	$300.00
	$4,200.00

Pennsylvania (1972)

Older Pennsylvanians	**$14,650.00**

Rhode Island (1974)

General fund	**$2,300.00**

South Carolina (2002)

Education lottery fund	**$868.24**

South Dakota (1989)

General fund	$371.81
Capital construction fund	$17.28
Property tax reduction fund	$935.31
Grant to human services	$1.76
	$1,326.16

Tennessee (2004)

Lottery for education account	$350.69
After school program	$8.92
	$359.61

TABLE 7.5

[From startup to 6/30/05, dollars in millions]

Texas (1992)

General revenue fund	$4,997.82
Foundation school fund	$7,629.34
Multicategorical teaching hospital	$100.00
Tertiary care facility account	$131.07
Health and Human Services Commission's graduate medical program	$40.00
	$12,898.23

Vermont (1978)

General fund	$212.46
Education fund	$128.70
	$341.16

Virginia (1988)

General fund (fiscal years 1989–1998)	$2,788.42
Direct aid to public education K-12 (fiscal years 1999-present)	$2,548.96
Literary fund (primarily for school construction additions and renovations)	$141.60
Debt set-off collection	$12.27
	$5,491.25

Washington (1982)

General fund	$1,838.11
Education funds	$374.22
Seattle Mariners Stadium (Safeco Field)	$33.88
King County Stadium and Exhibition Center (Qwest Field)	$47.39
	$2,293.60

West Virginia (1986)

Education	$773.72
Senior citizens	$328.30
Tourism	$318.33
Bonds covering profit areas	$0.00
General fund	$457.74
Other	$802.01
	$2,680.10

Wisconsin (1988)

Public benefit such as property tax relief	**$2,368.00**
Total - US	**$222,003.44**

SOURCE: Adapted from "Cumulative Lottery Contributions to Beneficiaries," in *NASPL: Where the Money Goes*, North American Association of State and Provincial Lotteries, 2006, http://www.naspl.org/index.cfm?fuseaction=content&PageID=10&PageCategory=37 (accessed September 6, 2006)

Commission, 1999, http://scholar.google.com/url?sa=U&q=http://www.nd.edu/~jstiver/FIN360/lottery.pdf) found that lottery revenues contribute from 0.41% to 4.07% of their states' general revenue (the average portion was approximately 2.2%).

TAXES AND OTHER WITHHOLDING FROM LOTTERY WINNINGS. Lottery winnings are usually taxable as personal income. All prizes greater than $600 are reported by the lotteries to the Internal Revenue Service. In general, the lottery agencies subtract taxes prior to awarding large prizes. For example, the New York lottery in 2006 withheld federal, state, and local income taxes on prizes greater than $5,000. The lottery withheld 25% for federal taxes and 6.85% for state taxes. An additional 3.65% was withheld if the winner was a New York City resident. Non-U.S. residents faced even higher tax withholding rates. In addition, the New York lottery was required by law to subtract past-due child support payments and collect repayment of public assistance from prizes of $600 or more.

In 2006 some states, such as South Carolina and Washington, offered tax-free jackpots. In these games, the actual prize is higher than the listed prize. The state lottery commission pays the winner the full amount advertised and then uses the unadvertised money to pay the taxes owed to the state and federal governments.

Education

Lottery proponents often advocate lotteries for their economic benefits to education. Some lotteries dedicate a portion of their profits toward K–12 or higher education. Opponents often argue, however, that these profits do not provide additional dollars for education but simply replace general fund dollars that would have been spent on education anyway.

Donald Miller, a mathematics professor at Saint Mary's College in Indiana, argued in "Schools Lose Out in Lotteries," (*USA Today*, April 15, 2004, http://www.usatoday.com/news/opinion/editorials/2004-04-14-miller_x.htm) that educational spending per student gradually decreases once a state starts a lottery. He examined data for twelve states that had enacted lotteries for education between 1965 and 1990. According to Miller, before lotteries were set up average education spending in those states increased each year by approximately $12 per student. In the years immediately following the initiation of the lotteries, the states increased their education spending on average by nearly $50 per student. However, the increase fell sharply in following years and eventually lagged behind states without lottery-generated education funds. Miller blamed legislators, who used lottery funds "to replace rather than add to existing sources of education funding."

THE HOPE SCHOLARSHIP. Begun in 1993, the Georgia lottery funds three educational programs: 1) the HOPE scholarship program; 2) a voluntary prekindergarten program; and 3) grants for training teachers in advanced technologies and capital for educational facilities. HOPE stands for Helping Outstanding Pupils Educationally. HOPE scholarships and grants are available to Georgia residents who enroll in certain programs at public and private institutions in the state. Students must have at least a B average to qualify for HOPE money and to maintain their eligibility in subsequent years. Most recipients are recent high school graduates who pursue college degrees.

At public colleges the HOPE scholarship pays for tuition and fees and provides a $300 book allowance per academic year. Room and board expenses are not covered. At private colleges the scholarship provides $3,000 per academic year to full-time students (who can also qualify for the Georgia Tuition Equalization Grant of $900 per academic year). Part-time students attending private colleges are eligible for $1,500 per academic year.

During its first twelve years of operation, the lottery provided approximately $3.58 billion to the HOPE scholarship program, $2.69 billion to the prekindergarten program, and more than $1.8 billion to the remaining programs.

As of August 2006 more than nine hundred thousand students had received HOPE scholarships. HOPE is one of the country's largest state-financed merit-based aid programs and is credited with significantly increasing the attendance of in-state residents at Georgia colleges. Similar programs include Kentucky's Educational Excellence Scholarship and Florida's Bright Futures Scholarship.

Social Effects

Lotteries are undeniably a cultural and social phenomenon—they operate on every continent except Antarctica. In the United States lotteries enjoy unprecedented popularity. They are legal in forty-two states and are generally considered a benign form of entertainment with two enormous selling points: they seem to offer a shortcut to the "American Dream" of wealth and prosperity, and they are a voluntary activity that raises money for the public good in lieu of increased taxes. Opposition to lotteries is generally based on religious or moral reasons. Some people consider all forms of gambling to be wrong, and state-sponsored lotteries may be particularly abhorrent to them.

The NGISC, in its final report of 1999, complained about the appropriateness of state governments pushing luck, instant gratification, and entertainment as alternatives to hard work, prudent investment, and savings. Such a message might be particularly troubling if it is directed to lower-income people.

POVERTY AND RACE/ETHNICITY. One of the most common criticisms leveled against state lotteries is that they unfairly burden the poor—that they are funded mostly by low-income people who buy tickets, but benefit mostly higher-income people. In economics terminology, a tax that places a higher burden on lower-income groups than higher-income groups (in terms of percentage of their income) is called "regressive." Although the lottery is not really a tax, many people consider it to be a form of voluntary taxation because the proceeds fund government programs. Economist Philip J. Cook, one of the co-authors of the National Gambling Impact Study Commission (NGISC) report, stated that "the tax that is built into the lottery is the most regressive tax we know."

Cook and Clotfelter had examined this issue at length in *Selling Hope: State Lotteries in America* (Harvard University Press, 1989). They found that lottery players with annual incomes of less than $10,000 spend more on lottery tickets ($597 per year) than any other income group. They also found that high school dropouts spend four times as much as college graduates, and that African-Americans spend five times as much as Caucasians. The NGISC, in its final report, expressed serious concern about the heavy reliance of lotteries upon less-educated, lower-income people. It also mentioned that an unusually large number of lottery outlets are concentrated in poor neighborhoods.

In response to these claims, the president of NASPL made the following points at a presentation in July 1999 to the National Conference of State Legislatures:

- The NGISC report does not provide any evidence that lotteries target their marketing to poor people.

- Marketing to poor people would be unwise from a business and political standpoint.

- People often buy lottery tickets outside of the neighborhoods in which they live.

- Many areas associated with low-income residents (for example, inner cities) are visited or passed through by higher-income shoppers and workers.

- High-income residential neighborhoods have relatively few stores and gas stations, making them less likely to have lottery outlets.

In 2001 researchers at the Vinson Institute of Government Studies at the University of Georgia reviewed a number of nationwide and state studies on the relationship between income and lottery participation. Joseph McCrary and Thomas J. Pavlak found that "the regressivity finding remains largely consistent throughout the literature" (*Who Plays the Georgia Lottery?*, 2002, http://www.cviog. uga.edu/store/item.php?item=51). Researchers cite a common belief among lower-income people that playing the lottery is their only chance to escape poverty.

In October 2002 the *Chicago Reporter* analyzed lottery sales in Illinois since 1997, comparing lottery sales figures around the state with income and demographic data from the 2000 census (Leah Samuel, *The Poor Play More*, http://findarticles.com/p/articles/ mi_m0JAS/is_9_31/ai_93451530). The ten zip codes with the highest lottery sales for the previous six fiscal years were all in Chicago. The residents of all ten zip codes had average incomes of less than $20,000 per year, compared with the city average of $24,000 per year. Eight of the zip code areas had unemployment rates in excess of the city average of 10%. Residents of half of the zip code areas were populated by at least 70% African-Americans. The newspaper found that average lottery sales per capita in the city's mostly African-American zip codes were 29% to 33% higher than in mostly white or Latino zip code areas.

The zip code with the highest lottery sales in the state, 60609, coincides with predominantly African-American and Latino low-income communities on the city's South Side. Residents of that zip code spent nearly $23 million on lottery tickets during fiscal year 2002. The newspaper also found that residents in poorer communities spent a larger portion of their incomes on lottery tickets than did people in more affluent neighborhoods. Lottery spending during fiscal year 2002 was $224 per person (or $1.57 for every $100 of income) in zip codes that were at least 70% African-American and $173 per person (or $0.46 for every $100 of income) in zip codes that were at least 70% Caucasian.

A similar study was reported by Robert Gebeloff in "Numbers Game: Who Really Pays for the Lottery," (*Newark Star-Ledger*, December 2005). The newspaper gathered data on lottery sales by zip code and compared that data to income and population data for each zip code from 2000 to 2004. The results clearly showed that those who lived in poorer areas bought far more lottery tickets than those living in wealthy ones. People who resided in zip codes where the average income was less than $52,151 spent an average of $250 per year on the lottery, while those who lived in zip codes with an average salary of $117,503 to $141,132 spent an average of $115 on lottery tickets per year. Residents of very wealthy neighborhoods—where the average salary was more than $141,132—spent $89 on lottery tickets each year. In addition, less wealthy neighborhoods had more lottery retailers per capita. The ratio of lottery retailers per five thousand people was 4 to 1 in low-income areas, compared with roughly 1.5 to 1 in wealthy neighborhoods.

Elizabeth A. Freund and Irwin L. Morris, two researchers at the University of Maryland, looked at the levels of relative income inequality created after a lottery was introduced in a state (*Social Science Quarterly*, December 2005). They discovered that lotteries add 10% to the increase of the average income disparity in a state. In other words, if people with less money grow 20% poorer relative to those with more money, then the addition of a lottery will exacerbate the problem by an additional 2% (10% of the total increase).

RACE/ETHNICITY OF LOTTERY BENEFICIARIES. In Georgia the Vinson Institute reported that African-Americans and less educated people are more likely to be active lottery players than Caucasians and more educated people. Proceeds from the Georgia lottery fund only education programs. If these programs provide more benefits to the poor than to the wealthy, it could be argued that this compensates for the regressive nature of the state lottery.

However, studies performed by Ross Rubenstein and Benjamin Scafidi (*National Tax Journal*, June 1, 2002) and by Christopher Cornwell and David Mustard (*The Distributional Impacts of Lottery Funded Merit-Based Aid*, 2001) have criticized Georgia's lottery for providing more benefits to white households than to minority households. Cornwell and Mustard claim that counties with the highest incomes and white populations receive significantly more HOPE college scholarships.

Researchers at the Vinson Institute argue that a county-by-county comparison of HOPE scholarship recipients is not appropriate because other factors affect these statistics—for example, whether a particular county contains a college or university. However, they did conclude that minorities in Georgia are "slightly less likely" than whites to get a HOPE scholarship.

In their latest research regarding the Georgia lottery, the Vinson Institute examined census data, polls, and other statistics from lottery inception through 1999 (*Review of Policy Research*, Winter 2003). They found that lottery play was inversely related to education level. In other words, people with fewer years of education played the lottery more often than those with more years of education. The study also found that lottery spending per person was highest in counties where African-Americans made up a larger percentage of the population.

Regarding the HOPE scholarship program, the researchers found that white students received a disproportionately high amount of the funds compared with African-American students. In 1999 white students made up 66% of the freshman class in Georgia, but accounted for 74% of all HOPE scholars. By contrast, 26% of all freshmen were African-Americans, yet they accounted for only 21% of HOPE scholars. The authors note that this disproportionate relationship was true for every year examined, back to 1994. However, they noted that the gap narrowed substantially over that time.

Analysis of Georgia's lottery-funded prekindergarten program provided completely different results. The Vinson Institute found that the rate of enrollment in the prekindergarten program is higher in lower-income areas of the state than in affluent areas. The researchers concluded that this particular lottery program is more beneficial to poorer people, African-Americans, and those who regularly play the lottery than to other groups in the state.

In another study published in the January 2004 issue of *Journal of Hispanic Higher Education*, a researcher from Saint Leo University in Florida found that minority and low-income students did not have proportionate access to higher education in lottery states ("State Lotteries: Their Effect on Equal Access to Higher Education").

COMPULSIVE GAMBLING AND "COGNITIVE DISTORTION." The vast majority of states operate lotteries, meaning they are easily accessible to large numbers of people. Surveys, including one conducted by the Pew Research Center in May 2006, have shown that lottery play is the most popular and widely practiced form of gambling in the United States. But does the combination of easy and widespread access and general public acceptance mean that lottery players are more likely to develop serious gambling problems?

The *Gambling Impact and Behavior Study: Report to the National Gambling Impact Study Commission* was conducted by researchers at the University of Chicago in 1999. The study concluded that there is a significant association between lottery availability and the prevalence of at-risk gambling within a state. At-risk gamblers are defined as those who gamble regularly and may be prone to a gambling problem. However, the study found that multivisit lottery patrons had the lowest prevalence of pathological and problem gambling among the gambling types examined.

The researchers also warned that the patron database used in their analysis was small, meaning that the findings may not apply universally. They note that lottery players who do have a problem may be less able to recognize it because lottery players tend to undercount their losses. Lottery players generally lose small amounts at a time, even though these small amounts may eventually total a very large amount. In other words, a casino gambler who loses thousands of dollars in a day might be more likely to admit to having a gambling problem than a lottery player who loses the same amount over a longer period of time.

In 2001 Canadian researchers studied students at McGill University to discover cognitive misconceptions of lottery gamblers (K. K. Hardoon, H. R. Baboushkin, J. L. Deverensky, and R. Gupta, *Journal of Clinical Psychology*, 2001). Sixty-three students were screened to determine their participation in gambling activities. Those with some gambling experience were given the South Oaks Gambling Screen, or SOGS test, which is used to determine the probability that a person has a gambling problem. (See Chapter 2.) All of the students were shown sixteen lotto tickets, each marked with a different sequence of six numbers. The sequences were random (for example, 1, 13, 19, 34, 40, 47); pattern (5, 10, 15, 20, 25, 30); long sequence (1, 2, 3, 4, 5, 6); or nonequilibrated or unbalanced (a series not covering the whole range of possible numbers, usually limited to either high or low numbers, such as 3, 5, 9, 12, 15, 17). The students were then asked to choose the twelve tickets they would most like to play in the lottery and to rank those tickets from best to worst. Random sequences were by far the most popular: more than half of the tickets selected by the students as their first, second, third, and fourth favorite choices contained random sequences. The second most popular choice was the pattern sequence.

The students were also asked to explain the reasoning behind their selections. Randomness was the reason given 78% of the time. The presence of significant numbers (for example, a birth date) was the second most popular reason (69.5%).

The researchers point out that all of the students' choices were irrational because every ticket has an equal chance of winning. However, those students who regularly played the lottery or participated in other gambling activities were more likely to display bias when choosing their favorite tickets. In other words, they had stronger opinions about what was "winnable" than did infrequent players and those who did not gamble. The probable pathological gamblers were found to have more illusions about control than all other participants. The authors concluded that there was "some level of cognitive distortion" demonstrated by all of the gamblers in the study.

THE FUTURE OF U.S. LOTTERIES

New State Lotteries?

As of August 2006, only eight states did not have lotteries: Alabama, Alaska, Arkansas, Hawaii, Mississippi, Nevada, Utah, and Wyoming. Hawaii and Utah permit no types of gambling and seem unlikely to amend their constitutions. Lotteries would be a long shot in Nevada because of the tremendous growth of casino gambling there. Alaskan politicians have shown minimal interest in a lottery. Though numerous state lottery bills have been introduced in the Alabama, Arkansas, and Mississippi legislatures, most of them died in committee and the rest were soundly defeated on the floor. For several years members of the Wyoming legislature have been pushing a bill to allow sale of Powerball tickets. The latest bill cleared a legislative committee in May 2006 and was expected to be introduced into the general legislature in January 2007.

Polls conducted in Alabama, Arkansas, Nevada, and Wyoming in the past few years show strong support for lotteries that would benefit education:

- An October 2004 poll performed by the Center for Governmental Services at Auburn University found 68.9% approval for a statewide lottery to benefit public education in Alabama. Some 55.1% of those polled "strongly supported" an educational lottery, while the rest only "supported" it.

- A poll conducted in the political science department at the University of Arkansas in October 2003 showed a 62% approval rating for a lottery to fund education in Arkansas. Twenty-seven percent "strongly approved" of such a measure, while 35% merely "approved."

- A *Reno Gazette-Journal* poll in February 2005 showed a 76% approval rating for a Nevada educational lottery. Support was slightly lower (63% approval) for a lottery that would only fund full-day kindergarten.

- A 2006 poll conducted by the *Casper-Star Tribune* reported that 62% of Wyoming residents were in favor of a Wyoming Powerball lottery.

Attempts at a National Indian Lottery

The Coeur d'Alene Indians of Idaho have been trying to start a national lottery since 1995. The National Indian Lottery would allow residents of all lottery states to dial a toll-free number at the reservation and register numbers to be played in each drawing. Players would pay using credit cards. While the plan was approved by the National Indian Gaming Commission, it has been tangled in lawsuits for years. As of August 2006, the Coeur d'Alene Tribal Council had not decided if it would continue to pursue the phone lottery.

"Jackpot Fatigue"

A major problem facing the lottery industry is called "jackpot fatigue." Lottery consumers demand higher and higher jackpots so they can stay excited about lotto games. However, individual states cannot increase jackpot sizes without either greatly increasing sales or decreasing the portion of lottery revenue going to public funds. The first option is difficult to achieve and the second is politically dangerous. Jackpot fatigue has driven increasing membership in multistate lotteries, such as Mega Millions and Powerball.

Pressure for Increased Revenue

Even as they cope with jackpot fatigue, many lotteries also face pressure to increase the amount of profit going to government programs. Several states are considering decreasing their lottery payout to raise much-needed funds. Opponents argue that cutting prize payouts will reduce sales, making it nearly impossible to increase state revenues.

CHAPTER 8
SPORTS GAMBLING

Wagering on sporting events is one of the oldest and most popular forms of gambling in the world. The ancient Romans gambled on chariot races, animal fights, and contests between gladiators. The Romans brought sports and gambling to Britain in the first century CE, where they have flourished for hundreds of years. Cockfighting, bear- and bullbaiting, wrestling, and footraces were popular sporting events for gambling throughout Europe during the sixteenth and seventeenth centuries. Horse races and boxing matches became popular spectator and betting sports during the eighteenth century. During the nineteenth and twentieth centuries, sporting events became more team-oriented and organized as rugby, soccer, and cricket grew in popularity.

Many early colonists to America brought their love of sports and gambling with them. Horse racing, in particular, became a part of American culture. However, the morals of the late eighteenth and early nineteenth centuries decreased popular support for legalized sports gambling. By 1910 almost all forms of gambling were illegal in the United States. This did not stop people from gambling on sports, however. The practice continued to flourish, and horse racing, in particular, managed to maintain some legal respectability as a betting sport.

Nevada legalized gambling again in 1931 and permitted sports wagering for two decades. Point-shaving scandals in college basketball and the exposure of the industry's underworld connections during a federal investigation led by Senator Estes Kefauver (D-TN) led to a crackdown during the 1950s. Legal sports gambling did not return to Nevada until 1975, when it was tightly licensed and regulated.

Today sports gambling in the United States can be broken down into three primary categories: 1) parimutuel betting, which is legal in forty-three states, on such events as horse and greyhound races and the ball game jai alai; 2) legal betting using a bookmaker, permitted only in Nevada; and 3) illegal betting.

SOCIAL ATTITUDES TOWARD SPORTS GAMBLING

The popularity of sports gambling is attributed to several factors, including a growing acceptance of gambling in general; intense media coverage of sporting events; and emerging technologies that make wagering easier. Americans can view a wide variety of sporting events from around the world via local and cable television stations, networks dedicated solely to sports, satellite services, and even the Internet. The latest scores can be sent directly to cellular phones. Sports bars and restaurants feature multiple television sets tuned into various sporting events.

In May 2006 the Pew Research Center released *Gambling: As the Take Rises, So Does Public Concern* by Paul Taylor, Cary Funk, and Peyton Craighill. As shown in Figure 2.2 in Chapter 2, the percentages of survey respondents who had gambled on sports were near the low end. Some 18% had bet in an office pool, 14% had bet on a professional sporting event, and 7% had bet on college sports. About 5% said they had bet on a horse race, and 3% had bet on a boxing match. Table 8.1 shows trends over time as reported by the Pew Research Center and the Gallup Poll for professional sports betting and horse racing. In 2003 participation was at thirty-year lows for all categories; in 2006 participation appeared as if it might be on the rise again.

The demographic makeup of those who bet on sports was slightly different from the demographic makeup of the average gambler. (See Table 2.3 in Chapter 2.) While 71% of those with some college education gambled, only 23% of them had bet on sports during the previous year. Similarly, 65% of college graduates gambled, but only 25% bet on sports; 66% of those with high school diplomas or less had gambled, but only 22% had bet on sports. African-Americans (24%) and whites (23%) were more likely than Hispanics (16%) to have bet on sports.

TABLE 8.1

Poll respondents' reported participation in sports gambling, selected years 1989–2006

	Yes %	No %	No opinion %
Bet on a professional sports event such as baseball, basketball, or football			
2006 Feb–Mar	14	86	*
2003 Dec 11–14	10	90	*
1999 Apr 30–May 23	13	87	—
1996 Jun 27–30	10	90	—
1992 Nov 20–22	12	88	—
1990 Feb 15–18	21	79	—
1989 Apr 4–9	22	78	—
Bet on a college sports event such as basketball or football			
2006 Feb–Mar	7	93	*
2003 Dec 11–14	6	94	*
1999 Apr 30–May 23	9	91	—
1996 Jun 27–30	7	93	—
1992 Nov 20–22	6	94	—
1990 Feb 15–18	11	89	—
1989 Apr 4–9	14	86	—
Bet on a boxing match			
2006 Feb–Mar	3	97	*
2003 Dec 11–14	2	98	*
1996 Jun 27–30	3	97	*
1992 Nov 20–22	6	94	—
1990 Feb 15–18	5	95	—
1989 Apr 4–9	8	92	—
Participated in an office pool on the World Series, Superbowl, or other game			
2006 Feb–Mar	18	82	*
2003 Dec 11–14	15	85	*
1999 Apr 30–May 23	25	75	—
1996 Jun 27–30	23	77	—
1992 Nov 20–22	22	78	—

*Less than 0.5%.

Note: 2006 figures are from Pew Research Center; data from all other years are from the Gallup Organization.

SOURCE: Adapted from Paul Taylor, Cary Funk, and Peyton Craighill, "What Kind of Bet Did You Place This Year?" in *Gambling: As the Take Rises, So Does Public Concern*, Pew Research Center, May 23, 2006, http://pewresearch.org/assets/social/pdf/Gambling.pdf (accessed September 6, 2006). Data from The Gallup Organization. Copyright © 1989 by The Gallup Organization. Reproduced by permission of The Gallup Organization.

TABLE 8.2

Poll respondents' opinion on sports betting, by level of interest in sports, 2006

	All adults	Follow sports news		
		Very closely	Somewhat closely	Not very/ not at all
	%	%	%	%
Approve	42	55	42	38
Disapprove	54	43	55	58
Don't know	4	2	3	4
	100	100	100	100
Number of respondents	2,250	383	646	1,216

SOURCE: Paul Taylor, Cary Funk, and Peyton Craighill, "Sports Fans Back Legalized Betting on Professional Sports," in *Gambling: As the Take Rises, So Does Public Concern*, Pew Research Center, May 23, 2006, http://pewresearch.org/assets/social/pdf/Gambling.pdf (accessed September 6, 2006)

While 67% of adults approved of legalized gambling in general in 2006, 50% of people approved of legalized off-track betting on horse races, down 4% from 1989. (See Figure 1.4 in Chapter 1.) Only 42% approved of legal betting on professional sports. In fact, this is the only gambling activity that a majority of Pew survey respondents did not find acceptable. As Table 8.2 shows, however, a higher percentage of sports fans approved of legalized betting on pro sports: 55% of adults who claimed to follow sports news very closely approved of legalized betting on pro sports, compared with only 38% of those who did not follow sports news very closely or at all.

PARI-MUTUEL GAMBLING

Pari-mutuel is a French term meaning "mutual stake." In pari-mutuel betting, all wagers on a particular event or race are combined into a pool that is split between the winning bettors, minus a percentage for the management. The larger the pool, the bigger the payoff. In pari-mutuel gambling, patrons bet against each other, not against the house. The principles of the pari-mutuel system were developed in France during the late nineteenth century by Pierre Oller.

The pari-mutuel system has been used for horse races in the United States since about 1875, but it did not really catch on until the 1920s and 1930s when an automatic odds calculator, a *totalizator*, came into use. The totalizator took money, printed betting tickets, and continuously calculated odds based on betting volume.

Previously, horse betting had been conducted mostly by bookmakers who were notoriously corrupt. In 1933 California, Michigan, New Hampshire, and Ohio legalized pari-mutuel gambling on horse racing as a means of regulating the industry and gaining some revenue. Dozens of states followed suit over the next decade. Pari-mutuel gambling was also adopted for greyhound racing and jai alai matches. More than forty U.S. states allowed pari-mutuel gambling as of 2006. A handful of states permit pari-mutuel gambling by law but do not have facilities or systems in place to conduct it. For example, pari-mutuel gambling on horse racing is permitted in Shelby County, Tennessee, but the state does not have a racing commission. Therefore, no pari-mutuel gambling takes place in Tennessee.

In pari-mutuel gambling the entire amount wagered is called the betting pool, the gross wager, or the *handle*. The system ensures that event managers receive a share of the betting pool, regardless of who wins a particular race or match. The management's share is called the *takeout*. The takeout percentage is set by state law and is usually about 20%.

Breakage refers to the odd cents not paid out to winning bettors because payoffs are rounded. For example, the payout on a $2 bet is typically rounded off in $0.20 increments. The cents left over are the breakage. Although breakage amounts to only pennies per bet, it adds up quickly with high betting volume. For example, California horse racetracks accumulated approximately $10.7 million in breakage in fiscal year 2005, according to the *Thirty-Fifth Annual Report of the California Horse-Racing Board: A Summary of Fiscal Year 2004–2005 Racing in California* (2005). Each state has it owns rules about breakage, but usually the funds are split between the state, the track operators, and the winning horse owners. Breakage is subtracted from the betting pool before payouts are made.

Pari-mutuel wagering can be performed in person at the event or, increasingly, at off-track betting (OTB) facilities. The New York legislature approved the state's first OTB operation in 1970. Some states also allow betting by telephone or Internet when an account is set up prior to bet placement. Many races are broadcast as they occur by televised transmission to in-state and out-of-state locations (including OTB sites). This process, known as *simulcasting*, allows intertrack wagering to take place. In other words, bettors at one racetrack can place bets there on races taking place at another racetrack.

A *race book* is an establishment (usually a room at a casino or a racetrack) in which intertrack wagering takes place on such pari-mutuel events as horse races and greyhound races. A race book typically features many television monitors that show races as they occur. Race books are included in many Nevada and Atlantic City, New Jersey, casinos as well as some tribal casinos. Figure 8.1 shows race book wagering statistics for Nevada casinos from 1996 to 2005. Slightly more than $537 million was wagered in Nevada race books during 2005.

According to statistics from the American Gaming Association, the total gross revenue (handle minus payout) on pari-mutuel gambling in the United States was $3.7 billion in 2005 (http://www.americangaming.org/Industry/factsheets/statistics_detail.cfv?id=7). Most of the money was bet on horse racing; lesser amounts were bet on greyhound racing and jai alai.

HORSE RACING

Horse racing has been a popular sport since the time of the ancient Greeks and Romans. It was popularized in western Europe in the Middle Ages when knights returned from the Crusades with fast Arabian stallions. These horses were bred with sturdy English mares to produce a new line of horses now known as Thoroughbreds. Thoroughbreds are tall, lean horses with long, slender legs. They are renowned for their speed and grace while running.

Thoroughbred racing became popular among the British royalty and aristocrats, earning it the nickname "Sport of Kings." The sport was transplanted to America during colonial times. Races were run on Long Island, New York, as far back as 1665, according to the Jockey Club, the governing body of Thoroughbred horse racing. However, the advent of organized Thoroughbred racing in the United States is attributed to Governor Samuel Ogle of Maryland, who staged a race "between pedigreed horses in the English style" in Annapolis, Maryland, in 1743. The Annapolis Jockey Club, which sponsored the race, later became the Maryland Jockey Club. Among its members were George Washington and Thomas Jefferson.

Thoroughbred breeding was prominent in Maryland and Virginia until the Civil War (1861–65), when many operations were moved to Kentucky. Thoroughbred racing had already grown popular throughout the agricultural South. In 1863 the Saratoga racecourse opened in northern New York. It is considered the oldest Thoroughbred flat track in the country. (A flat track is one with no hurdles or other obstacles for a racing horse to jump over.) The Jockey Club, which maintains the official breed registry for Thoroughbred horses in North America, was established in 1894 in New York City.

Horse racing remained popular in the United States until World War II (1941–45), when it was severely curtailed. The decades since the war have seen a sharp decline in the popularity of horse racing. Three reasons are commonly mentioned:

- Competition increased from other entertainment venues and leisure activities, such as theme parks, shopping malls, and television.

- The horse-racing industry avoided television coverage of races during the 1960s for fear it would keep people away from the tracks. (This is now seen as a failure to take advantage of a major marketing tool.)

- The legalization of state lotteries and casinos created competition for gambling dollars.

However, while attendance declined, the amount of money gambled on horse races increased overall. As shown in Figure 8.2, the pari-mutuel handle from Thoroughbred horse racing was $15.2 billion in 2003, up from $9.4 billion in 1990. It dropped slightly to $14.8 billion in 2005. Nearly 88% of the amount gambled during 2005 was bet at OTB facilities. Analysts believe that attendance at live racing will continue to decline as more OTB opportunities become available.

Thoroughbred Racetracks and Races

About ninety Thoroughbred racetracks of varying sizes operate throughout the country. Some are open seasonally, while those in warm climates are open year-round. Some are owned by the government, and some are owned by private and

FIGURE 8.1

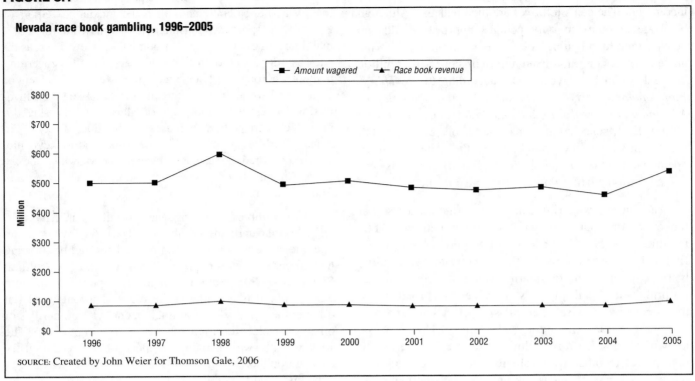

Nevada race book gambling, 1996–2005

Legend: ■ *Amount wagered*　▲ *Race book revenue*

SOURCE: Created by John Weier for Thomson Gale, 2006

FIGURE 8.2

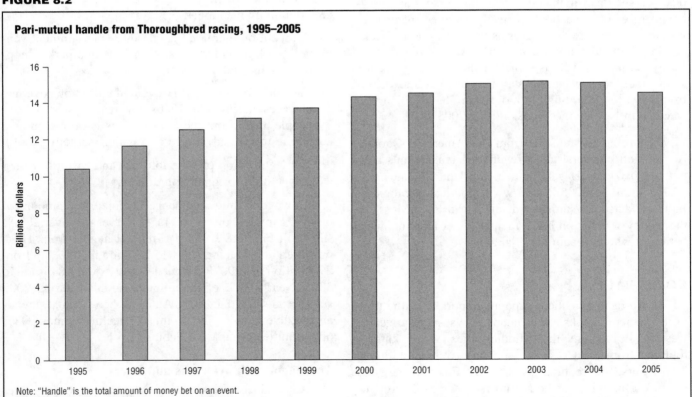

Pari-mutuel handle from Thoroughbred racing, 1995–2005

Note: "Handle" is the total amount of money bet on an event.

SOURCE: "U.S. Pari-Mutuel Handle," in *Fact Book*, The Jockey Club, 2006, http://www.jockeyclub.com/factbook.asp?section=8 (accessed September 6, 2006)

TABLE 8.3

Thoroughbred horse races by state or Canadian province, 2005

State/province	Number of races	Gross purses*	Starters	Starts	Average field	Average starts per runner
Arizona	2,020	$15,394,256	3,078	16,060	8.0	5.2
Arkansas	560	$13,934,100	1,847	4,910	8.8	2.7
California	5,012	$169,694,057	7,877	37,672	7.5	4.8
Colorado	253	$1,994,800	665	2,107	8.3	3.2
Delaware	1,214	$37,209,840	3,276	8,928	7.4	2.7
Florida	3,732	$81,504,048	7,851	31,322	8.4	4.0
Georgia	10	$365,000	68	68	6.8	1.0
Idaho	27	$178,300	186	190	7.0	1.0
Illinois	2,970	$70,627,593	4,665	23,405	7.9	5.0
Indiana	1,074	$13,198,400	2,894	9,686	9.0	3.3
Iowa	707	$13,116,587	1,277	5,345	7.6	4.2
Kansas	253	$1,521,450	834	2,013	8.0	2.4
Kentucky	2,556	$80,064,081	6,938	22,140	8.7	3.2
Louisiana	3,352	$72,031,436	6,999	29,878	8.9	4.3
Maryland	1,834	$42,296,000	4,541	14,598	8.0	3.2
Massachusetts	1,146	$12,133,700	1,399	8,921	7.8	6.4
Michigan	964	$10,485,982	1,287	7,048	7.3	5.5
Minnesota	585	$10,628,100	1,275	4,787	8.2	3.8
Montana	182	$421,750	351	1,184	6.5	3.4
Nebraska	932	$6,586,242	1,480	8,012	8.6	5.4
Nevada	30	$125,566	104	166	5.5	1.6
New Hampshire	0	$0	0	0	0.0	0.0
New Jersey	1,141	$41,549,276	2,977	8,626	7.6	2.9
New Mexico	1,453	$24,061,777	2,584	11,954	8.2	4.6
New York	3,745	$154,404,075	6,566	29,161	7.8	4.4
North Carolina	18	$300,000	95	115	6.4	1.2
North Dakota	103	$306,106	301	741	7.2	2.5
Ohio	3,226	$25,424,600	5,476	27,023	8.4	4.9
Oklahoma	905	$8,963,630	2,421	8,295	9.2	3.4
Oregon	740	$2,562,622	1,212	5,384	7.3	4.4
Pennsylvania	3,681	$49,313,112	6,278	30,348	8.2	4.8
South Carolina	20	$535,000	142	169	8.5	1.2
Tennessee	6	$325,000	46	46	7.7	1.0
Texas	1,868	$27,132,150	4,043	16,418	8.8	4.1
Virginia	427	$12,145,250	1,920	3,680	8.6	1.9
Washington	1,002	$11,096,804	1,750	7,750	7.7	4.4
West Virginia	4,472	$73,306,275	9,156	39,630	8.9	4.3
Wyoming	37	$68,450	127	268	7.2	2.1
Total	**52,257**	**$1,085,005,415**				
Canada						
Alberta	1,151	$13,045,701	1,692	8,740	7.6	5.2
British Columbia	798	$12,591,501	1,049	5,877	7.4	5.6
Manitoba	590	$4,961,352	883	4,607	7.8	5.2
Ontario	2,466	$82,139,695	3,712	20,620	8.4	5.6
Saskatchewan	233	$660,791	414	1,752	7.5	4.2
Total	**5,238**	**$113,399,040**				

*Purses include monies not won and returned to state breeder or other funds.

SOURCE: "2005 Analysis of Races by State or Province," in *Fact Book*, The Jockey Club, 2006, http://www.jockeyclub.com/factbook/factbook06/compare%2005.htm (accessed September 6, 2006). Data from Equibase Company, LLC.

public companies. Thoroughbred horse racing in the United States is controlled by a relatively small group of players. Two publicly traded companies, Churchill Downs and Magna Entertainment, along with the New York City Off-Track Betting Corporation (NYCOTB) and the New York Racing Association, control much of the business. The New York Racing Association is a not-for-profit group that controls the Belmont, Saratoga, and Aqueduct racetracks. Analysts predict that the industry will continue to undergo consolidation, with corporations taking over most of the business.

The three most prestigious Thoroughbred races in the United States are the Kentucky Derby at the Churchill Downs track in Kentucky, the Preakness Stakes at Pimlico in Maryland, and the Belmont Stakes at Belmont Park in New York. The races are held over a five-week period during May and June of each year. A horse that wins all three races in one year is said to have won the Triple Crown. Only eleven horses have ever captured the Triple Crown, most recently a horse named Affirmed in 1978.

According to the Jockey Club, there were 52,257 Thoroughbred horse races in 38 states during 2005. (See Table 8.3.) California hosted the most events, with 5,012 races, followed by West Virginia (4,472), New York (3,745), Florida (3,732), and Pennsylvania (3,681). The

FIGURE 8.3

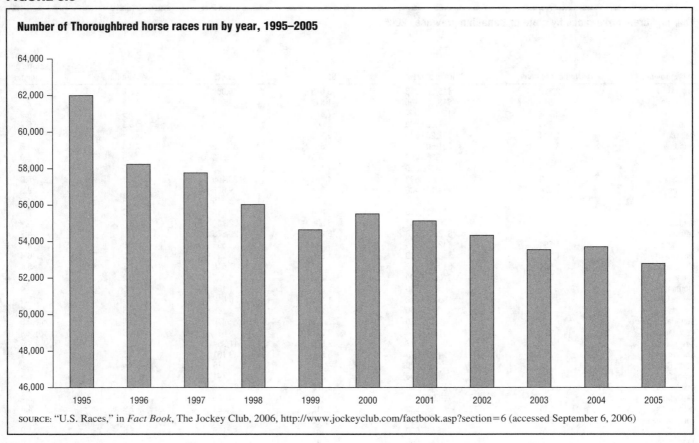

Number of Thoroughbred horse races run by year, 1995–2005

SOURCE: "U.S. Races," in *Fact Book*, The Jockey Club, 2006, http://www.jockeyclub.com/factbook.asp?section=6 (accessed September 6, 2006)

total gross purses amounted to more than $1 billion. The gross purse is the amount awarded to the owners of the winning horses. California racetracks had the highest gross purse of nearly $170 million, followed by New York ($154 million), Florida ($82 million), Kentucky ($80 million), and West Virginia ($73 million). As shown in Figure 8.3, the number of Thoroughbred races held each year has steadily declined since the early 1990s.

Non-Thoroughbred Horse Racing

Although Thoroughbred horse racing is the most popular, other types of horse racing are attractions for pari-mutuel wagering. In harness racing, specially trained horses trot or pace rather than gallop. Usually, the horse pulls a two-wheeled cart, or *sulky*, carrying a jockey who controls the reins. Sometimes the jockey is seated on the horse rather than in a sulky. Harness racing is performed by standardbred horses, which are shorter, more muscled, and longer in body than Thoroughbreds. The National Association of Trotting Horse Breeders in America established the official registry for standardbred horses in 1879. At the time, Thoroughbred horses were the favorite of high society; standardbred racing became popular among the common folk. As of 2006 thirty-seven licensed harness racetracks offered pari-mutuel betting, according to the United States Trotting Association http://www.ustrotting.

com/trackside/trackfacts/tracksbystate.cfm. Harness racing is also an attraction at state and county fairs, although not all allow wagering.

A third type of horse known for racing is the quarter horse, so named because of its high speed over distances of less than a quarter of a mile. Quarter horses were originally bred by American colonists to be both hardworking and athletic. The American Quarter Horse Association reported that in 2006 races were conducted at eighty-four separate meets, which lasted from a mere two days of racing at some local fairs to 200 race days offered at the Los Alamitos Race Course in Los Alamitos, California (http://www.aqha.com/aqharacing.com/schedule/06USARaceDates051506.pdf).

Arabian horses are considered the only purebred horses on the race circuit. They race at about fifteen tracks in the United States.

Betting on Horse Races

The betting pool for a particular horse race depends on how much is wagered by bettors on that race. Each wager affects the odds. The more money bet on a horse, the lower that horse's odds and the potential payoff becomes. The payout for winning tickets is determined by the amount of money bet on the winner in relation to the amount bet on all the other horses in that particular race.

FIGURE 8.4

Distribution of the horse racing takeout dollar in California, 2005

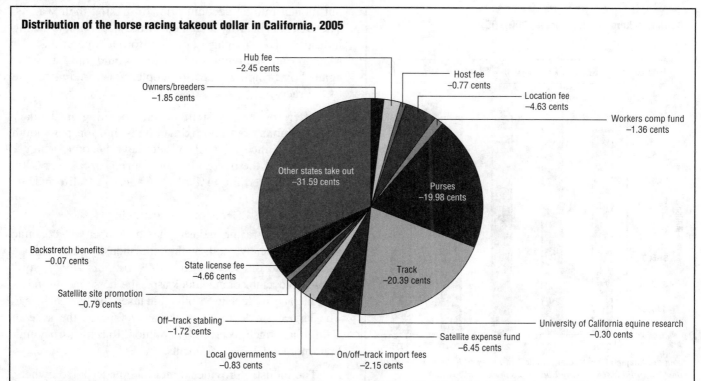

SOURCE: Adapted from "The Takeout Dollar in California: Where It Goes and How It's Used," in *Thirty-fifth Annual Report of the California Horse Racing Board: A Summary of Fiscal Year 2004–2005 Racing in California*, California Horse Racing Board, 2006, http://www.chrb.ca.gov/annual_reports/2005_annual_report.pdf (accessed September 6, 2006)

First, the takeout is subtracted from the betting pool. This money goes toward track expenses, taxes, and the purse. Most states also require that a portion of the takeout be put into breeder incentive funds to encourage horse breeding and health in the state. Figure 8.4 shows the breakdown of each takeout dollar in California. (Note: In this graphic, "other states takeout" refers to wagering fees that are paid to betting facilities in other states that take bets on California races.) After the takeout and the breakage are subtracted from the betting pool, the remaining money is divided by the number of bettors to determine the payoff, or return, on each wager.

The odds on a particular horse winning first, second, or third place are estimated on the morning of a race and then constantly recalculated by computer during the betting period before the race. The odds are posted on a display, or tote board, and on television screens throughout the betting area. The tote board also tallies the total amount paid into each pool. Bettors can wager that a particular horse will win (come in first), place (come in first or second), or show (come in first, second, or third). The payoff for a win is higher than payoffs for place or show, because the latter two pools have to be split more ways. For example, the show pool must be split between all bettors who selected win, place, or show. The approximate payoffs for a $2 winning ticket on horses of various odds are shown in Table 8.4.

TABLE 8.4

Money paid out on a successful $2 pari-mutuel bet

Odds	$2 bet returns	Odds	$2 bet returns
1–10	$2.20	3–1	$8.00
1–5	$2.40	7–2	$9.00
2–5	$2.80	4–1	$10.00
1–2	$3.00	9–2	$11.00
3–5	$3.20	5–1	$12.00
4–5	$3.60	6–1	$14.00
1–1	$4.00	7–1	$16.00
6–5	$4.40	8–1	$18.00
7–5	$4.80	9–1	$20.00
3–2	$5.00	10–1	$22.00
8–5	$5.20	12–1	$26.00
2–1	$6.00	15–1	$32.00
5–2	$7.00	20–1	$42.00

SOURCE: "How Much Do I Win?" in *Daily Racing Form*, Spring 2004, http://www.drf.com/row/fan_ed/winning-techniques-2004.pdf (accessed September 26, 2004)

Betting on horse races is considered more a game of skill than a game of chance. Professional racing bettors spend many hours observing individual horses and consider previous race experience when they make their picks. This gives them some advantage over bettors who pick a horse based on whim—because they like its name, for example. Although bettors do not play directly against

FIGURE 8.5

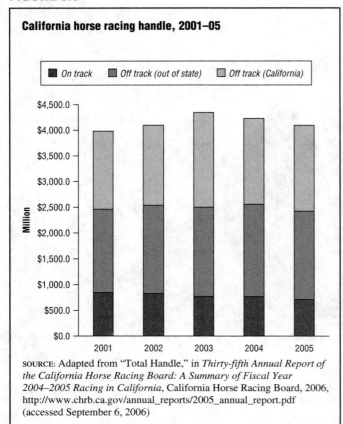

California horse racing handle, 2001–05

Legend: ■ On track ■ Off track (out of state) ■ Off track (California)

(Y-axis: Million — $0.0 to $4,500.0; X-axis: 2001, 2002, 2003, 2004, 2005)

SOURCE: Adapted from "Total Handle," in *Thirty-fifth Annual Report of the California Horse Racing Board: A Summary of Fiscal Year 2004–2005 Racing in California*, California Horse Racing Board, 2006, http://www.chrb.ca.gov/annual_reports/2005_annual_report.pdf (accessed September 6, 2006)

each other, an individual bettor's skill does affect other bettors because the odds are based on the bets of all gamblers.

Horse Racing in California

California led the nation in 2005 in terms of the number of races held and the purses paid to winning horses. The state has allowed pari-mutuel gambling on horse races since 1933, when a constitutional amendment was passed by the voters. California has six privately owned racetracks and nine racing fairs. Racing fairs are county and state fairs—often held at racetracks—where wagering on horse races is one of many fair events. The fairs usually last only a week or two and are conducted several times a year. Gamblers can also bet on horse races at twenty simulcast facilities in the state.

The Thirty-Fifth Annual Report of the California Horse-Racing Board (2005) reveals that the industry grossed $4.2 billion during fiscal year 2005, the highest of any state in the country. Figure 8.5 shows the handle broken down by on-track, off-track, and out-of-state wagers. Only 17% ($726 million) of all wagers occurred at the track during 2005. The vast majority of wagers were placed at off-track locations. Winning bettors received 80% of the betting pool, or $3.4 billion. The state received revenues of $44 million.

In August 2001 California legalized advanced-deposit wagering (ADW), which permits betting over the telephone and Internet. To do this, gamblers must put money into an account prior to making their wagers. The idea was heartily endorsed by the state's horse-racing industry. The manager of California operations for Magna Entertainment said racing would only flourish again "by bringing races to people, not bringing people to the races."

After the new system began operating in January 2002, gamblers bet approximately $4 million per month via ADW. Since then ADW bets have become a bigger percentage of the overall handle. During fiscal year 2005 ADW accounted for 11% of all wagers in California.

The Economic Effects of Horse Racing

The horse-racing industry has a number of economic effects on society, both within the industry and without. According to the Jockey Club's *Online Fact Book* (http://www.jockeyclub.com/factbook.asp), the horse-racing industry generates more than $1 billion in taxes and fees each year. The largest single recipient during 2005 was the state of California, which received $44 million. Racetracks pay millions more to local governments.

The industry provides direct income to horse owners, trainers, and jockeys through purses. California tracks paid out the highest gross purse for the year ($170 million), and New York paid out the highest average purse per race ($41,229). The largest portion of a Thoroughbred race purse (typically 60%) goes to the owner of the first-place horse. The owner is responsible for paying the horse's trainer and jockey. The owners of the horses finishing second and third typically receive around 20% and 12%, respectively, of a race purse. Harness track purses paid out during 2005 totaled approximately $315 million. New Jersey had by far the highest gross purse ($73 million) and the highest average purse per race ($16,983).

The racing industry also supports a large business in horse breeding. In 1962 Maryland was the first state to establish a program to encourage breeders within the state through direct money payments. The practice spread quickly to other states involved in horse racing.

Figure 8.6 is a flow chart developed by researchers at the University of Maryland (*Economic Impact of Horse Racing in Maryland*, 1999) to show the economic impact of horse racing. They determined that the sport's main impact is not the cash flows between the wagering public, the racetracks and OTBs, the horse owners, jockeys, breeders, and trainers, and the regulatory government agencies. The researchers saw that cash flow as cash transfers. The true economic effects of the industry, they said, occur outside the industry from expenditures on goods and services.

Racetrack and OTB operators spend money on land, labor, and other goods and services from various businesses. Horse owners, breeders, and trainers spend money

FIGURE 8.6

Maryland horse racing industry flow chart

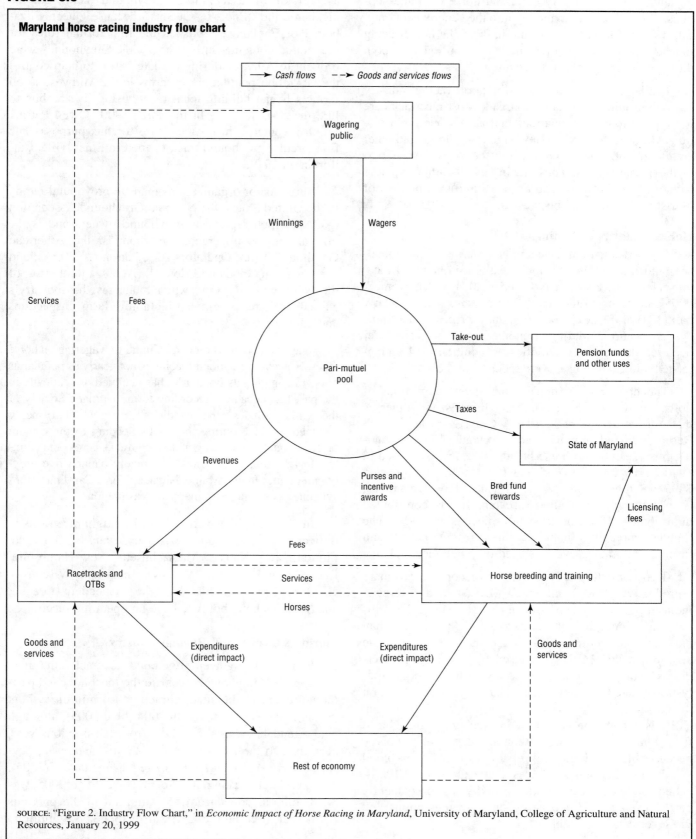

SOURCE: "Figure 2. Industry Flow Chart," in *Economic Impact of Horse Racing in Maryland*, University of Maryland, College of Agriculture and Natural Resources, January 20, 1999

on land, labor, veterinary care, and horse feed and supplies. All of these pump money into the general economy. The Jockey Club estimated that in 2005 the horse-racing industry created the equivalent of 1.4 million jobs both directly and indirectly in the United States.

Unlike the casino industry, the horse-racing industry has only a minor impact on tourism. Most racetracks are not typical tourist destinations that attract overnight visitors who would spend money on lodging, food, and other entertainment. The exceptions are the races held as part of the Triple Crown. Those racing events attract visitors from all over the world and bring a significant number of tourist dollars to local businesses.

Horse Fatalities and Injuries

Horse racing does have a price in terms of horse fatalities and injuries. For example, California had 320 racehorse fatalities between November 2004 and November 2005, according to the state's horse-racing board. Nearly half (154) of the deaths occurred during races. Ninety-nine deaths occurred during training, and the remainder occurred during other activities. In addition, 514 racing-related injuries to horses were reported in the state.

The horse-racing industry has invested millions of dollars in veterinary research on injuries and illnesses that affect racehorses. The Grayson-Jockey Club Research Foundation, the leading private source of funding for research into horse health issues, was founded in 1940. For 2005, the foundation says, it allocated $895,948 toward twenty-one projects at twelve universities that conduct equine research. It has contributed more than $12 million to such projects since 1983. The foundation receives financial support from donations and from special racing events staged by horse racetracks.

Two horse health issues of major concern are mare reproductive loss syndrome (MRLS) and exercise-induced pulmonary hemorrhage (EIPH). MRLS is an illness that killed 30% of Kentucky foals (horses less than one year old) during 2001. Since then, scientists have determined that MRLS is caused by eastern tent caterpillars, which can find their way into horse food. Analysts estimate that MRLS has had an economic impact on the horse-racing industry of $336 million to $500 million. EIPH is a common condition in racehorses: they bleed from the lungs during strenuous exercise, probably because increased blood pressure ruptures tiny blood vessels in their lungs. Horses that experience EIPH—called *bleeders*—can be temporarily or permanently barred from racing depending on state regulations and the severity of the problem.

GREYHOUND RACING

Greyhounds are mentioned in many ancient documents. English noblemen used greyhounds to hunt rabbits, a sport known as *coursing*. Greyhound racing got the nickname the "Sport of Queens" because Queen Elizabeth I of England established the first formal rules for greyhound coursing during the 1500s. Greyhounds were brought to America during the late 1800s to help control the jackrabbit population on farms in the Midwest. Soon farmers began holding local races, using live rabbits to lure the dogs to race. In the early 1900s Owen Patrick Smith invented a mechanical lure for this purpose. The first circular greyhound track opened in Emeryville, California, in 1919.

Three major organizations manage greyhound racing in the United States: the National Greyhound Association (NGA), which represents greyhound owners and is the official registry for racing greyhounds; the American Greyhound Track Operators Association (AGTOA); and the American Greyhound Council (AGC), a joint effort of the NGA and AGTOA, which manages the industry's animal welfare programs, including farm inspections and adoptions.

Wagering on greyhounds is similar to wagering on horse races. However, greyhound racing is not nearly as popular as horse racing, and its popularity has declined dramatically in the past few decades. According to the Humane Society of the United States, the handle from greyhound racing declined by 45% during the 1990s, leading to the closure or cessation of live racing at sixteen tracks across the country. In addition, eight states specifically banned live greyhound racing: Idaho, Maine, Nevada, North Carolina, Pennsylvania, Vermont, Virginia, and Washington.

In 2005 greyhounds raced at thirty-eight racetracks in thirteen states: Alabama, Arizona, Arkansas, Colorado, Florida, Iowa, Kansas, Massachusetts, New Hampshire, Rhode Island, Texas, West Virginia, and Wisconsin. Greyhound racing is also legal in Connecticut, Oregon, and South Dakota, but they have no operating racetracks.

Florida's Greyhound-Racing Industry

Florida has eighteen greyhound racetracks, the most of any state. Greyhound races are the most attended pari-mutuel event in the state, attracting 1.6 million visitors during fiscal year 2005 (July 2004–June 2005), although paid attendance was down 12% from the previous year, according to the *Division of Pari-mutuel Wagering Seventy-Fourth Annual Report: Fiscal Year 2004-- (2005).* The greyhound-racing handle in fiscal year 2005 was $448 million, down from $509 million in the previous fiscal year. (See Figure 8.7.) Purses totaled $29 million.

Greyhound racetracks paid $13 million to the state during fiscal year 2005, accounting for 49% of the state's revenue from pari-mutuel gambling. The taxes paid to the state declined by 19% from the previous year.

FIGURE 8.7

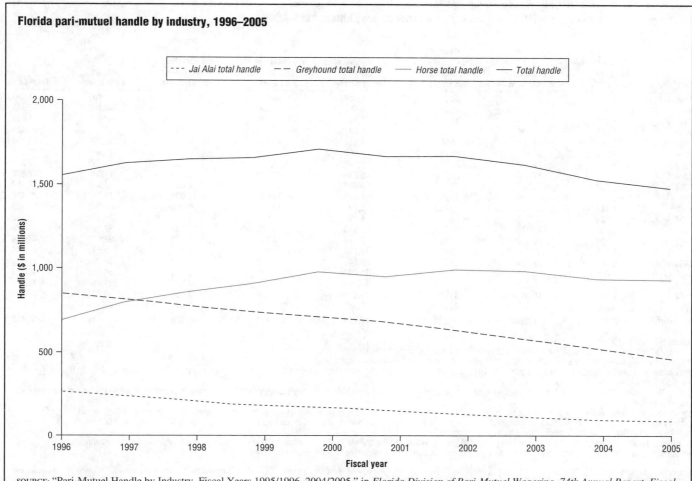

Florida pari-mutuel handle by industry, 1996–2005

Legend: - - - Jai Alai total handle — — Greyhound total handle —— Horse total handle —— Total handle

Y-axis: Handle ($ in millions) — 0, 500, 1,000, 1,500, 2,000

X-axis: Fiscal year — 1996, 1997, 1998, 1999, 2000, 2001, 2002, 2003, 2004, 2005

SOURCE: "Pari-Mutuel Handle by Industry, Fiscal Years 1995/1996–2004/2005," in *Florida Division of Pari-Mutuel Wagering, 74th Annual Report, Fiscal Year 2004–2005*, Florida Department of Business and Professional Regulation, Division of Pari-Mutuel Wagering, December 2005, http://www.myflorida.com/dbpr/pmw/annual_reports/ar0405.pdf (accessed September 6, 2006)

The Economic Effects of Greyhound Racing

According to the AGC Web site (http://www.agcouncil.com/racing.cfm?page=3), breeding farms and racing kennels represented an investment of more than $150 million and pumped $96 million per year into local economies. AGC valued the nation's racing greyhounds at more than $200 million. In addition, it said that greyhound tracks around the country employed more than 14,000 people and raised nearly $100 million per year in tax revenue. The tracks were credited with donating more than $11.7 million per year to charities and community causes.

Concerns about Greyhound Welfare

The National Coalition against Legalized Gambling claims that there were more than seventy-five well-documented cases of cruelty and abuse in the greyhound industry during the 1990s involving thousands of dogs that were shot, starved, abandoned, or sold to research laboratories. Because of the work of animal rights groups such as the Humane Society, the cruelty of the greyhound industry was revealed to the American public. Many greyhound-racing organizations changed the way they treated greyhounds and initiated adoption programs for dogs that were too old to race. The practice of killing unsuccessful greyhounds, however, is still very much alive. The Greyhound Protection League (http://www.greyhounds.org) compiles statistics on what it says are the number of greyhounds bred, adopted, and killed each year. (See Table 8.5. Note that the figures are not exact—many are estimates.) The league claims that more than 600,000 greyhound puppies and adult dogs were killed by the industry from 1986 to 2005. During the same period 164,275 greyhounds were adopted. The organization alleges that the racing industry overbreeds greyhounds in the hopes of producing winners, leading to the destruction of thousands of unwanted puppies each year. A racing greyhound's career is typically over at the age of four years, well below its average lifespan of twelve years, meaning that thousands of adult dogs are also destroyed each year when they are no longer able to race.

According to the Florida Department of Business and Professional Regulation, almost all of that state's

TABLE 8.5

Racing greyhound breeding statistics and estimated number of dogs killed, 1986–2005

Year	Number of litters born (NGA)	Estimated number born	Dogs individually registered to race (NGA)	Farm puppies culled before racing	Estimated greyhounds adopted[b]	Estimated dogs retained for breeding	Racing dogs killed	Total killed
2005	4,300	28,036	26,207	1,829	14,600	1,500	10,107	11,936
2004	4,977	32,450	26,262	6,187	14,500	1,600	10,162	16,349
2003	5,171	33,714	26,277	7,437	14,500	1,800	9,977	17,414
2002	5,205	33,936	27,142	6,794	14,000	1,800	13,142	19,936
2001	5,015	32,698	26,797	5,901	13,000	1,800	11,997	17,898
2000	5,234	34,126	26,464	7,662	13,000	2,000	11,464	19,126
1999	5,266	34,334	27,059	7,275	13,000	2,000	12,059	19,334
1998	5,034	32,822	26,036	6,786	13,000	2,000	11,036	17,822
1997	5,192	33,852	28,025	5,827	12,500	2,000	13,525	19,352
1996	5,438	35,456	28,877	6,579	12,000	2,000	13,977	21,456
1995	5,749	37,483	31,688	5,795	10,000	2,100	19,588	25,383
1994	6,232	40,633	34,746	5,887	8,500	2,200	24,046	29,933
1993	6,805	44,369	39,139	5,230	6,000	2,500	30,639	35,869
1992	7,690	50,139	38,023	12,116	3,000	2,500	32,523	44,639
1991	8,049	52,479	38,430	14,049	1,000	3,500	33,930	47,979
1990	9,473	61,764	38,615	23,149	650	3,200	34,765	57,914
1989	7,690	50,139	38,443	11,696	450[c]	3,000	34,993	46,689
1988	7,979	52,023	37,784	14,239	300	2,750	34,734	48,973
1987	7,638	49,800	33,021	16,779	200	2,500	30,321	47,100
1986	6,688	43,606	30,219	13,387	75	2,000	28,144	41,531
Total[a]	124,825	813,859	629,254	184,604	164,275	44,750	421,129	606,633

Notes:

Litters: As reported by the National Greyhound Association (NGA), the U.S. registry organization.

Total born: Derived by multiplying the total number of litters by an average of 6.52 pups per litter.

Individuals registered to race: As reported by the NGA in The Greyhound Review, the official industry publication. Each owner must pay an additional fee to the NGA to have a greyhound individually registered.

Culled: This column shows the total number of young dogs that disappear annually between birth and individual registration by 18 months of age. Few puppies or young dogs are ever delivered to rescue groups.

[a]To arrive at an estimated eighteen-year total of greyhounds killed, one must also subtract the number of dogs still in the racing system (approximately 38,000), the number of puppies/youngsters currently at farms approximately 26,000) and the breeding stock required to produce thousands of litters a year (about 500 males and 3,000 females).

[b]A liberal estimate of figures from those in the adoption community.

[c]Organized, large-scale adoption efforts did not take place until the mid 1990s. During the late 1980s it is estimated that only a few hundred dogs made it into adoptive homes nationwide. During the previous 50 years of dog racing, all greyhounds that were not used for breeding were routinely destroyed.

SOURCE: Adapted from "A. Where Do Those Puppies Go?" and "B. Thousands More Greyhounds That Are Registered to Race Disappear Annually," in *Know the Facts about Greyhound Racing*, Greyhound Protection League, 2006, http://www.greyhounds.org/gpl/contents/exploit.html (accessed September 6, 2006)

greyhound tracks actively sponsor greyhound adoption programs, and many have on-site adoption booths. The tracks are required to pay 10% of the credit they receive for uncashed winning tickets to organizations that promote or encourage greyhound adoptions. These mandatory contributions amounted to $202,206 during fiscal year 2005. AGC estimates that racetracks nationwide donate $2 million per year to greyhound adoption efforts.

JAI ALAI

Jai alai is a court game in which players bounce a ball against the wall and catch it using a long curved basket, or *cesta*, that is strapped to the wrist. The term *jai alai* (pronounced "hi-lie") comes from the Spanish Basque phrase for "merry festival." The first permanent jai alai arena, called a *fronton*, was built in Florida in 1924.

The game's scoring system has been adjusted over the years to make it more attractive to gamblers. Typical games include eight players, with two players competing for a point at one time. The game continues until one player obtains seven points. Win, place, and show positions are winning bets, just as in horse racing.

Jai alai peaked in popularity during the early 1980s, when more than $600 million was wagered on the sport. By fiscal 2005 the total handle had declined to $87 million. (See Figure 8.7.)

In 2006 only five frontons in Florida offered pari-mutuel gambling on jai alai. (Other frontons in the United States—in Connecticut and Rhode Island—had closed by 2003.) Paid attendance in Florida was 270,253 in fiscal year 2005, down from 360,340 the year before. The state received almost $540,000 in taxes and fees from the jai alai industry in 2005.

THE FUTURE OF PARI-MUTUEL GAMBLING

Decreasing Popularity and Decreasing Income

Pari-mutuel gambling is decreasing in popularity as it faces more and more competition from other gambling options, particularly casinos. The horse-racing industry experienced a 40% decline in attendance during the 1990s, so

FIGURE 8.8

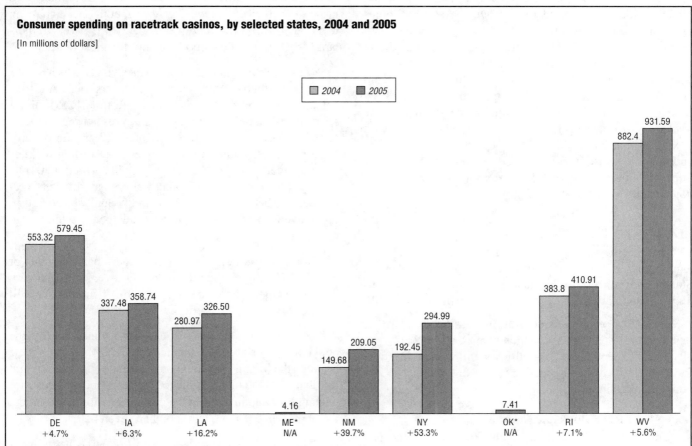

Consumer spending on racetrack casinos, by selected states, 2004 and 2005

[In millions of dollars]

☐ 2004 ■ 2005

	DE +4.7%	IA +6.3%	LA +16.2%	ME* N/A	NM +39.7%	NY +53.3%	OK* N/A	RI +7.1%	WV +5.6%
2004	553.32	337.48	280.97		149.68	192.45		383.8	882.4
2005	579.45	358.74	326.50	4.16	209.05	294.99	7.41	410.91	931.59

*There are no 2004 statistics for Maine and Oklahoma because racetrack casinos in these states only became operational in 2005.

SOURCE: "State by State Consumer Spending on Racetrack Casinos, 2004 vs. 2005," in *2006 State of the States: The AGA Survey of Casino Entertainment*, American Gaming Association, 2006, http://www.americangaming.org/assets/files/2006_Survey_for_Web.pdf (accessed September 6, 2006). Reprinted with permission from the American Gaming Association. All rights reserved.

racetracks found it increasingly difficult to attract a large enough betting pool to afford to run races. According to the Jockey Club, the number of Thoroughbred races run each year in the United States fell from 74,071 in 1989 to 52,257 in 2005, a decrease of 29%. Figure 8.3 illustrates the decline over the period 1995 to 2005. Total handle grew from $9.39 billion in 1990 to $14.56 billion in 2005, an increase of 55%, but inflation during the same period drove up costs of goods and services by 49%, according to the Bureau of Labor Statistics (http://data.bls.gov/cgi-bin/cpicalc.pl).

Attempts to Attract New Gamblers

Gambling industry analysts say horse races have a relatively small hard-core group of attendees, most of whom are older people. The industry is trying to attract a larger and younger fan base (twenty-five to forty-five years old) with disposable income. Some racetracks have tried to become entertainment venues by offering food courts, malls, and music concerts. Although these attractions may increase attendance, the newcomers do not necessarily gamble. Meanwhile, devoted race fans complain that such promotions are too distracting and draw attention away from the racing.

Increasingly, pari-mutuel facilities are offering other gambling choices to patrons. Nine states had slot machines and/or video lottery terminals at their racetracks during 2006: Delaware, Iowa, Louisiana, Maine, New Mexico, New York, Oklahoma, Rhode Island, and West Virginia. Racetrack casinos, or *racinos*, have been a huge success. According to the American Gaming Association's annual assessment of the industry (2006), consumer spending at racetrack casinos increased from $2.1 billion in 2001 to $3.1 billion in 2005, a jump of 49%. As Figure 8.8 shows, gamblers in West Virginia wagered almost a third of the revenue brought in by racetrack casinos nationwide in 2005.

Most of Florida's racetracks and jai alai frontons have card rooms in which gamblers wager on card games, mainly poker. According to the annual report of the Florida Division of Pari-mutuel Wagering, gross revenue in the state's card rooms was $38 million in fiscal year 2005. The card rooms contributed more than $4 million in taxes and fees to state and local governments.

In 2003 the Florida State Assembly amended the state constitution to allow slot machines at Florida pari-mutuel establishments. The counties in which the pari-mutuel tracks reside are required to approve the slot machines by referendum. Broward County residents approved slot machines at two failing horse tracks, one dilapidated dog track, and a jai-alai fronton in 2004. Construction was nearly complete on racino facilities at the dog track and one horse track in late 2006. In August, however, the First District Court of Appeals in Tallahassee ruled that the tracks could not open because of disputed signatures on a petition that launched the 2004 Broward County referendum. The case was expected to reach the Florida Supreme Court. Construction of the racino facilities was not suspended, however.

LEGAL SPORTS GAMBLING

Besides the sports involved in pari-mutuel gambling, legal sports gambling is extremely limited in the United States. Only one state, Nevada, allows high-stakes gambling on such sports as football, basketball, and baseball.

In 1992 Congress passed the Professional and Amateur Sports Protection Act, which banned sports betting in all states except those that already allowed it in some form (Delaware, Montana, Nevada, New Mexico, Oregon, and Washington).

Sports and Race Books in Nevada

Sports books are establishments that accept and pay off bets on sporting events. They are legal only in Nevada. Bettors must be over age twenty-one and physically present in the state.

According to the Nevada Gaming Control Board, 183 locations in the state were licensed to operate sports books and/or race books in August 2006. More than half of them were in Las Vegas, and most were operated by casinos. The typical casino book is a large room with many television monitors showing races and games from around the world. Most casinos have combined race/sports books, although the betting formats are usually different. Race-book betting is mostly of the pari-mutuel type, while sports-book betting is by bookmaking.

Bookmaking

Bookmaking is the common term for the act of determining odds and receiving and paying off bets. The person performing the service is called the bookmaker, or *bookie*. Bookmaking has its own lingo, which can be confusing to those who are not familiar with it. For example, a "dollar" bet is actually a $100 bet, a "nickel" bet is a $500 bet, and a "dime" bet is a $1,000 bet. To place a bet with a bookmaker, the bettor "lays down," or pays, a particular amount of money to win a particular payoff.

Bookmakers make money by charging a commission called *juice* or *vigorish*. Although the exact origins of the word are not known, *Merriam-Webster's Dictionary* suggests that vigorish may be derived from the Ukrainian word *vygrash* or the Russian word *vyigrysh*, both of which mean winnings or profit. In any event, vigorish is a very important and very misunderstood concept for most bettors.

Most gambling literature describes vigorish as a 4.55% commission that a bookie earns from losers' bets. A different interpretation of vigorish comes from J. R. Martin, a sports handicapper (a person who analyzes betting odds and gives advice to bettors) who operates a Web site on professional sports gambling. Statistically, according to Martin, only bettors who win exactly half of their bets pay exactly 4.55% in vigorish. Other bettors pay different percentages. A bettor must win 53% of all equally sized bets to break even, Martin says. However, this bettor would wind up paying a vigorish of at least 4.82%.

Some sports bets are simple wagers based on yes or no logic. Examples include under and over bets, in which a bettor wagers that a particular game's final score will be under or over a specific number of points.

Most sports bets are based on the "line" set by the bookmaker. For example, the line for an NFL football game between the Miami Dolphins and the Tennessee Titans might say that the Dolphins are picked by seven points. A bettor picking the Dolphins to win the game wins money only if the Dolphins win the game by more than seven points.

The line does not reflect a sport expert's assessment of the number of points by which a team will win. Rather, it is a concept designed to even up betting, to ensure that the bookmaker gets bets on both sides. This reduces the bookie's financial risk. Bookmakers will change lines if one side receives more betting action than the other. The skill of sports gambling comes in recognizing the accuracy of the line. Experienced bettors choose games in which they believe the posted lines do not accurately reflect the expected outcomes. This gives them an edge.

The odds for most licensed sports books in Nevada are set by Las Vegas Sports Consultants, Inc. Formerly owned by SportsLine.com, Inc., the company was purchased in November 2003 by a group of private investors in Las Vegas.

Developments in Legal Sports Gambling in Nevada

Nevada legalized gambling during the Great Depression of the 1930s as a means of raising revenue. During that time, Charles McNeil, a Chicago securities analyst, developed the handicapping system, in which bookmakers establish the betting line. The new system provided incentive for gamblers to bet on the underdog in a contest and made gambling more appealing. During the 1940s the Nevada legislature legalized off-track betting on horses, and sports and race books were popular in the state's casinos.

FIGURE 8.9

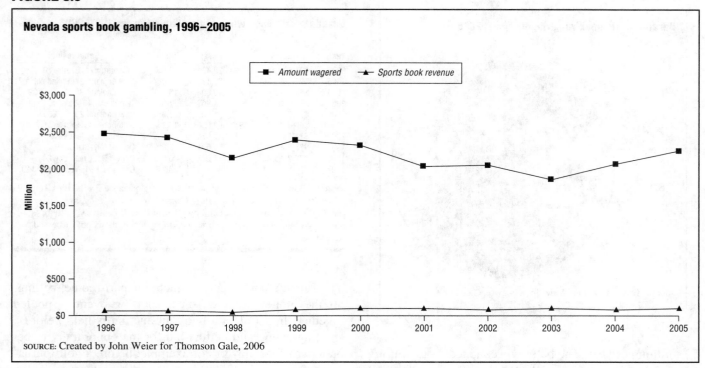

Nevada sports book gambling, 1996–2005

Legend: ■ Amount wagered ▲ Sports book revenue

SOURCE: Created by John Weier for Thomson Gale, 2006

Then in 1950 and 1951 a series of Senate hearings led by Senator Kefauver investigated the role of organized crime in the gambling industry. The televised hearings focused the nation's attention on gangsters, corrupt politicians, and legal and illegal gambling. One of the results was the passage of a 10% federal excise tax on "any wager with respect to a sports event or a contest." Because of the tax, the casino sports books, which were making only a small profit, were forced to shut down.

In 1974 the federal excise tax was reduced to 2%, and the sports books slowly made a comeback. Frank "Lefty" Rosenthal, a renowned handicapper, is credited with popularizing the sports book in Las Vegas during the 1970s. The 1980s were boom years for the sports and race books: in 1983 the federal excise tax was reduced to 0.25%. Jimmy "the Greek" Snyder brought some legitimacy to sports gambling through his appearances on televised sports shows. The amount of money wagered in the Nevada sports books increased dramatically until the mid 1990s, when it began to level off.

Money and Games

As shown in Figure 8.9, Nevada's sports books had a betting handle of $2.3 billion during 2005. This was up from $2.1 billion in the previous fiscal year, but down from $2.5 billion in 1996. After $2.1 billion was paid out to gamblers, the sports books had revenue of $126 million in 2005, up from $81 million in 1996.

According to the Nevada Gaming Commission and Gaming Control Board, football wagers accounted for 32% of the state's sports book wagering during 2005. (See Figure 8.10.) Basketball accounted for 30% of wagering, baseball 21%. Other sports and parlay bets were far less popular. A parlay bet is a combination bet in which the bettor selects the winners of two or more events. Every selection must be correct for the bettor to win the wager.

Football's share of sports betting was around 40% during every year from 1996 to 2004, but lost some ground to parlay betting in 2005. The Super Bowl alone generated $94.5 million in wagers in 2006, as shown in Table 8.6. The NCAA Division I college basketball tournament known as "March Madness" is another big sports-book betting event. Betting volume for the 2006 tournament was estimated to be $90 million in Nevada.

Industry experts estimate that one-third of the bets placed in the Nevada sports books are on college sporting events. Wagering is not allowed on high school sporting events or Olympic events. Nevada law also restricts the sports books to wagering on events that are athletic contests: betting is not allowed on related events, such as who will win most valuable player awards.

Options Outside Nevada

OREGON. As of August 2006 Oregon operated two sports betting games as part of its lottery. Proceeds from the Sports Action game, which began operation in 1989, go to the state's Intercollegiate Athletic and Academic Scholarship Fund. The game has earned more than $30 million for the fund since it was started, averaging about

FIGURE 8.10

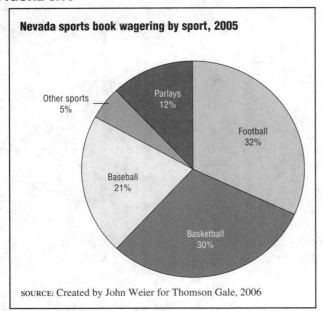

Nevada sports book wagering by sport, 2005

Other sports 5%

Parlays 12%

Football 32%

Baseball 21%

Basketball 30%

SOURCE: Created by John Weier for Thomson Gale, 2006

TABLE 8.6

Nevada sports book wagering on Super Bowls, 1997–2006

Year	Wagers	Win/(loss)	Win %	Game results
2006	$94,534,372	$8,828,431	9.3%	Pittsburgh 21, Seattle 10
2005	$90,759,236	$15,430,138	17.0%	New England 24, Philadelphia 21
2004	$81,242,191	$12,440,698	15.3%	New England 32, Carolina 29
2003	$71,693,032	$5,264,963	7.3%	Tampa Bay 48, Oakland 21
2002	$71,513,304	$2,331,607	3.3%	New England 20, St. Louis 17
2001	$67,661,425	$11,002,636	16.3%	Baltimore 34, N.Y. Giants 7
2000	$71,046,751	$4,237,978	6.0%	St. Louis 23, Tennessee 16
1999	$75,986,520	$2,906,601	3.8%	Denver 34, Atlanta 19
1998	$77,253,246	$472,033	0.6%	Denver 31, Green Bay 24
1997	$70,853,211	$2,265,701	3.2%	Green Bay 35, New England 21

SOURCE: "Summary of Nevada Sports Book Performance for the Last Ten Super Bowls," in *Nevada Gambling Control Board Press Release: Super Bowl 2006*, State of Nevada Gaming Control Board, February 7, 2006, http://www.gaming.nv.gov/documents/pdf/pr_06superbowl.pdf (accessed September 6, 2006)

$2 million per year. The betting is conducted only during the football season on selected professional football games. Because professional football leagues restrict the use of their trademarked names, lottery officials refer to teams by location only (for example, Denver vs. Miami). The state passed a law in 2005 that would eliminate the Sports Action lottery game by July 2007. In a second lottery game, Scorecard, bettors win money if they correctly pick a number that matches the last digit of the scores from selected professional football games.

DELAWARE. Delaware tried a sports lottery in 1976 based on games of the National Football League. The league sued for trademark violation but eventually lost the case. The sports lottery, which was called Scorecard, proved to be unpopular with bettors and unprofitable for the state. It was abandoned after only one football season. A task force was set up in 2002 to investigate the feasibility of reinstating a sports lottery game. The group's report to the Delaware General Assembly in 2003 estimated that a legal sports lottery could raise approximately $13 million for the state. In 2005 legislation was introduced to give the state lottery permission to create a pari-mutuel betting game. The bill was soundly defeated. In addition, Governor Ruth Ann Minner, who was in office in 2006, was opposed to expanded gambling in Delaware, making it unlikely that a sports lottery would be initiated while she was in office. The expansion of sports betting is also opposed by the National Football League, National Basketball Association, National Hockey League, Major League Baseball, and National Collegiate Athletic Association (NCAA).

MONTANA. The State of Montana allows five types of sports gambling: sports pools, Calcutta pools, fantasy sports leagues, sports tab games, and fishing derbies.

Calcutta pools operate much like pari-mutuel betting: all the money wagered on a sporting event is pooled together. In a Calcutta pool, an auction is held before a sporting event, and bettors bid for the opportunity to bet on a particular player. For example, before a golf tournament, the pool participants bid against each other for the right to bet on a particular golfer. The money collected during the auction becomes the wagering pool. It is divided among the "owners" of the best finishing players and the pool sponsor. Calcutta pools are most often associated with rodeos and golf tournaments.

Fantasy sports leagues are games in which the participants create fictitious teams composed of actual professional athletes. Each team wins points based on its performance against other teams in the league over a designated time period. Team performance is based on the actual performance of the selected athletes during real sporting events. The points collected by each participant in the league can be exchanged for cash or merchandise paid for by membership fees collected from each participant.

A sports tab game is one in which players purchase a numbered tab from a game card containing one hundred tabs with different number combinations. Bettors win money or prizes if their numbers match those associated with a sporting event—for example, digits in the winning team's final score. The cost of a sports tab is limited by law to less than $5. Operators of sports tab games (except charities) are allowed to take no more than 10% of the total amount wagered to cover their expenses (charities are allowed to take 50%). Sports tab sellers must obtain a license from the state and pay licensing fees and gaming taxes.

OTHER STATES. Other states that offer limited sports gambling are Washington, which permits $1 bets on race cars, and New Mexico, where small bets on bicycle races are legal. Office pools on sporting events are legal in a few states as long as the operator does not take a commission. Despite these examples of sports betting in other parts of the United States, though, the big money in legal sports gambling is in Nevada.

ILLEGAL SPORTS GAMBLING

The American Gaming Association estimated in 2005 that Nevada sports books account for less than 4% of all sports gambling in the country, so the vast majority of sports bets are illegal. This makes it difficult to assess exactly how much money is involved.

Illegal sports gambling encompasses a wide variety of activities. Most illegal bets on sporting events have been placed with bookies, although Internet gambling and office pools have also been popular. In addition, some "sporting" events, illegal in themselves, are popularly associated with gambling—for example, cockfighting and dog fighting.

The Link to the Nevada Sports Books

Most illegal books use the odds posted by the Nevada sports books because these are well publicized. Nevada sports books also provide illegal bookies with a means for spreading the risk on bets: illegal bookies who get a lot of action on one side of a bet often bet the other side with the Nevada sports books to even out the betting.

Transmitting gambling information across state lines for the purpose of placing or taking bets is illegal. News items about point spreads (the predicted scoring difference between two opponents) can be reported for informational and entertainment purposes only, but betting lines are still published by many U.S. newspapers. The Newspaper Association of America, which represented 87% of daily-circulation papers in the country in 2006, defends the practice as free speech protected under the First Amendment of the Constitution. The association claims that readers want to see the lines for informational purposes—to learn which teams are favored to win—and not necessarily for betting purposes. While the NCAA has argued that a ban on all college sports wagering would pressure newspapers to stop publishing point spreads, the American Gaming Association has countered that betting lines would still be accessible through independent sports analysts, offshore Internet gambling sites, and other outlets.

The Link to Organized Crime

Illegal sports gambling has long been associated with organized crime in the United States. During the 1920s and early 1930s mobsters set up organized bookmaking systems across the country, including two illegal wire services, Continental Wire Service and Trans America Wire, which operated under the direction of gangster Al Capone. The legal wire service, Western Union, was prohibited by law from transmitting race results until races were officially declared over. Sometimes this declaration did not take place for several minutes after the race finish, so mobsters reported the winners on the illegal wire services to prevent bettors from taking advantage of these delays by posting winning bets before the official results were wired.

During the 1950s the federal government cracked down on organized crime and eventually drove mobsters out of the Nevada casino industry. As the casinos were taken over by corporations, organized crime strengthened its hold on illegal bookmaking. Although law enforcement officials acknowledge that many "independent" bookies operate throughout the country, the big money in illegal sports gambling is still controlled by organized crime.

ANIMAL FIGHTING

Gambling on animal fights has a long history in the United States, despite its unsavory reputation. Most staged animal fights involve cocks (male chickens, or roosters) or dogs specially bred and trained. Although such fighting is usually associated with rural areas, urban police reports about cockfighting and dog fighting have increased in recent years as the "sport" has become popular among street gangs. Animal fights are of particular concern to law enforcement authorities because large amounts of cash and weapons are usually present.

No official national statistics are available on animal fighting. However, Pet-Abuse.com, a Web site operated by a nonprofit organization in New York, collects and documents information about animal abuse cases. As of September 2006 the Web site's database included some 670 documented cases of animal fighting.

Cockfighting

In the wild, cocks fight and peck one another to establish a hierarchy within their social order. These altercations rarely lead to serious injury. Fighting cocks, by contrast, are specially bred and trained by humans to be as aggressive as possible. They are given stimulants, steroids, and other drugs to heighten their fighting nature. Sharp spikes, called *gaffs*, are attached to their legs. The cocks are thrown into a pit from which they cannot escape. They slash and peck at one another, often until death. Spectators wager on the outcome of these fights. Cockfighting was banned by most states during the 1800s.

According to the Humane Society of the United States, cockfighting was legal only in Louisiana and parts of New Mexico in 2004. In 2006 the Louisiana State Senate passed a bill to ban cockfighting in Louisiana, but it was dropped by the state House of Representatives.

Cockfighting was a felony in seventeen states and a misdemeanor offense in thirty-one others, although states differ in their treatment of cockfight spectators and those caught in possession of birds for fighting. The federal Animal Welfare Act prohibits the interstate transport of birds for cockfighting into states with laws against cockfighting.

Because cockfighting is still legal in some parts of the United States, in Mexico and the Caribbean, and in many Asian countries, a commercial breeding industry operates in the United States. The industry is represented by a national organization, the United Gamefowl Breeders Association, and similar groups at the state level. These groups call themselves agricultural organizations; the Humane Society has accused them of promoting cockfighting.

The database maintained by Pet-Abuse.com lists dozens of documented cases of cockfighting in the United States since the beginning of this decade. For example, in June 2005 in Sevierville, Tennessee, the Federal Bureau of Investigations broke up a cockfighting ring, known as the Del Rio, one of the oldest and largest in the country. About 300 birds and more than 700 spectators were discovered in the raid. Individual bets were said to be as high as $30,000. According to officials, it was common to have 250 fights per night at that location, resulting in dozens of dead chickens; 143 people were charged in the incident.

In February 2006 police in San Luis Obispo County, California, raided what they believed to be a fighting cock breeding center. The law enforcement officials uncovered nearly 900 birds that were likely intended for fighting. The officers also found gaffs that cockfighting promoters strap onto the cocks' legs, but no evidence of a fighting ring on the premises. Three people were arrested for raising fighting cocks. The birds were put under the protection of the county's animal-control unit.

Dog Fighting

Spectators huddle around pits or small, boarded arenas to watch dog fights. They place bets on the outcome of the contests, which can go on for hours, sometimes to the death.

Dogs are specially bred and trained for such fights—the American pit bull terrier is the most common breed because of its powerful jaws. Authorities report that the dogs are often draped in heavy chains to build muscle mass and systematically deprived of food and water. Stolen and stray pet dogs and cats are commonly used as bait to train the fighters. The smaller animals are stabbed or sliced open and thrown to the fighting dogs to enhance their blood lust. Dogs are often drugged to increase their aggressiveness.

Dog fighting is illegal in all fifty states. According to the Humane Society of the United States, people could possess dogs for the purpose of fighting in Georgia, Idaho, and Nevada. Dog fighting is a felony in all states with the exception of Idaho and Wyoming, where dog fighting is a misdemeanor.

Dog-fighting rings are often intermingled with other criminal activities. For example, in May 2005 Louisiana authorities broke up one of the larger dog-fighting rings in the state. Police said more than 140 dogs were seized from two kennels in the rural towns of Church Point and Franklinton. The owners of the kennels had been under investigation for money laundering and drug dealing when authorities uncovered the dog-fighting ring. Four people were arrested.

Dog fighting is not limited to southern states and rural areas. According to T. J. Pignataro in "Betting on Cruelty" (*Buffalo News*, February 2004), drug and weapons raids by police accidentally uncovered well-organized dog-fighting operations around Buffalo, New York. Authorities reported that thousands of dollars in cash and other valuables, such as car titles, guns, and drugs, were commonly wagered at the dogfights. They also described gruesome scenes in which owners chopped off the heads of dogs that disgraced them by losing or backing down during a fight. Trash bags full of mangled pit bulls have also been found by city authorities in vacant fields or along city streets.

THE EFFECTS OF ILLEGAL SPORTS GAMBLING ON SOCIETY

Money and Crime

Because the vast majority of sports gambling that occurs in this country is illegal, it is difficult to determine its economic effects. However, the only people definitely benefiting from illegal sports gambling are the bookmakers. Large bookmaking operations overseen by organized crime groups take in billions of dollars each year. The betting stakes are high and the consequences for nonpayment can be violent. Small independent bookies typically operate as entrepreneurs, taking bets only from local people they know well. Illegal bookmaking cases reported in the media range from multimillion-dollar enterprises to small operations run by one person.

Sports Tampering

Sports tampering is officially defined by the U.S. Criminal Code as follows: "To unlawfully alter, meddle in, or otherwise interfere with a sporting contest or event for the purpose of gaining a gambling advantage." The most common form is point shaving, which occurs when a player deliberately limits the number of points scored by his or her team in exchange for payment of some sort. For example, if a basketball player purposely misses a free throw in exchange for a fee that player is participating in a point-shaving scheme.

Gambling has led to some famous sports scandals, mostly in college basketball games. However, any link between an athlete and gambling gives rise to suspicions about the integrity of the games in which that athlete participates.

The professional baseball player Pete Rose is an example. On September 11, 1985, at Riverfront Stadium in Cincinnati, Ohio, Rose broke Ty Cobb's all-time hit record. Before the end of the decade, however, Rose was under investigation by the commissioner of Major League Baseball and by federal prosecutors for betting on sporting events and associating with known bookies. He agreed to leave baseball, and the case was dropped. At the time Rose denied ever betting on baseball games. However, in January 2004 he admitted that he had bet on baseball games while he managed the Cincinnati Reds during the late 1980s.

THE INTEGRITY OF COLLEGE SPORTS. The popularity of sports gambling among college students leads to suspicions that athletes, coaches, and officials associated with collegiate sports could be wagering on the very games in which they are participating. In May 2004 the extent of gambling among college athletes was examined in "Pushing the Limits: Gambling among NCAA Athletes," in *The Wager*, which is published by the Harvard Medical School and the Massachusetts Council on Compulsive Gambling. The article summarized the findings of two major studies: the NCAA's *National Study on Collegiate Sports Wagering and Associated Health Risks* and the Harvard School of Public Health's *Correlates of College Student Gambling in the United States*. The Harvard study had been published in the *Journal of American College Health* in 2003.

Table 8.7 compares the findings of the studies. The NCAA study examined gambling activities by students during the previous twelve months. The other study asked students about gambling during the current school year. The results indicate that approximately one-quarter of the

TABLE 8.7

Comparison of statistics from the National Collegiate Athletic Association (NCAA) and the Harvard School of Public Health College Alcohol Study (CAS) on gambling by student-athletes, 2004

Study	Student athletes who gamble on anything		Student athletes who gamble on any sport		Student athletes who gamble on college sports		Student athletes who gamble on the Internet	
	Women	Men	Women	Men	Women	Men	Women	Men
NCAA	47%	69%	10%	35%	6%	21%	2%	6%
CAS*	33%	57%	10%	33%	6%	26%	2%	5%

*CAS student athletes self-reported that they played or practiced intercollegiate sports.

SOURCE: "Table 1. Comparison between NCAA and CAS Statistics on Student-Athletes Who Gamble," in "Pushing the Limits: Gambling among NCAA Athletes," in *The Wager*, vol. 9, no. 21, May 26, 2004. Data from Harvard School of Public Health College Alcohol Study (CAS), Harvard School of Public Health, Boston, MA, 2004, and Executive Summary for the National Study on Collegiate Sports Wagering and Associated Health Risks, National Collegiate Athletic Association, Indianapolis, IN, 2004.

male student athletes had gambled on college sporting events.

The NCAA opposes both legal and illegal sports gambling in the United States. Bylaw 10.3 of the NCAA prohibits staff members and student athletes from engaging in gambling activities related to college and professional sporting events. It also forbids them from providing any information about collegiate sports events to persons involved in organized gambling activities.

The NCAA opposes sports gambling for the following reasons:

- It attracts organized crime.

- The profits fund other illegal activities, such as drug sales and loan-sharking.

- Student athletes who become involved can become indebted to bookies, leading to point-shaving schemes.

CHAPTER 9

INTERNET GAMBLING

Internet gambling is a relatively new phenomenon. The first gambling Web sites launched in the mid 1990s and soared in popularity, particularly in the United States. Millions of Americans have gambled online, even though the practice is illegal. Christiansen Capital Advisors, which provides gambling analysis and management services, estimated that Internet gambling generated nearly $11.9 billion worldwide in 2005, up from $5.7 billion in 2003.

Exact figures on Internet gambling revenue are not known because the sites are not permitted to operate within the United States and because most of the countries that do allow them to operate do not collect or report revenue statistics. According to *An Analysis of Internet Gambling and Its Policy Implications* by David Stewart (American Gaming Association, 2006), two-thirds of Internet gambling operations are located in small Caribbean and Central American countries that provide little or no government oversight of the industry.

Many Internet gambling sites either do not pay taxes to their home countries or pay lower taxes than land-based gambling establishments. For example, according to the AGA analysis, the tiny island of Antigua in the Caribbean was the headquarters for 536 gambling sites, the most of any country. The sites were only required to pay 3% of their gambling revenues (winnings after payout to customers) to the government of Antigua with a ceiling of $50,000 per month. Other popular locations included Central and South America, Canadian Native American reservations, and the British Isles.

Unlike most land-based casinos, the vast majority of Internet gambling sites are operated by small, virtually unknown companies. While a land-based casino could cost several hundred million dollars and require hundreds of employees, an online casino can be set up and operated by a handful of people for an initial investment of a few million dollars. The relatively low setup and operating costs make the businesses very profitable and allow them to offer higher payoffs to winners than land-based casinos.

The future of Internet gambling in the United States remains uncertain. Under the Unlawful Internet Gambling Enforcement Act (UIGEA), which became law in 2006, banks and credit-card companies would be committing a crime if they transferred Americans' money to Internet gambling sites. Though serious Internet gamblers will likely find ways of transferring funds to online casinos and card rooms, lawmakers hope the law will turn casual gamblers away. As of late 2006, many of the larger, publicly traded Internet gambling companies, such as PartyPoker, had stopped accepting American customers altogether to avoid any conflicts with the U.S. government.

THE DEVELOPMENT OF INTERNET GAMBLING

Online gambling would not exist without the Internet, which is a vast network of hundreds of millions of computers in more than a hundred countries. It is not operated by any one business or government but is a cooperative venture in which many companies, organizations, and individuals choose to participate by making their computers part of the network. The Internet has been evolving since the 1960s, when researchers at the U.S. Department of Defense tried to link computers located far from each other. Today the Internet allows computer users at millions of locations around the world to share information and data. Computer Industry Almanac (http://www.c-i-a.com) estimated that slightly more than one billion people worldwide had Internet access by the end of 2005. That number is expected to grow to nearly two billion by 2011.

As soon as the Internet was opened to commercial enterprise, Web sites were developed to sell goods and services to the public. According to the Pew Internet &

American Life Project (http://www.pewinternet.org), as of June 2005 about 67% of American adults who access the Internet had purchased a product online.

No consensus exists on when the first Internet casino began operating and who started it. However, it is generally agreed that the first online casinos began operating sometime in 1995 or 1996. Among the first was Intercasino, based in Antigua, which has positioned itself as one of the leaders in Internet gambling. In 1996 the country legalized and licensed online gambling sites. The companies that operate these Web sites are trade-zone corporations—foreign-owned corporations operating in specific areas of the country as if they were on foreign soil. In Antigua, trade-zone corporations cannot produce products for domestic consumption, so Antiguans are not allowed to participate in online gambling with any trade-zone companies located there.

Various agencies and private entities have attempted to estimate the extent of the online gambling industry, including the National Gambling Impact Study Commission (NGISC), the U.S. Department of Justice (DOJ), and such industry researchers as Christiansen Capital Advisors and Bear Stearns & Co. While their estimates differ, these analysts agree that the growth of online gambling has been phenomenal. In 1997 there were fifty to sixty Internet casinos in operation, most based in the Caribbean, which earned approximately $300 million to $350 million. By 2000 an estimated 600 to 700 sites were operating and revenues approached $2 billion. By 2005 about 2,500 online casinos were estimated to exist, and revenues had jumped to $11.9 billion.

ONLINE GAMES

The AGA analysis showed that sports book betting constituted roughly one-third (35%) of all Internet gambling in 2005, totaling about $4.2 billion. Casino games brought in $3 billion, which equated to 25% of the $11.9 billion online gambling market. Online poker accounted for roughly 18% of all online gambling revenue in 2005. Poker was growing in popularity at a faster rate than any other type of online gambling, however. In 2000 online poker sites, such as PartyPoker, racked up $82 million in revenue. By 2005 poker sites worldwide were thought to have revenues of $2 billion. The rest of online gaming revenue, about $2.7 billion, came from the sale of lottery tickets, pari-mutuel race betting, and other games.

Casino sites offer many of the same games available in land-based casinos, such as poker, blackjack, roulette, and slot machines. Bet denominations range from pennies to thousands of dollars. Poker Web sites have card rooms where players compete against each other rather than against the house. This is an example of person-to-person, or *P2P*, betting. To make a profit on these sites, the casino operators take a small percentage of the winning hand.

Online casino games operate in much the same way as the electronic games found in actual casinos. Both depend on random number generators: real slot machines have a computer chip built in; online games have random number generators written into their programming. While slot-machine payoff percentages at actual casinos are dictated by the state in which they are located, online payoffs are not. However, online providers who never have winners would not have return customers, so their programs are designed to pay out a particular percentage. Online games are particularly appealing to people who enjoy card games because the betting limits are much lower than they are in actual casinos. For example, an online gambler can play blackjack for $1 per hand, while many land-based casinos set a $10- or $25-per-hand minimum.

Some sites require players to download software onto their personal computers. The software still runs through a program at the Web site, so the user must be online to play. Other games are played right at the Web site. Many use high-technology software that allows players to gamble in virtual reality: they can "look" around the table or around the casino room. Players can even "chat" with each other via online messaging during a game. Both of these effects make online gambling more interactive for the user.

Many sites offer free play to introduce visitors to the types of games offered and to give them a chance to practice. Visitors who decide to play for money must register, open an account, and deposit money into that account. This requires input of personal information, including name and address. The user usually sets up a user name and password for future access. Money is transferred to the gambling site via credit or debit card, through an account with an online bank or payment service, or via electronic check or wire transfer.

Most online sites offer bonuses of 5% to 20% of the amount of the initial deposit. These bonuses usually require that the gambler wager an amount two to three times the size of the bonus. Other sites offer prizes, such as trips, for repeat business. Winnings are typically deposited into the user's online account or paid via a certified check mailed to the winner.

ONLINE GAMBLERS

A May 2006 survey by the Pew Research Center (Paul Taylor, Cary Funk, and Peyton Craighill, *Gambling: As the Take Rises, So Does the Public Concern*) revealed that very few American adults have gambled for money on the Internet: only 2% of adults polled had participated in online gambling in the previous twelve months. Though this number is small, the number of people who gambled online doubled from 1996, when a Gallup organization poll reported that only 1% of Americans gambled online.

In February 2006 the Harris Poll (http://www.harris interactive.com) interviewed 2,985 adults in the United States and 2,074 adults in Great Britain and asked them about their online gambling habits. The results generally fell in line with the Pew survey's results. The Harris poll revealed that most people who gambled online did it frequently. Some 2% of those surveyed in the United States played online poker once a month, as opposed to 1% who played online poker once a year. In addition, 1% gambled at an online casino once a month. Fewer than 0.5% reported gambling at an online casino only once a year.

According to the Harris Poll, there was not much difference between the level of online play in Great Britain and the United States. Adults in Great Britain tended to go online to bet on sports more than Americans. Three percent of adults in Great Britain reported betting on sports online once a month, as opposed to fewer than 0.5% of Americans.

Peter D. Hart Research Associates and Luntz Maslansky Strategic Research conducted a more extensive poll of online gaming habits in the United States in 2005, which was presented in *2006 State of the States: The AGA Survey of Casino Entertainment* (http://www.americangaming.org/assets/files/2006_Survey_for_Web.pdf). The poll found that nearly 4% percent of Americans gambled online in 2005, which was twice the percentage of those who had gambled online the year before. Online gamblers were much more likely than the average casino customer to be male, under the age of thirty, and have a college degree. (See Figure 9.1, Figure 9.2, and Figure 9.3.) Of casino gamblers, 53% were male. Only 9% were twenty-one to twenty-nine, and 28% had four-year college degrees. Of online gamblers, 68% were male, and 43% were between the ages of twenty-one and twenty-nine. In addition, 35% of online gamblers had four-year college degrees; 41% had incomes of $75,000 or more. (See Figure 9.4.)

According to the poll, 38% of those who gambled online in 2005 had started betting online a year before, and 32% said they had started one to two years before. The largest number of online gamblers (80%) reported playing poker against other people in the previous year. Nearly as many online gamblers (78%) played casino games for money, and far fewer people (56%) placed bets on sports online. Out of those people who played poker online, nearly two-thirds (65%) said that Texas Hold 'Em was their favorite game, followed by seven-card stud (13%), five-card draw (13%), and Omaha (8%). For online casino gamblers, people reported playing blackjack (78%) most often, followed by video poker (65%), slot machines (60%), roulette (37%), and craps (29%).

THE LEGAL ISSUES

Regulating any activity on the Internet has turned out to be a political and legal headache for authorities. Every country wants jurisdiction (the authority to enforce its

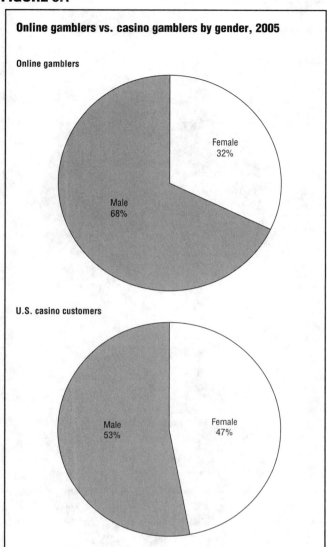

FIGURE 9.1

Online gamblers vs. casino gamblers by gender, 2005

Online gamblers

Female 32%

Male 68%

U.S. casino customers

Male 53%

Female 47%

SOURCE: "Online Gamblers: Who Are They? Gender," in *2006 State of the States: The AGA Survey of Casino Entertainment*, American Gaming Association, 2006, http://www.americangaming.org/assets/files/2006_Survey_for_Web.pdf (accessed September 6, 2006). Data from Peter D. Hart Research Associates, Inc. and Luntz, Maslansky Strategic Research. Reprinted with permission from the American Gaming Association. All rights reserved.

own laws) over content that its citizens can access over the Internet. This has proved to be difficult, however, because the Internet has no boundaries. A business based on a host computer might be legal in the country in which it is physically located but illegal in other countries where it can be accessed over the Internet.

Most countries restrict gambling activity much less than the United States does, but in this country the individual states and not the federal government regulate gambling. Although there are federal antigambling laws, they defer to the Tenth Amendment of the U.S. Constitution, which guarantees the rights of the states to govern their own affairs. Every state allows or disallows different

FIGURE 9.2

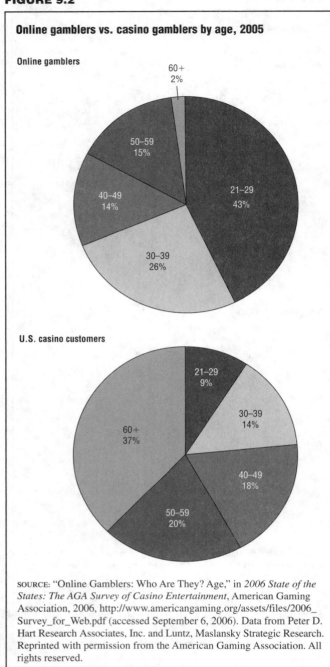

Online gamblers vs. casino gamblers by age, 2005

Online gamblers

U.S. casino customers

FIGURE 9.3

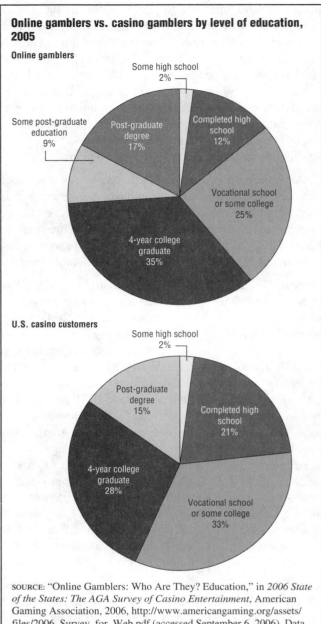

Online gamblers vs. casino gamblers by level of education, 2005

Online gamblers

U.S. casino customers

forms of gambling. Utah and Hawaii, for example, prohibit all types of gambling. Commercial casino gambling is legal in eleven states. Pari-mutuel wagering on horse or dog races is legal in more than forty states. Gambling on sporting events through a bookmaker is legal only in Nevada. Internet gambling, however, is not subject to state boundaries. A user in any state can access online gambling sites operated from countries around the world where gambling is legal.

Determining jurisdiction is a major problem for authorities. Does online gambling occur at the location where the Web site is hosted or at the location where the gambler is located? The U.S. Department of Justice has said that gambling occurs in both places. The problem grows even more complicated when one or the other is not on U.S. soil. Although an international treaty with extradition rights could settle such matters, it is unlikely that one would be written and signed.

Various forms of gambling are legal in many parts of Europe, Central and South America, the Caribbean, Australia, and New Zealand. Most of those areas have set up regulatory measures that are similar to the laws regulating

FIGURE 9.4

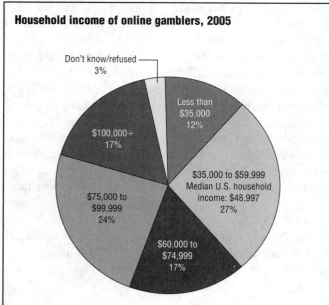

Household income of online gamblers, 2005

- Don't know/refused 3%
- Less than $35,000 12%
- $35,000 to $59,999 Median U.S. household income: $48,997 27%
- $60,000 to $74,999 17%
- $75,000 to $99,999 24%
- $100,000+ 17%

SOURCE: "Online Gamblers: Who Are They? Household Income," in *2006 State of the States: The AGA Survey of Casino Entertainment*, American Gaming Association, 2006, http://www.americangaming.org/assets/files/2006_Survey_for_Web.pdf (accessed September 6, 2006). Data from Peter D. Hart Research Associates, Inc. and Luntz, Maslansky Strategic Research. Reprinted with permission from the American Gaming Association. All rights reserved.

land-based casinos in the United States. For example, in June 2001 the Australian Senate passed the Interactive Gambling Act, which prohibits online casinos in the country from taking bets from Australians. The law has provisions allowing interactive sports gambling and wagering services. Foreign residents can gamble at the Australia-based online casinos unless their governments sign up to be excluded from the program. In 2005 the parliament of the United Kingdom passed the Gaming Act, which set up regulations and licensing procedures for online casinos. Though online casinos in Britain were required to pay higher taxes than such companies pay in Caribbean countries, many analysts believe that Internet casino operations will flock to Great Britain because of the advanced communications infrastructure, the stable political environment, and the educated workforce.

Federal Laws

In 1961 President John F. Kennedy signed the Interstate Wire Act—widely known as "the Wire Act"—which makes it a crime to use telephone lines ("wire communication") in interstate or foreign commerce for the placement of sports bets or even to transmit information assisting in the placement of bets on sporting events. The act applies only to the gambling business, not to gamblers themselves.

In February 2001 the Harvard Medical School's *Weekly Addiction Gambling Education Report* examined the legal issues involved in Internet gambling, particularly criticisms of the Wire Act ("Gambling on the Internet: Crossing the Interstate Wire"). It found that many legal experts say the law does not directly apply or is too ambiguous to apply to offshore Internet gambling sites because:

- The Internet did not exist when the act was made law.
- Gambling Web sites maintained on offshore computers are not under U.S. jurisdiction.
- Internet service providers do not fall under the definition of wire communications facilities (particularly those associated with satellite and mobile-phone transmissions).
- The law specifically mentions only sports betting, not casino games.
- Prosecutors cannot prove that online gambling sites "knowingly" transmit bets from U.S. citizens, because the physical location of online gamblers cannot be determined.

The states have interpreted the Wire Act to mean that online wagering is illegal if it occurs to or from any state in which gambling is illegal. In 1999 the issue was addressed by the New York Supreme Court in *People v. World Interaction Gaming Corp.* (WL 591955 NY Sup. Ct. July 22, 1999). The state of New York brought suit against World Interactive Gaming Corporation (WIGC) and Golden Chips Casino for offering online gambling to residents of New York. Golden Chips Casino operated a legal land-based casino in Antigua. The company was wholly owned by WIGC, a Delaware-based corporation with corporate offices in New York. The suit alleged that the casino had installed interactive software on its computer servers in Antigua that allowed Internet users around the world to gamble. The online casino was advertised on various Internet sites and in U.S. gambling magazines, both of which were accessible to New York residents.

Users had to wire money to a bank account in Antigua and type in their permanent address prior to play. Only users who entered addresses within states that permitted land-based gambling, such as Nevada, were allowed to play, so a user who entered a New York address was not granted permission. However, the suit alleged that the barrier was easily overcome by typing in an out-of-state address, because the software had no way of checking the physical location of the user. The state did not consider this a "good faith effort" to keep New Yorkers from gambling, as required by law.

WIGC argued that the federal and state laws in question did not apply to an offshore casino operated in full compliance with the law in the country in which it was located. The court ruled in favor of the state, saying that the act of entering the bet and transmitting the betting information originated in New York and constituted illegal gambling activity. The legality of gambling in Antigua was not an issue.

Furthermore, the court said, the gambling activity violated three federal laws: the Wire Act; the Foreign Travel or Transportation in Aid of Racketeering Enterprising Act (U.S. Code, § 1952), known as "the Travel Act"; and the Interstate Transportation of Wagering Paraphernalia Act (U.S. Code, § 1953), known as "the Paraphernalia Act." The Travel Act prohibits the use of "any facility in interstate or foreign commerce" with intent to promote any unlawful activity. The Paraphernalia Act is specific to gambling activity, prohibiting the interstate or foreign transmission of any item for use "in (a) book-making; or (b) wagering pools with respect to a sporting event; or (c) in a numbers, policy, *bolita*, or similar game." WIGC violated this law, the court ruled, because it had used the U.S. mail to send literature to potential investors and to send computers to the Antigua operations.

One issue was still not settled yet: which types of gambling sites were covered by the Wire Act? The Wire Act only states that people cannot make sports bets over communication lines. In 2002 the Appeals Court for the Fifth Circuit ruled in *In regarding MasterCard International, Inc.,* (313 F.3d 257) that the Wire Act applies specifically to online sports gambling (also known as sports books) and not to online casinos or poker sites.

During the late 1990s federal prosecutors went after the operators of offshore sports books that had taken bets from U.S. citizens via the Internet and telephone. In March 1998 they charged twenty-one people with conspiring to violate the Wire Act. Ten pleaded guilty to that charge, and three pleaded guilty to related misdemeanor charges. Seven could not be apprehended and are considered fugitives. The last defendant, a U.S. citizen named Jay Cohen, decided to stand trial. Cohen operated a sports book called World Sports Exchange in Antigua. The prosecution in the case argued that Cohen solicited U.S. customers through U.S. newspaper and magazine advertisements, encouraging them to contact World Sports Exchange via a toll-free telephone number and Internet site to place sports bets. On February 28, 2000, Cohen was convicted of conspiracy to violate the Wire Act and seven substantive violations of the Wire Act. He was sentenced to twenty-one months in prison and assessed a fine of $5,000.

In 2001 U.S. agents arrested Jeff D'Ambrosia and Duane Pede, who were the principle owners of Gold Medal Sports, a sports book Web site that operated out of Curaçao. Both pleaded guilty to violating the Wire Act by accepting bets online from people on U.S. soil. They were sentenced to five years in jail and were forced to pay $1.4 million in back taxes.

Despite these arrests, many online sports books operating outside the United States continued to openly market their Webs sites to Americans and allow Americans to place bets. In 2006 the Department of Justice cracked down once again on the owners of Internet sports book sites when it arrested David Carruthers, who was the chief executive of Costa Rican–based BetOnSports. Federal agents arrested Carruthers when he changed planes in Dallas. He was charged with violating the Wire Act, committing mail fraud, and a host of other felonies. Carruthers, who is a British citizen, was awaiting trial as of August 2006. After the arrest, BetOnSports shut down the division of its operations that took bets from U.S. gamblers and fired Carruthers. Other arrests were made of BetOnSports executives, but Carruthers was the most high profile. He was an outspoken opponent of U.S. federal legislation designed to eliminate online gambling.

In 2003 Antigua and Barbuda claimed that the stance the United States took on online gambling was in violation of several free trade agreements laid down by the World Trade Organization—a multinational trading organization with limited power that sets up and enforces trading agreements between its members. When they appealed to the WTO in an effort to end U.S. restrictions, Antigua and Barbuda maintained that thousands of jobs in their nation depended on online gambling and that the United States was harming their economy by attempting to restrict access by U.S. citizens. The WTO ruled against the United States in 2004, claiming that several U.S. laws regarding online gambling violated WTO free-trade agreements. After two years of talks, the United States refused to change its position on online gambling. Antigua and Barbuda approached the WTO again, and in July 2006 the WTO convened a panel to further investigate U.S. laws regarding online gambling.

THE UNLAWFUL INTERNET GAMBLING ENFORCEMENT ACT. Politicians have long recognized the shortcomings of the Wire Act to address modern gambling technologies. The NGISC recommended in 1999 that Congress enact federal legislation that would prohibit wire transfers from U.S. banks to online gambling sites or their banks.

Some form of Internet gambling legislation has been circulating around Congress since 1995, when Senator Jon Kyl (R-AZ) introduced a bill to amend the Wire Act to specifically prohibit online gambling via the Internet and satellite technologies. It would have allowed individual states to permit online forms of gambling already legal in their states (such as lotteries and casino games), while prohibiting forms that were not (chiefly sports gambling). Considered by many to be virtually impossible to enforce, it did not gain popular support. It failed to pass in 1997 and 1999 as well.

In following years other legislation was proposed in Congress by Kyl and by Jim Leach (R-IA), Bob Goodlatte (R-VA), Michael Oxley (R-OH), and John LaFalce (D-NY) and in the Senate by Richard Shelby (R-AL) and Dianne Feinstein (D-CA). In most of the later bills the focus had shifted to outlawing the use of credit cards or electronic payment services to pay for online gambling.

The Unlawful Internet Gambling Enforcement Act (H.R. 4411) found broad approval in November 2005. Rather than regulate the behavior of individuals, it was intended to prohibit credit-card companies from making transactions with online gambling establishments and to authorize the Secretary of the Treasury to prohibit any future, unforeseen payment methods that might be used for online gambling. With exceptions for online pari-mutuel betting facilities in the United States as well as tribal betting already in place, it was passed by Congress and signed by President Bush on October 9, 2006.

Even after it became law, many questions remained about how it would be enforced. It was clear that banks and credit-card companies could no longer transfer money directly to online casinos or poker sites, such as PartyPoker—it would be a crime to do so. However, whether banks and credit-card companies could transfer money for gambling to online payment processors, such as NETeller, was considerably murkier. Many online gamblers set up accounts with payment processors, which function as online banks, and then transfer money in and out of online casinos. While the new law would prohibit U.S. banks and credit-card companies from sending money to payment processors that deal exclusively with casinos, the law is less clear about payment processors that cater to a wide array of businesses and to payment processors or casinos that are in other countries or are privately held: foreign businesses are not regulated by U.S. law, and privately held companies are not required by law to divulge publicly how they make money. Many people believe that those determined to gamble online will find a way, probably by going to foreign, private payment processors and casinos.

State Laws

Both Hawaii and Utah outlaw any acts of gambling within state borders, which by default includes Internet gambling. According to the AGA's 2006 analysis of Internet gambling, attorneys general in Florida, Kansas, Minnesota, Oklahoma, and Texas maintained the position that online wagering is illegal in their states and in violation of existing laws. In New Jersey the courts ruled that online gambling violates state laws. Massachusetts had a law on the books that specifically forbids gambling transactions over phone lines, which has been interpreted to include online gambling. Seven states have enacted laws specifically prohibiting aspects of Internet gambling:

- Illinois prohibits anyone from establishing, maintaining, or operating an Internet gambling site and prohibits making a wager by means of the Internet.

- Louisiana prohibits the operation of an Internet gambling business and providing computer services to Web sites primarily engaged in gambling businesses.

- Oregon law forbids the collection of Internet gambling debts through credit-card payments, checks, or electronic fund transfers. Credit-card providers are not held liable for debts incurred by Internet gamblers.

- South Dakota prohibits anyone engaged in a gambling business from using the Internet to take bets and prohibits anyone from establishing an Internet gambling business in the state. The law does not apply to the state's licensed casinos.

- Nevada made it illegal to make or take an Internet bet within the state in 1997.

- Indiana's law states that anyone who operates a gambling Web site or who assists in the operation of such a site commits a felony.

- Washington had the toughest state law against online gambling (as of August 2006). Anyone caught gambling online in Washington can be convicted of committing a class C felony, which means that Internet gambling is legally as egregious an offense as possessing child pornography.

Credit Cards

In 1997 and 1998 a California woman named Cynthia Haines charged more than $70,000 in online gambling losses to her credit cards. Providian National Bank, which issued the cards, sued her for nonpayment. In June 1998 Haines countersued the bank, claiming that it had engaged in unfair business practices by making profits from illegal gambling activities. At that time all casino gambling was illegal in California. Haines's lawyers argued that her debt was void because it arose from an illegal contract. Providian ultimately settled out of court, forgave her debt, and paid $225,000 of her attorney's fees. The company decided to no longer accept online gambling transactions.

The settlement caught the attention of other major credit-card issuers. Nonpayment of outstanding credit-card charges results in serious losses, called *charge-offs* in the industry. Faced with the potential for massive charge-offs and legal uncertainties, many card issuers—including Bank of America, Capital One Bank, Chase Manhattan, Citibank, Direct Merchants, Fleet, and MBNA—stopped accepting financial transactions from online gambling sites. Issuers that do accept online gambling transactions generally delay payment of part or all of the money to the online sites for several months in case the user decides to dispute the charges.

FIGURE 9.5

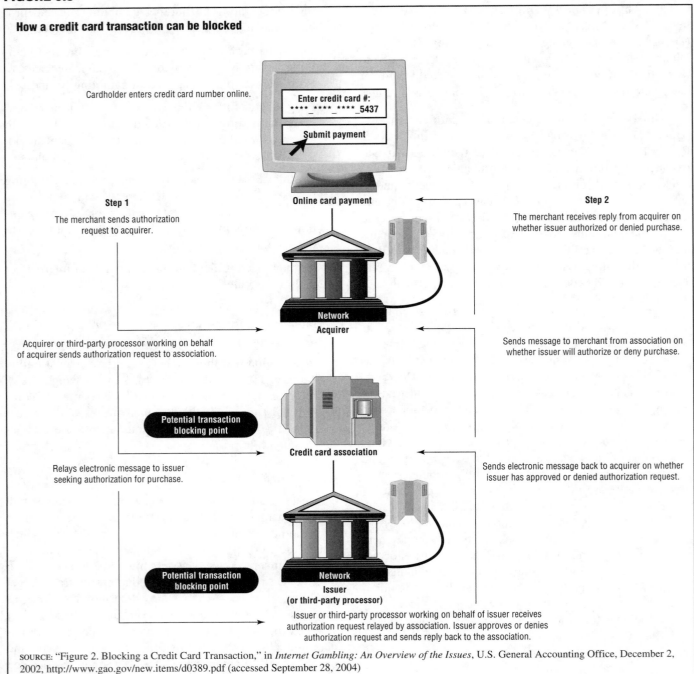

How a credit card transaction can be blocked

Cardholder enters credit card number online.

Enter credit card #:
**** _ **** _ **** _ **5437**

Submit payment

Online card payment

Step 1

The merchant sends authorization request to acquirer.

Network
Acquirer

Acquirer or third-party processor working on behalf of acquirer sends authorization request to association.

Potential transaction blocking point

Credit card association

Relays electronic message to issuer seeking authorization for purchase.

Potential transaction blocking point

Network
Issuer
(or third-party processor)

Issuer or third-party processor working on behalf of issuer receives authorization request relayed by association. Issuer approves or denies authorization request and sends reply back to the association.

Step 2

The merchant receives reply from acquirer on whether issuer authorized or denied purchase.

Sends message to merchant from association on whether issuer will authorize or deny purchase.

Sends electronic message back to acquirer on whether issuer has approved or denied authorization request.

SOURCE: "Figure 2. Blocking a Credit Card Transaction," in *Internet Gambling: An Overview of the Issues*, U.S. General Accounting Office, December 2, 2002, http://www.gao.gov/new.items/d0389.pdf (accessed September 28, 2004)

All of the major credit-card companies—Discover, American Express, Visa, and MasterCard—have enacted measures to restrict the use of their cards for Internet gambling (*Internet Gambling: An Overview of the Issues*, Government Accountability Office, December 2002). Discover and American Express do so primarily by preventing Internet gambling sites from becoming merchants in the first place. All potential merchants are screened, and existing merchants are spot-checked to make sure they are not engaged in online gambling. Visa and MasterCard are issued by a large network of financial institutions that have credit-card associations, which set policies for member institutions and provide the computer systems used to process financial transactions. The associations have a coding system that merchants must use to distinguish the different types of transactions. It was refined in 1998 so that online gambling sites have to enter a special two-part code that tells the issuer the nature of their business and gives the issuer a chance to deny authorization. Figure 9.5 shows how an online gambling transaction can be blocked at various points.

The coding system, however, does not distinguish between legal and illegal transactions. For example, Americans visiting countries in which online gambling is legal may find their credit cards rejected there when they try to gamble over the Internet. The coding system has also been tricked by unscrupulous merchants who entered the wrong code for their businesses, according to the credit-card associations.

Because credit-card transactions were blocked at online gambling sites, merchants and gamblers turned to alternative payment systems, called online payment providers. These services allow customers to transfer money from their credit cards into accounts that can then be debited to pay for a variety of online goods and services, including gambling. Money going to and from these intermediary accounts is not easily traced. Online payment providers include PayPal, NETeller, FirePay, and ECash. Some credit-card associations are refusing to do business with online payment providers unless they receive assurances that money will not be transferred to Internet gambling sites.

In 2002 and 2003 the online payment network PayPal paid millions of dollars to settle allegations that the company violated the Patriot Act during 2001 and early 2002 by processing online gambling transactions from U.S. citizens. The Patriot Act (officially titled Uniting and Strengthening America by Providing Appropriate Tools Required to Intercept and Obstruct Terrorism Act of 2001) forbids the electronic transmission of funds known to be associated with criminal acts. PayPal stopped handling online gambling transactions in November 2002.

In 2006 the Unlawful Internet Gambling Enforcement Act forbade banks and credit-card companies from transferring money to both Internet gambling sites and online payment processors strongly associated with virtual casinos. However, identifying payment processors that deal primarily with casinos is not a simple task. This is especially true if the payment provider is a private corporation with no financial transparency. Even if all such payment providers are identified, large European banks could open gambling services to people in the United States.

Federal Crackdown on Advertising

Under the Interstate Wire Act, advertisements for online gaming are illegal in the United States. Media outlets that run advertisements for online gambling are aiding and abetting the gambling Web sites, according to the Department of Justice, yet online gambling companies have advertised extensively online, in magazines and newspapers, and on television. In 2003 the DOJ mounted an offensive against the U.S. media to stop the proliferation of such advertisements. One salvo was a letter to the National Association of Broadcasters in which it outlined its views on advertising for online gambling outfits.

Then in 2004 the department intervened when Discovery Communications agreed to run $3.85 million in ads for Paradise Poker, mostly during *World Poker Tour* episodes on the Travel Channel. Discovery Communications aired $600,000 worth of ads and refused to air the rest. Before Paradise Poker could recover the remainder of the balance paid to Discovery for the ads (about $3.25 million), the Department of Justice seized the money. Its obvious message was that online gambling sites that advertised in the United States could have their ads canceled and their assets seized.

In April 2004 major Internet search engines, including Yahoo and Google, announced that they would no longer display ads for online gambling sites that targeted U.S. citizens. The companies reportedly acted to head off plans by the DOJ to pursue legal action against them. Many other Web sites did not heed the department's warning. For example, in 2005 the parent company of *The Sporting News* was forced to surrender $4.2 million in advertising revenue after running ads for several online gambling sites. The company also agreed to spend $3 million to create and run antigambling advertisements online. The Department of Justice also intervened in 2005 when *Esquire* magazine ran ads for the Costa Rican poker site Bodog.com. *Esquire* agreed not to run any more online casino ads.

THE EFFECTS OF ONLINE GAMBLING

Because the Internet gambling medium is relatively new, a limited number of studies have been conducted to determine its effects on people and their gambling habits. Economic factors are also difficult to assess because most online gambling sites operate in foreign countries with little government oversight.

Economics

Unlike traditional casinos, online gambling sites are not licensed or taxed by state governments. Therefore, they provide no revenue for social and educational programs. The primary financial beneficiaries are the online gambling companies themselves, the foreign countries in which they are located, and the companies that process their financial transactions.

Other businesses that benefit directly or indirectly from online gambling include Internet service providers, phone and cable companies, nongambling Web sites that feature advertisements for online gambling sites, and software companies. Major software providers to online gambling sites include WagerLogic, Boss Media, Microgaming Systems, and World Gaming.

Mobile phone companies expect cellular gambling to become commonplace in the future, particularly for phones with video streaming. Ladbrokes and William Hill are traditional British bookmakers that accept wagers via cellular phones using wireless application protocol. The company Eurobet launched wireless betting in 2000. Other companies, such as Slotland.com, allow people to play slots and win jackpots on their mobile phones. In May 2006 industry analysts at Juniper Research predicted that gambling via cellular phone would grow from a $2 billion business in 2006 to a $23 billion business by 2011 (http://www.juniperresearch.com/shop/viewpressrelease.php?pr=4).

The economic effects of online gambling are discussed by Ryan D. Hammer in "Does Internet Gambling Strengthen the U.S. Economy? Don't Bet on It" (*Federal Communications Law Journal*, December 2001). Hammer argues that people who do not gamble on the Internet suffer financially from online gambling. The high costs of litigation and unpaid bills, he notes, are passed on by credit-card companies to other consumers in the form of higher interest rates and fees. Taxpayer money also funds federal and state lawsuits against online gambling sites. State governments receive no licensing fees or tax revenue from online gambling sites but must fund treatment programs for pathological gamblers, a growing number of whom are online gamblers. The federal government collects income taxes from the big winners of lotteries and traditional casino games, but no taxes are collected from online gambling winners.

Money Laundering

Law enforcement agencies are very concerned about the possible use of online gambling businesses for money laundering—the transfer of money gained via illegal means through third parties to purposely make its origins obscure. According to Deputy Assistant Attorney General John G. Malcolm, once the money has been stashed with an online casino, criminals can use the games themselves to transfer money to their associates (testimony at a hearing of the Senate Banking, Housing, and Urban Affairs Committee, April 29, 2003, http://banking.senate.gov/03_03hrg/031803/malcolm.htm). Some criminals set up private tables at online casino sites and then intentionally lose their money to business associates at the table. In other instances, the casino is part of the crime organization, so all the criminal has to do is lose money to the casino.

The factors that make online gambling susceptible to money laundering, officials say, include the speed and anonymity with which financial transactions take place and the offshore locations of the gambling companies. Many financial analysts believe the risk is low when credit cards are used because credit-card transactions are closely monitored and recorded. Now that credit card use is illegal in online gambling, other, less traceable payment methods may become popular.

Compulsive Gambling

Experts say that the fast pace and instant gratification associated with online gambling make it more addictive than other types of gambling. Online gambling is quite different from traditional casino gambling, because it is a solitary and anonymous activity. Casino gambling, by contrast, is a social activity, usually conducted in the company of family or friends. The Council on Compulsive Gaming of New Jersey has estimated that 90% to 95% of online gamblers gamble alone. Online gamblers who contact the organization for help are usually younger than traditional gamblers and have built up large amounts of debt in a shorter time than traditional gamblers.

In March 2002 George T. Ladd and Nancy M. Petry, researchers at the University of Connecticut at Farmington, released the results of a study of Internet gamblers ("Disordered Gambling among University-Based Medical and Dental Patients: A Focus on Internet Gambling," *Psychology of Addictive Behaviors*). Between August 1999 and September 2000 they surveyed patients seeking free or reduced-cost services at the university's health and dental clinics. All of the 389 patients who completed the questionnaires in full reported gambling at some point in their lives. About 90% had gambled in the previous year, and 42% had gambled in the previous week. Only 8% of the respondents had gambled online during their lifetimes. However, 4% gambled online on a weekly basis. The younger respondents were more likely to have Internet gambling experience than the older respondents: the median age of the online gamblers was 31.7 years, compared with 43.5 years for traditional gamblers. Ethnicity also made a difference. Non-Caucasians made up only 16% of the total group surveyed but nearly 36% of the Internet gamblers.

All participants were given the South Oaks Gambling Screen (SOGS), a standard series of questions used to determine the probability that a person has a gambling problem. Results showed that the mean SOGS score of online gamblers was 7.8, compared with 1.8 for those who had no online gambling experience. Researchers categorized all respondents into levels depending on their SOGS scores. Level 1 gamblers had SOGS scores of 0–2 and were considered not to have a gambling problem. Level 2 gamblers had SOGS scores of 3–4 and were considered probable problem gamblers. Level 3 gamblers had SOGS scores of 5 or greater and were considered probable pathological gamblers.

Internet gamblers were much more likely to have gambling problems than non–Internet gamblers. Slightly more than 74% of Internet gamblers were rated at Levels 2 or 3, compared with less than 22% of the traditional gamblers.

Petry reported the results of a follow-up study in 2006 ("Internet Gambling: An Emerging Concern in Family Practice Medicine," *Family Practice*, August 2006). In this study, 1,414 adults in health-clinic waiting areas were given the SOGS test. Some 6.9% of adults reported ever gambling on the Internet and 2.8% said they gambled online frequently. Of those who gambled frequently, nearly two-thirds (65.9%) were categorized as problem gamblers, as compared with 29.8% of those who reported ever gambling on the Internet and 7.6% of those who were classified as non–Internet gamblers. The researchers then retrieved the medical records for those who participated in the study and found that Internet gamblers had poorer mental and physical health than those who did not.

In detailing the first study, Ladd and Petry wrote that "the availability of Internet gambling may draw individuals who seek out isolated and anonymous contexts for their gambling behaviors." While problem gamblers might be able to resist traveling to another state to casinos, they would find online gambling more difficult to avoid because Internet sites are always open and accessible.

Underage Gambling

In January 2001 the American Psychiatric Association was already warning the public about Internet gambling. In a public health advisory, it noted that because online sites are not regulated, no measures were being taken to prevent underage gamblers from participating. It considered children and teenagers, who already play non-gambling games on the Internet, at significant risk of being lured to gambling sites. It also noted that few safeguards were in place to ensure the fairness of the Internet games or to establish exactly who had responsibility for operating them.

The U.S. Federal Trade Commission (FTC) also issued a warning to parents about children and online gambling. A Consumer Alert released in June 2002 said it was too easy for kids, particularly teenagers, to access online gambling sites. The agency complained that many nongambling game-playing sites popular with kids contain links to gambling sites. The agency had examined 100 Internet gambling sites and found that 20% had no warnings at all to children and many lacked measures to block minors from gambling.

Each year the Annenberg Public Policy Center at the University of Pennsylvania releases the National Annenberg Risk Survey of Youth. In 2005 researchers interviewed 900 young people aged fourteen to twenty-two and asked them about their gambling habits, specifically with regard to Internet gambling. The survey found that some 16% of young people gambled on a weekly basis, and 44.2% gambled on a monthly basis in 2005. Just 1.6% gambled online on a weekly basis in 2005, but this figure was up considerably from 0.9% in 2004. A much higher percentage (14.2%) gambled online on a monthly basis. Those in post-secondary educational programs gambled online the most. Some 2.4% of young people in post-secondary school programs gambled online, as opposed to 1.3% of high school students and 1.4% of young people not in school at all.

IMPORTANT NAMES AND ADDRESSES

Alaska Department of Revenue
333 Willoughby Ave., 11th Fl.
Juneau, AK 99811
(907) 465-2300
FAX: (907) 465-2389
E-mail: bill_corbus@revenue.state.ak.us
URL: http://www.revenue.state.ak.us/

American Gaming Association
1299 Pennsylvania Ave. NW, Ste. 1175
Washington, DC 20004
(202) 552-2675
FAX: (202) 552-2676
E-mail: info@americangaming.org
URL: http://www.americangaming.org/

Annenberg Public Policy Center of the University of Pennsylvania
3535 Market St., Ste. 200
Philadelphia, PA 19104-3309
(215) 898-9400
FAX: (215) 898-7116
URL: http://www.annenbergpublic
policycenter.org/

Arizona Department of Racing
1110 W. Washington, Ste. 260
Phoenix, AZ 85007
(602) 364-1700
FAX: (602) 364-1703
E-mail: ador@azracing.gov
URL: http://www.azracing.gov/

Arizona Lottery
PO Box 2913
Phoenix, AZ 85062
(480) 921-4400
URL: http://www.arizonalottery.com/

Arkansas Racing Commission
PO Box 3076
Little Rock, AR 72203
(501) 682-1467
FAX: (501) 682-5273
E-mail: shelby.mccook@dfa.state.ar.us
URL: http://www.arkansas.gov/dfa/racing/

Birmingham Racing Commission
1000 John Rogers Dr., Ste. 102
Birmingham, AL 35203
(205) 838-7470
FAX: (205) 838-7471
URL: http://www.birminghamracing
commission.com/

Boyd Gaming
2950 Industrial Rd.
Las Vegas, NV 89109
(702) 792-7200
URL: http://www.boydgaming.com

California Horse Racing Board
1010 Hurley Way, Ste. 300
Sacramento, CA 95825
(916) 263-6000
FAX: (916) 263-6042
E-mail: IngridF@chrb.ca.gov
URL: http://www.chrb.ca.gov/

California Lottery
600 N. Tenth St.
Sacramento, CA 95814
(916) 323-7095
1-800-568-8379
URL: http://www.calottery.com/

Christiansen Capital Advisors, LLC
170 Sawyer Rd.
New Gloucester, ME 04260
(207) 688-4500
E-mail: jaypaw@maine.rr.com
URL: http://www.cca-i.com/

Colorado Division of Gaming
1881 Pierce St., Ste. 112
Lakewood, CO 80214
(303) 205-1355
FAX: (303) 205-1342
URL: http://www.revenue.state.co.us/
Gaming/home.asp

Colorado Lottery
212 W. Third St., Ste. 210
Pueblo, CO 81003
(719) 546-2400

FAX: (719) 546-5208
URL: http://www.coloradolottery.com/
home.cfm

Connecticut Division of Special Revenue
PO Box 310424
Newington, CT 06131-0424
(860) 594-0500
FAX: (860) 594-0509
E-mail: dosr@po.state.ct.us
URL: http://www.ct.gov/dosr/site/default.asp

Connecticut Lottery Corporation
270 John Downey Dr.
New Britain, CT 06051
(860) 348-4000
FAX: (860) 348-4015
E-mail: ctlottery@po.state.ct.us
URL: http://www.ctlottery.org/

Delaware Department of Agriculture, Delaware Thoroughbred Racing Commission
2320 S. DuPont Hwy.
Dover, DE 19901
(302) 698-4500
E-mail: mark.davis@state.de.us
URL: http://www.state.de.us/deptagri/
thoroughbred/index.shtml

Delaware Lottery
1575 McKee Rd., Ste. 102
Dover, DE 19904
(302) 739-5291
FAX: (302) 739-6706
URL: http://lottery.state.de.us

DC Lottery and Charitable Games Control Board
2101 Martin Luther King Jr. Ave. SE
Washington, DC 20020
(202) 645-8000
URL: http://lottery.dc.gov

Florida Department of Business and Professional Regulation, Division of Pari-mutuel Wagering
1940 N. Monroe St., Ste. 50
Tallahassee, FL 32399

(850) 488-9130
E-mail: callcenter@dbpr.state.fl.us
URL: http://www.myflorida.com/dbpr/pmw/
index.shtml

Florida Lottery
250 Marriott Dr.
Tallahassee, FL 32301
(850) 487-7725
E-mail: asklott@flalottery.com
URL: http://www.flalottery.com/

The Gallup Organization
901 F St. NW
Washington, DC 20004
(202) 715-3030
1-877-242-5587
FAX: (202) 715-3041
E-mail: sarah_van_allen@gallup.com
URL: http://www.gallup.com

Gamblers Anonymous
PO Box 17173
Los Angeles, CA 90017
(213) 386-8789
FAX: (213) 386-0030
E-mail: isomain@gamblersanonymous.org
URL: http://www.gamblersanonymous.org/

Georgia Lottery Corporation
250 Williams St., Ste. 3000
Atlanta, GA 30303
(404) 215-5000
E-mail: media@galottery.org
URL: http://www.galottery.com/

Greyhound Protection League
PO Box 669
Penn Valley, CA 95946
1-800-446-8637
URL: http://www.greyhounds.org/

Harrah's Entertainment
2100 Caesars Palace Dr.
Las Vegas, NV 89109
(702) 407-6000
URL: http://www.harrahs.com

Hoosier Lottery
Pan Am Plaza
201 S. Capitol Ave., Ste. 1100
Indianapolis, IN 46225
1-800-955-6886
E-mail: playersupport@hoosierlottery.com
URL: http://www.in.gov/hoosierlottery/

Idaho Lottery
1199 Shoreline Ln., Ste. 100
Boise, ID 83702
(208) 334-2600
E-mail: info@idaholottery.com
URL: http://www.idaholottery.com/

Idaho State Police Racing Commission
PO Box 700
Meridian, ID 83680
(208) 884-7080
FAX: (208) 884-7098

E-mail: jack.baker@isp.idaho.gov
URL: http://www.isp.state.id.us/race/index.html

Illinois Gaming Board
160 N. LaSalle, Ste. 300
Chicago, IL 60601
(312) 814-4700
FAX: (312) 814-4602
URL: http://www.igb.state.il.us/

Illinois Lottery
101 W. Jefferson St.
Springfield, IL 62702
1-800-252-1775
E-mail: lotteryinfo@revenue.state.il.us
URL: http://www.illinoislottery.com/

Illinois Racing Board
100 W. Randolph, Ste. 7-701
Chicago, IL 60601
(312) 814-2600
E-mail: IRB.Info@illinois.gov
URL: http://www.state.il.us/agency/irb/

Indiana Gaming Commission
115 W. Washington St.
South Tower, Ste. 950
Indianapolis, IN 46204
(317) 233-0046
FAX: (317) 233-0047
URL: http://www.in.gov/gaming/

Indiana Horse Racing Commission
150 W. Market St., Ste. 530
Indianapolis, IN 46204
(317) 233-3119
FAX: (317) 233-4470
URL: http://www.in.gov/ihrc/

Institute for Problem Gambling
955 S. Main St.
Middletown, CT 06457
(860) 343-5500
FAX: (860) 347-3183
URL: http://www.gamblingproblem.net/

**International Gaming Institute,
University of Nevada at Las Vegas**
4505 Maryland Pkwy.
PO Box 456037
Las Vegas, NV 89154
(702) 895-3903
FAX: (702) 895-1135
E-mail: hosinfo@unlvedu.org
URL: http://www.unlvedu.org

Iowa Lottery
2323 Grand Ave.
Des Moines, IA 50312
(515) 725-7900
E-mail: wmaster@ialottery.com
URL: http://www.ialottery.com/

Iowa Racing and Gaming Commission
717 E. Court, Ste. B
Des Moines, IA 50309
(515) 281-7352
FAX: (515) 242-6560

E-mail: irgc@iowa.gov
URL: http://www.state.ia.us/irgc/

Jockey Club
40 E. 52nd St.
New York, NY 10022
(212) 371-5970
FAX: (212) 371-6123
URL: http://www.jockeyclub.com/

Kansas Lottery
128 N. Kansas Ave.
Topeka, KS 66603
(785) 296-5774
E-mail: lotteryinfo@kslottery.net
URL: http://www.kslottery.com

Kansas Racing and Gaming Commission
700 SW Harrison, Ste. 420
Topeka, KS 66603
(785) 296-5800
FAX: (785) 296-0900
E-mail: krgc@ksracing.org
URL: http://www.kansas.gov/krc/

Kentucky Horse Racing Authority
4063 Iron Works Pkwy., Bldg. B
Lexington, KY 40511
(859) 246-2040
FAX: (859) 246-2039
E-mail: lisa.underwood@ky.gov
URL: http://www.khra.ky.gov

Kentucky Lottery
1011 W. Main St.
Louisville, KY 40202
(502) 560-1500
E-mail: custsrvs@kylottery.com
URL: http://www.kylottery.com

Louisiana Gaming Control Board
9100 Bluebonnet Centre Blvd., Ste. 500
Baton Rouge, LA 70809
(225) 295-8450
FAX: (225) 295-8479
E-mail: trudy.fuselier@dps.state.la.us
URL: http://www.dps.state.la.us/lgcb/

Louisiana Lottery Corporation
555 Laurel St.
Baton Rouge, LA 70801
(225) 297-2000
URL: http://www.louisianalottery.com

**Maine Harness Racing Promotion
Board**
State House, Station 28
Augusta, ME 04333
(207) 287-3221
E-mail: info@maineharnessracing.com
URL: http://www.maineharnessracing.com/

Maine State Lottery
10 Water St.
Hallowell, ME 04347
(207) 287-3721
1-800-452-8777
URL: http://www.mainelottery.com/

Maryland Racing Commission
500 N. Calvert St.
Second Fl., Rm. 201
Baltimore, MD 21202
(410) 230-6330
FAX: (410) 333-8308
E-mail: racing@dllr.state.md.us
URL: http://www.dllr.state.md.us/racing/

Maryland State Lottery Agency
1800 Washington Blvd., Ste. 330
Baltimore, MD 21230
(410) 230-8800
E-mail: paffairs@msla.state.md.us
URL: http://www.mdlottery.com

Massachusetts State Lottery Commission
60 Columbian St.
Braintree, MA 02184
(781) 849-5555
E-mail: webmaster@masslottery.com
URL: http://www.masslottery.com/

Massachusetts State Racing Commission
1 Ashburton Pl., Rm. 1313
Boston, MA 02108
(617) 727-2581
FAX: (617) 727-6062
E-mail: racing.commission@state.ma.us
URL: http://www.state.ma.us/src/

MGM Mirage
3600 Las Vegas Blvd. S
Las Vegas, NV 89109
(702) 693-7120
URL: http://www.mgmmirage.com/

Michigan Gaming Control Board
1500 Abbott Rd., Ste. 400
East Lansing, MI 48823
(517) 241-0040
FAX: (517) 241-0510
E-mail: MGCBweb@michigan.gov
URL: http://www.michigan.gov/mgcb

Michigan Lottery
101 E. Hillsdale
PO Box 30023
Lansing, MI 48909
(517) 335-5600
FAX: (517) 335-5644
E-mail: milottery@michigan.gov
URL: http://www.michigan.gov/lottery

Michigan Racing Commission
PO Box 30773
Lansing, MI 48909
(517) 335-1420
URL: http://www.michigan.gov/mda

Minnesota Gambling Control Board
1711 W. County Road B, Ste. 300 S.
Roseville, MN 55113
(651) 639-4000
URL: http://www.gcb.state.mn.us/index.html/

Minnesota Racing Commission
1100 Canterbury Rd.
PO Box 630

Shakopee, MN 55379
(952) 496-7950
FAX: (952) 496-7954
E-mail: richard.krueger@state.mn.us
URL: http://www.mnrace.commission.
state.mn.us/

Minnesota State Lottery
2645 Long Lake Rd.
Roseville, MN 55113
(651) 297-7456
E-mail: lottery@mnlottery.com
URL: http://www.lottery.state.mn.us/index.html

Mississippi Gaming Commission
PO Box 23577
Jackson, MS 39225
(601) 576-3800
1-800-504-7529
FAX: (601) 576-3929
URL: http://www.mgc.state.ms.us/

Missouri Gaming Commission
3417 Knipp Dr.
PO Box 1847
Jefferson City, MO 65102
(573) 526-4080
FAX: (573) 526-1999
E-mail: PublicRelation@mgc.dps.mo.gov
URL: http://www.mgc.dps.mo.gov/

Missouri Lottery
1823 Southridge Dr.
PO Box 1603
Jefferson City, MO 65109
(573) 751-4050
FAX: (573) 751-5188
URL: http://www.molottery.com/

**Montana Department of Livestock—
Board of Horse Racing**
PO Box 200512
Helena, MT 59620
(406) 444-4287
FAX: (406) 444-1929
E-mail: livemail@state.mt.us
URL: http://mt.gov/liv/HorseRacing/index.asp

Montana Gambling Control Division
2550 Prospect Ave.
PO Box 201424
Helena, MT 59620
(406) 444-1971
E-mail: gcd@mt.gov
URL: http://www.doj.state.mt.us/
department/gamblingcontroldivision.asp

Montana Lottery
2525 N. Montana Ave.
Helena, MT 59601
(406) 444-5825
FAX: (406) 444-5830
E-mail: montanalottery@mail.com
URL: http://www.montanalottery.com/

Multi-State Lottery Association
4400 NW Urbandale Dr.
Urbandale, IA 50322

(515) 453-1400
URL: http://www.musl.com/

**National Association of Fundraising
Ticket Manufacturers**
1360 Energy Park Dr., Ste. 210
St. Paul, MN 55108
(651) 644-4710
FAX: (651) 644-5904
E-mail: MaryMagnuson@naftm.org
URL: http://www.naftm.org/

National Center for Responsible Gaming
PO Box 14323
Washington, DC 20044-4323
(202) 552-2689
E-mail: contact@ncrg.org
URL: http://www.ncrg.org/

**National Coalition Against Legalized
Gambling**
100 Maryland Ave. NE, Rm. 311
Washington, DC 20002
1-800-664-2680
E-mail: ncalg@ncalg.com
URL: http://www.ncalg.org/

National Council on Problem Gambling, Inc.
216 G Street NE, Ste. 200
Washington, DC 20002
(202) 547-9204
1-800-522-4700
FAX: (202) 547-9206
E-mail: ncpg@ncpgambling.org
URL: http://www.ncpgambling.org/

National Indian Gaming Association
224 Second St. SE
Washington, DC 20003
(202) 546-7711
FAX: (202) 546-1755
E-mail: info@indiangaming.org
URL: http://www.indiangaming.org/

National Indian Gaming Commission
1441 L St. NW, Ste. 9100
Washington, DC 20005
(202) 632-7003
FAX: (202) 632-7066
E-mail: info@nigc.gov
URL: http://www.nigc.gov/

Nebraska Lottery
301 Centennial Mall S
PO Box 98901
Lincoln, NE 68509
(402) 471-6100
E-mail: lottery@nelottery.com
URL: http://www.nelottery.com/

Nebraska State Racing Commission
301 Centennial Mall S, Sixth Fl.
PO Box 95014
Lincoln, NE 68509
(402) 471-4155
FAX: (402) 471-2339
E-mail: Diane.Vandeun@racing.ne.gov
URL: http://www.horseracing.state.ne.us/

Nevada Gaming Commission and State Gaming Control Board
1919 College Pkwy.
Carson City, NV 89706
(775) 684-7750
FAX: (775) 687-5817
E-mail: gcbpers@gcb.nv.gov
URL: http://gaming.nv.gov

New Hampshire Lottery
PO Box 1208
Concord, NH 03302
(603) 271-3391
1-800-852-3324
FAX: (603) 271-1160
E-mail: webmaster@lottery.state.nh.us
URL: http://www.nhlottery.org/

New Hampshire Pari-mutuel Commission
78 Regional Dr., Bldg. 2
Concord, NH 03301
(603) 271-2158
FAX: (603) 271-3381
URL: http://www.racing.nh.gov

New Jersey Casino Control Commission
Arcade Bldg.
Tennessee Avenue & Boardwalk
Atlantic City, NJ 08401
(609) 441-3799
FAX: (609) 441-3329
E-mail: communications@ccc.state.nj.us
URL: http://www.state.nj.us/casinos/

New Jersey Lottery
PO Box 041
Trenton, NJ 08625
(609) 599-5800
FAX: (609) 599-5935
E-mail: publicinfo@lottery.state.nj.us
URL: http://www.state.nj.us/lottery/

New Jersey Racing Commission
140 E. Front St., Fourth Fl.
PO Box 088
Trenton, NJ 08625
(609) 292-0613
FAX: (609) 599-1785
URL: http://www.nj.gov/oag/racing/index.html

New Mexico Gaming Control Board
4900 Alameda Blvd. NE
Albuquerque, NM 87113
(505) 841-9700
FAX: (505) 841-9725
E-mail: gcb.is@nm.us
URL: http://www.nmgcb.org/

New Mexico Lottery
PO Box 93130
Albuquerque, NM 87199
(505) 342-7600
E-mail: custservice@nmlottery.com
URL: http://www.nmlottery.com/

New Mexico Racing Commission
4900 Alameda NE, Ste. A
Albuquerque, NM 87113

(505) 222-0700
FAX: (505) 222-0713
E-mail: rosemary.leeder@state.nm.us
URL: http://nmrc.state.nm.us/

New York Lottery
PO Box 7500
Schenectady, NY 12301
(518) 388-3300
URL: http://www.nylottery.org/index.php

New York State Racing and Wagering Board
1 Broadway Center, Ste. 600
Schenectady, NY 12305
(518) 395-5400
E-mail: info@racing.state.ny.us
URL: http://www.racing.state.ny.us/

North American Association of State and Provincial Lotteries
2775 Bishop Rd., Ste. B
Willoughby Hills, OH 44092
(216) 241-2310
FAX: (216) 241-4350
E-mail: info@naspl.org
URL: http://www.naspl.org/

North Carolina Department of Crime Control and Public Safety, Alcohol Law Enforcement Division, Bingo Licensing Section
4704 Mail Service Center
Raleigh, NC 27699
(919) 733-3029
URL: http://www.nccrimecontrol.org/
Index2.cfm?a=000003,000005,000077

North Dakota Lottery
600 E. Boulevard Ave., Dept. 125
Bismarck, ND 58505
(701) 328-1574
E-mail: ndlottery@nd.gov
URL: http://www.ndlottery.org

North Dakota Office of Attorney General, Gaming Division
600 E. Boulevard Ave., Dept. 125
Bismarck, ND 58505
(701) 328-4848
1-800-326-9240
FAX: (701) 328-3535
URL: http://www.ag.state.nd.us/Gaming/
Gaming.htm

Ohio Lottery Commission
615 W. Superior Ave.
Cleveland, OH 44113
(216) 787-3200
1-800-686-4208
URL: http://www.ohiolottery.com

Ohio State Racing Commission
77 S. High St., 18th Fl.
Columbus, OH 43215
(614) 466-2757
FAX: (614) 466-1900

E-mail: Sam.Zonak@rc.state.oh.us
URL: http://www.racing.ohio.gov

Oklahoma Horse Racing Commission
2401 NW 23rd St., Ste. 78
Oklahoma City, OK 73107
(405) 943-6472
FAX: (405) 943-6474
E-mail: ohrc@socket.net
URL: http://www.ohrc.org/

Oregon Lottery
500 Airport Rd. SE
PO Box 12648
Salem, OR 97309
(503) 540-1000
FAX: (503) 540-1001
E-mail: lottery.webcenter@state.or.us
URL: http://www.oregonlottery.org/

Oregon Racing Commission
800 NE Oregon St., Ste. 310
Portland, OR 97232
(971) 673-0207
FAX: (971) 673-0213
E-mail: jodi.hanson@state.or.us
URL: http://racing.oregon.gov

Penn National Gaming
825 Berkshire Blvd., Ste. 200
Wyomissing, PA 19610
(610) 373-2400
FAX: (610) 373-4966
E-mail: corporate@pngaming.com
URL: http://www.pngaming.com

Pennsylvania Lottery
2850 Turnpike Industrial Dr.
Middletown, PA 17057
(717) 986-4699
FAX: (717) 986-4767
URL: http://www.palottery.state.pa.us

Pennsylvania State Horse Racing Commission
2301 N. Cameron St.
Agriculture Bldg., Rm. 304
Harrisburg, PA 17110
(717) 787-1942
FAX: (717) 346-1546
URL: http://www.agriculture.state.pa.us/
agriculture/cwp/view.asp?a=3&q=128999

Pet-Abuse.Com
PO Box 5
Southfields, NY 10975-0005
1-888-523-PETS
info@pet-abuse.com
URL: http://www.pet-abuse.com/

Pew Research Center
1615 L Street NW, Ste. 700
Washington, DC 20036
(202) 419-4300
FAX: (202) 419-4349
E-mail: info@pewresearch.org
URL: http://www.pewresearch.org/

Public Gaming Research Institute, Inc.
225 Crossroads Blvd., Ste. 425
Carmel, CA 93923
(425) 985-3159
1-800-493-0527
FAX: 1-800-657-9340
E-mail: info@publicgaming.org
URL: http://www.publicgaminginter
national.com/

Rhode Island Department of Business
Regulation, Division of Racing and Athletics
233 Richmond St.
Providence, RI 02903
(401) 222-6541
FAX: (401) 222-6131
E-mail: RacingAthleticsInquiry@dbr.state.ri.us
URL: http://www.dbr.state.ri.us/

Rhode Island Lottery
1425 Pontiac Ave.
Cranston, RI 02920
(401) 463-6500
FAX: (401) 463-5669
URL: http://www.rilot.com/

South Carolina Education Lottery
PO Box 11949
Columbia, SC 29211
(803) 737-2002
FAX: (803) 737-2005
URL: http://www.sceducationlottery.com/

South Dakota Commission on Gaming
1320 E. Sioux Ave.
Pierre, SD 57501
(605) 773-6050
FAX: (605) 773-6053
E-mail: gaminginfo@state.sd.us
URL: http://www.state.sd.us/drr2/reg/gaming/

South Dakota Lottery
207 E. Capitol
PO Box 7107
Pierre, SD 57501
(605) 773-5770
FAX: (605) 773-5786
E-mail: lottery@state.sd.us
URL: http://www.sdlottery.org/

Station Casinos, Inc.
PO Box 29500
Las Vegas, NV 89126
(702) 797-7040
URL: http://www.stationcasinos.com

Tennessee Lottery
PO Box 23470
Nashville, TN 37202
(615) 324-6500
URL: http://www.tnlottery.com

Texas Lottery Commission
PO Box 16630
Austin, TX 78761
(512) 344-5000
1-800-375-6886
FAX: (512) 344-5080

E-mail: customer.service@lottery.state.tx.us
URL: http://www.txlottery.org/

Texas Racing Commission
PO Box 12080
Austin, TX 78711
(512) 833-6699
FAX: (512) 833-6907
E-mail: caking@txrc.state.tx.us
URL: http://www.txrc.state.tx.us/

U.S. Department of Justice
950 Pennsylvania Ave. NW
Washington, DC 20530-0001
(202) 514-2000
E-mail: AskDOJ@usdoj.gov
URL: http://www.usdoj.gov/

U.S. Trotting Association
750 Michigan Ave.
Columbus, OH 43215
1-877-800-USTA
FAX: (614) 228-1385
E-mail: customerservice@ustrotting.com
URL: http://www.ustrotting.com/

Vermont Lottery Commission
1311 U.S. Rte. 302—Berlin
Ste. 100
Barre, VT 05641
(802) 479-5686
FAX: (802) 479-4294
E-mail: staff@vtlottery.com
URL: http://www.vtlottery.com/

Vermont Racing Commission
Service Bldg.
128 Merchants Row
Rutland, VT 05701
(802) 786-5050
FAX: (802) 786-5052
URL: http://www.vermont.gov/tools/
whatsnew2/index.php?topic=Boards
AndCommissions& id=151&v=Article

Virginia Department of Charitable
Gaming
101 N. 14th St., 17th Fl.
Richmond, VA 23219
(804) 786-1681
FAX: (804) 786-1079
E-mail: webmaster@DCG.Virginia.gov
URL: http://www.dcg.state.va.us/

Virginia Lottery
900 E. Main St.
Richmond, VA 23219
(804) 692-7000
FAX: (804) 692-7102
URL: http://www.valottery.com/

Virginia Racing Commission
10700 Horsemen's Rd.
New Kent, VA 23124
(804) 966-7400
FAX: (804) 966-7418
E-mail: Kimberly.Carter@VRC.Virginia.gov
URL: http://www.vrc.virginia.gov/

Washington Horse Racing
Commission
6326 Martin Way, Ste. 209
Olympia, WA 98516
(360) 459-6462
FAX: (360) 459-6461
E-mail: whrc@whrc.state.wa.us
URL: http://www.whrc.wa.gov/

Washington's Lottery
PO Box 43000
Olympia, WA 98506
(360) 664-4720
FAX: (360) 664-2630
E-mail: director's_office@lottery.wa.gov
URL: http://www.walottery.com

Washington State Gambling
Commission
PO Box 42400
Olympia, WA 98504
(360) 486-3440
1-800-345-2529
FAX: (360) 486-3629
URL: http://www.wsgc.wa.gov/

West Virginia Lottery
PO Box 2067
Charleston, WV 25327
(304) 558-0500
1-800-982-2274
FAX: (304) 558-3321
E-mail: mail@wvlottery.com
URL: http://207.97.205.154/20th_ann.aspx

West Virginia Racing
Commission
106 Dee Dr.
Charleston, WV 25311
(304) 558-2150
FAX: (304) 558-6319
E-mail: oliver8@saintjoes.net
URL: http://www.wvf.state.wv.
us/racing/

Wisconsin Division of Gaming
205 W. Beltline Hwy.
Madison, WI 53713
(608) 270-2555
URL: http://www.doa.state.wi.us/gaming/
index.asp

Wisconsin Lottery
PO Box 8941
Madison, WI 53708
(608) 261-4916
URL: http://www.wilottery.com/

Wyoming Pari-mutuel
Commission
Hansen Bldg.
2515 Warren Ave., Ste. 301
Cheyenne, WY 82002
(307) 777-5928
FAX: (307) 777-3681
E-mail: flamb@state.wy.us
URL: http://parimutuel.state.wy.us/

RESOURCES

Several resources useful to this book were published by companies and organizations within the gambling industry. Most notable are *Harrah's Survey '06: Profile of the American Casino Gambler*; *Charity Gaming in North America, 2004 Annual Report* by the National Association of Fundraising Ticket Manufacturers; and *2006 State of the States: The AGA Survey of Casino Entertainment* and *An Analysis of Internet Gambling and Its Policy Implications* by the American Gaming Association. The National Indian Gaming Association (NIGA) published *An Analysis of the Economic Impact of Indian Gaming in 2004* (2005). The NIGA's resource library also provided excellent information about tribal gambling.

Informative resources from industry analysts include publications from Christiansen Capital Advisors, LLC, including *Past as Prologue. E-gambling: What Does the Future Hold?* (2005) by Sebastian Sinclair and *The Gross Annual Wager of the United States: 2003* (2004) by Eugene Martin Christiansen and Sebastian Sinclair. The Pew Research Center provided valuable insight into the industry in *Gambling: As the Take Rises, So Does Public Concern* (2006) by Paul Taylor, Cary Funk, and Peyton Craighill.

Information on particular gambling markets was obtained from *Indian Country Today*, the *Las Vegas Review-Journal*, the *Las Vegas Sun*, the *Detroit News*, the Biloxi *SunHerald*, the *Reno Gazette-Journal*, and the *Miami Herald*. The *Christian Science Monitor*, the *New York Times*, Salon.com, *USA Today*, the *Wall Street Journal*, and the *Washington Post* were useful in reporting on a variety of gambling topics.

Many Internet sites were helpful, particularly those of the state regulatory agencies that oversee gambling. Useful commercial sites include http://www.vegas.com, which describes the basics of sports betting. The Web site of the Las Vegas Convention and Visitors' Authority, at http://www.lasvegas24hours.com, contains an excellent gaming guide, with instructions to many casino games. J. R. Martin publishes gambling advice at http://www.professionalgambler.com, including *A Crash Course in Vigorish, and It's Not 4.55%*. I. Nelson Rose, a professor of law at Whittier Law School, maintains a Web site (http://www.gamblingandthelaw.com) that is a valuable resource for historical and legal information on gambling. Gambling Law U.S. (http://www.gambling-law-us.com) is maintained by attorney Chuck Humphrey; it provides a detailed listing of all the state and federal gambling laws as well as those laws that affect gambling indirectly. The National Council Against Legalized Gambling (http://www.ncalg.org) provides the latest news updates on gambling and politics around the United States.

Several publications of the U.S. Government Accountability Office, the investigative arm of Congress, were used in preparation of this book, including *Indian Issues: Improvements Needed in Tribal Recognition Process* (November 2, 2001) and *Internet Gambling: An Overview of the Issues* (December 2, 2002).

The FBI Law Enforcement Bulletin provided information on the effects of gambling on crime across the United States. *Occupational Outlook Handbook* (http://www.bls.gov/oco/), a publication of the Bureau of Labor Statistics, provided information on career opportunities in the gaming industry. Information on gambling policy and legislation is available from the National Conference of State Legislatures. The Legislative Analyst's Office, which provides fiscal and policy advice to the California legislature, has published information papers on gambling on tribal lands.

The Greyhound Protection League and the Humane Society of the United States provided important information on the history and status of animal racing and fighting in this country. Additional statistics on animal fighting were obtained from the Web site http://www.pet-abuse.com. With regard to the horse-racing industry, the Jockey Club, the U.S. Trotting Association, and the *Daily Racing Form* issue informative materials.

The Gallup Organization and the Harris Poll provide valuable results from recent polls regarding gambling in the United States. Another helpful resource is *Illegal Sports Bookmakers* (2003, http://www.unc.edu/~cigar/papers/Bookie4b.pdf) by Koleman S. Strumpf of the University of North Carolina at Chapel Hill. The Society for Human Resource Management and a Vault.com report entitled "Employees Placing Their Bets" (February 28, 2006) provided valuable information about gambling in the workplace. The Annenberg Public Policy Center of the University of Pennsylvania compiles information each year detailing the gambling habits of young people in their teens and twenties. Insights into the effects of tribal gambling were obtained from *Background to Dream: Impacts of Tribal Gaming in Washington State* (2002) by Cheryl King and Casey Kanzler, which was published in collaboration with the First American Education Project.

Scientific and educational publications devoted to problem gambling were invaluable to this book. They include the *Weekly Addiction Gambling Education Report (WAGER)*, which is published by Harvard Medical School and the Massachusetts Council on Compulsive Gambling, as well as *CrossCurrents* and the *Journal of Gambling Issues*, both of which are published by the Centre for Addiction and Mental Health in Toronto, Ontario, Canada. Rachel A. Volberg, with Gemini Research, Ltd., wrote *Gambling and Problem Gambling in Nevada* (2002) and *Gambling and Problem Gambling in Arizona* (2003). Other scholarly journals referenced for this publication include the *American Journal of Geriatric Psychiatry*, the *American Journal of Psychiatry*, the *Journal of Risk and Uncertainty*, and *Social Science Quarterly*.

Organizations devoted to problem gambling that provided helpful data and information include Gamblers Anonymous (http://www.gamblersanonymous.org), the National Center for Responsible Gaming (http://www.ncrg.org), and the National Council on Problem Gambling (http://www.ncpgambling.org).

The Final Report of the National Gambling Impact Study Commission (1999, http://govinfo.library.unt.edu/ngisc/reports/fullrpt.html) is a critical reference for information about the effects of gambling on society. The report is based on information submitted by many researchers.

INDEX

Page references in italics refer to photographs. References with the letter t following them indicate the presence of a table. The letter f indicates a figure. If more than one table or figure appears on a particular page, the exact item number for the table or figure being referenced is provided.

A

Abramoff, Jack, 75
Addiction. *See* Problem gamblers
Adolescents, 21, 123
Adult entertainment, 70
Adult gamblers, 19–21
Advanced-deposit wagering, 100
Advertising
    Internet gambling, 121
    Las Vegas, 70
Age
    casino gamblers, 32(*t*3.1), 74,
        74(*t*6.6)
    Internet gambling, 123
American Gaming Association, 73
American Psychiatric Association, 7
Ancient civilization, 1
Animal fighting, 2, 109–110
Animal welfare
    cockfighting, 109–110
    dogfighting, 110
    greyhounds, 103–104, 104*t*
    racehorses, 102
Anne, Queen, 2
Antidepressant drugs, 25
Antigua, 113, 117–118
Armed forces, U.S., 18
Arrests
    illegal gambling, 16
    Missouri Gaming Division, 71*t*
    by type of crime, 17*t*
Atlantic City, New Jersey, 40, 70–71
Avoyelles Parish, Louisiana, 64

B

Bally Technology, 15
Bankruptcy, 72–73
BetOnSports, 118
BIA (Bureau of Indian Affairs), 54
Blood sports, 2, 109–110
Bookmaking
    illegal sports gambling, 109
    legal sports gambling, 106–107
    organized crime, 16
Boyd Gaming Corporation, 14
Bureau of Indian Affairs (BIA), 54
Business. *See* Commercial casinos; Small
    businesses
Butterworth, Seminole Tribe of Florida v.,
    53

C

CAACE (Connecticut Alliance against
    Casino Expansion), 59
*Cabazon Band of Mission Indians,
    California v.*, 5, 53
California
    horse racing, 99*f*, 100, 100*f*
    Native American tribal casinos, 60–61
    Proposition 1A, 5
California Nations Indian Gaming
    Association (CNIGA), 58, 60
*California v. Cabazon Band of Mission
    Indians*, 5, 53
Canada, 97*t*
Capone, Al, 109
Card games
    casinos, 28
    consumer spending on poker, 35*f*
    frontier gambling, 3
    history, 2
    poker, 36*f*, 114
    Texas Hold 'Em, 32
Carruthers, David, 118

Casino Reinvestment Development
    Authority (CRDA), 70–71
Casinos
    comp programs, 33, 35
    consumer spending, 28*f*, 38*t*
    corporate owners, 4, 13–15
    crime, 71–72
    definition, 27
    demographics, gambler, 30–32
    economic and social effects of, 65
    education level of gamblers, 31(*f*3.4)
    employment, 67–70
    gamblers' favorite games, 34*t*
    games, 28–29
    government revenue, 65–67
    history, 3, 27
    income of gamblers, 32(*t*3.2)
    Internet casino sites, 114
    life stage of gamblers, 32(*t*3.1)
    locations, by category and state,
        29*f*–30*f*
    Nevada, 3–4, 38*f*, 39*t*
    occupations, 68*t*
    odds against gamblers, 29–30
    online *vs.* casino gamblers, by age,
        116(*f*9.2)
    online *vs.* casino gamblers, by
        educational attainment, 116(*f*9.3)
    online *vs.* casino gamblers, by gender,
        115*f*
    outside Nevada, history of, 4
    problem gamblers, 73
    public opinion, 28, 31(*f*3.3), 63, 64*t*
    receipts, 27
    social aspects, 32
    states whose residents made the most
        trips, 33*f*, 34*f*
    tourism, 70–72
    underage gambling, 74, 74(*t*6.6)
    See also Commercial casinos; Native
        American tribal casinos

Charitable gambling
    receipts and proceeds, 18*f*
    state oversight and fees, 17–18
Christianity, 2, 3
Churchill Downs, 15
Clark County, Nevada, 39–40
Classification of gambling games, 53–54
CNIGA (California Nations Indian Gaming
    Association), 58, 60
Coeur d'Alene Tribe, 92
Cognitive behavior therapy, 24–25
Cognitive distortion, 91–92
Cohen, Jay, 118
College sports, 111, 111*t*
Colonial America, 2, 77
Colorado
    casino revenue, 51*f*
    commercial casinos, 50–51
Commercial casinos
    Colorado, 50–51, 51*f*
    corporate owners and operators, 4, 13–15
    employment, 67–68
    gambling industry, 15
    government revenue, 65–66
    Illinois, 46–47, 47(*t*4.8)
    Indiana, 45–46, 47(*t*4.7)
    Iowa, 49–50, 50*f*
    jobs, by state, 69*f*
    Louisiana, 42, 44–45, 45*t*, 46*f*
    Michigan, 48–49, 49*f*
    Mississippi, 43*t*
    Missouri, 47–48, 48(*f*4.4), 48(*f*4.5)
    Nevada, 37–40
    New Jersey, 40
    revenue, 37
    South Dakota, 51–52, 52*f*
    states, 37
    tax revenue, by state, 66*f*
    top 20 casino markets, 40*t*
    tribal-commercial ventures, 57–58
Comps, 33, 35
Compulsive gambling. *See* Pathological
    gamblers; Problem gamblers
Connecticut, 59–60, 60*f*, 60*t*
Connecticut Alliance against Casino
    Expansion (CAACE), 59
Consumer behavior, 33
Consumer spending
    casino gaming, 28*f*, 38*t*
    poker, 35*f*
    racetrack casinos, 105*f*
Continental Wire Service, 109
Convenience gambling. *See* Retailers
Convenience stores, 15
Corporations. *See* Commercial casinos
Costello, Frank, 4
Counseling, 24–25

Court cases
    *California v. Cabazon Band of Mission
      Indians*, 5, 53
    *In regarding MasterCard International,
      Inc.*, 118
    Oneida Tribe of Indians v. Wisconsin, 53
    *People v. World Interaction Gaming
      Corp.*, 117–118
    *Seminole Tribe of Florida v.
      Butterworth*, 53
Cowlitz Tribe, 59
CRDA (Casino Reinvestment Development
    Authority), 70–71
Credit cards, 119–121, 120*f*
Crime
    arrests, by type of crime, 17*t*
    arrests made by Missouri Gaming
      Division, 71*t*
    casino communities, 71–72
    See also Illegal gambling; Organized crime
Crusades, 2
Customer service, 33

D

D'Ambrosia, Jeff, 118
Davis, Gray, 60
Deadwood, South Dakota, 51–52
Definitions
    casino, 27
    gambling, 1
    problem gamblers, 22
Demographics
    adult gamblers, 19–20, 21*t*
    casino gamblers, 30–32
    lottery players, 83–84
    sports gamblers, 93–94
Detroit, Michigan, 49, 74(*t*6.6)
Dice games, 1, 2
Discovery Communications, 121
Dogs
    fighting, 110
    greyhound racing, 102–104, 104*t*

E

Economic effects
    casino jobs, 69*f*, 70*f*
    casinos, 65
    commercial casinos tax revenue, by
      state, 66*f*
    employment at casinos, 67–70
    government revenue from casinos, 65–67
    greyhound racing, 103
    horse racing, 100–101
    Internet gambling, 121–122
    lotteries, 85–86, 88
    tourism, 70–71
    tribal casinos, 63–65
Education, 89, 90–91
Edwards, Edwin, 44, 74

EIPH (Exercise-induced pulmonary
    hemorrhage), 102
El Gordo, 82
Elizabeth I, Queen, 2
Employment
    casino occupations, 68*t*
    commercial casinos, 67–68, 69*f*
    Native American tribal casinos, 68–70
    tribal gaming jobs creation, 70*f*
England, 2, 3
Enterprise control
    charities, 17–18, 18*f*
    corporations, 13–15
    government, 18–19
    illegal, 16
    small businesses, 15–16
Europe, 82, 85
Euthanasia, 103, 104*t*
Exercise-induced pulmonary hemorrhage
    (EIPH), 102

F

Family entertainment, 70
Fatalities and injuries, horse, 102
Federal government
    gambling involvement, 18
    Internet gambling laws, 117–118
    Native American tribal casino
      regulation, 54
Federal Trade Commission (FTC), 123
Fees. *See* Taxes and fees
Flamingo Hotel and Casino, 4, 37
Florida
    greyhound racing, 102–104
    jai alai, 104
    pari-mutuel handle, by industry, 103*f*
    racetrack casinos, 105–106
Football, 107, 108*t*
Foreign Travel or Transportation in Aid of
    Racketeering Enterprising Act, 118
Foxwoods Casino, 59
FTC (Federal Trade Commission), 123

G

Gamblers
    adults, 19–20
    casino gambler demographics, 30–32
    casino trips, by state, 33*f*, 34*f*
    casinos and consumer behavior, 33
    demographics, 21*t*
    education level of casino gamblers,
      31(*f*3.4)
    favorite games, 34*t*
    income of casino gamblers, 32(*t*3.2)
    Internet gamblers, household income of,
      117*f*
    Internet gambling, 114–115
    Internet gambling, credit card use for,
      119–121

life stage of casino gamblers, 32(*t*3.1)
lottery players, 83–85
odds against, in casino games, 29–30
online *vs.* casino gamblers, by educational attainment, 116(*f*9.3)
online *vs.* casino gamblers, by gender, 115*f*, 116(*f*9.2)
sports gamblers, 93–94, 94(*t*8.1)
by type of game, 20(*f*2.2), 20(*f*2.3)
Gamblers Anonymous
    origins, 6–7
    recovery program, 24
    self-assessment questionnaire, 22, 22(*t*2.5)
    twelve-step program, 24*t*
Gamblers Fallacy, 30
Gaming machines
    casinos, 28–29
    convenience gambling, 16
    corporations, 15
    military, 18
    slot machines, 30, 74
Georgia, 89, 90–91
Gold Medal Sports, 118
Golden Chips Casino, 117
Government gambling enterprises, 18–19
Grayson-Jockey Club Research Foundation, 102
Great Awakening, 2
Great Britain, 115
Greyhound Protection League, 103
Greyhound racing, 102–104, 104*t*
GTECH Corporation, 15

H
Haines, Cynthia, 119
Handicapping system, 106
Harrah's Entertainment, 14
Helping Outstanding Pupils Educationally (HOPE) scholarships, 89, 90–91
Hickok, Wild Bill, 3, 51
High rollers, 33, 35
History
    casinos, 27
    gambling, 1–5
    Internet gambling, 113–114
    lotteries, 77–79
    Louisiana gambling, 42, 44
    Medieval period, 1–2
    Mississippi gambling, 40–42
    Native American tribal casinos, 53
    Nevada casinos, 3–4, 37
    public opinion on historical gambling events, 8*f*
    sports gambling, 93
Holliday, Doc, 3
HOPE scholarship, 89, 90–91
Horse racing
    betting, 98–100

California, 99*f*, 100, 100*f*
    economic effects, 100–101
    Maryland industry flow chart, 101*f*
    non-thoroughbred, 98
    thoroughbred racing, 95, 96(*f*8.2), 97–98, 97*t*, 98*f*
Hotlines, 73
Hughes, Howard, 4
Hurricane Katrina, 42, 45

I
Illegal gambling
    cockfighting, 109–110
    criminals, 16
    Mississippi, 42
    organized crime, 4, 37, 71
    sports gambling, 109, 110–111
Illinois, 46–47, 47(*t*4.8)
In regarding MasterCard International, Inc., 118
Income
    casino gamblers, 32(*t*3.2)
    Internet gamblers, 117*f*
    lottery participation, 90
Indian Gaming Regulatory Act, 5, 53–54, 57
Indiana, 45–46, 47(*t*4.7)
Injuries, horse, 102
Internal Revenue Service, 18, 18*t*, 88–89
International issues
    Internet gambling, 113, 116–118, 117–118
    lotteries, 82
Internet gambling
    businesses, 16
    credit card use, 119–121
    economic effects, 121–122
    federal laws, 117–118
    gamblers, 114–115
    history, 5, 113–114
    household income of gamblers, 117*f*
    money laundering, 122
    online *vs.* casino gamblers, by age, 116(*f*9.2)
    online *vs.* casino gamblers, by educational attainment, 116(*f*9.3)
    online *vs.* casino gamblers, by gender, 115*f*
    problem gamblers, 122–123
    state laws, 115–116
Internet Gambling Prohibition Act (proposed), 75
Interstate Transportation of Wagering Paraphernalia Act, 118
Interstate Wire Act, 117–118, 121
Investments, 15
Iowa
    casino revenue, 50*f*
    commercial casinos, 49–50
    Gambling Treatment Program, 73, 74(*t*6.5)

J
Jackson, Andrew, 3
Jai alai, 104
James I, King, 2, 77
Jurisdiction issues, 116

K
Kennedy, John F., 117
Kentucky Derby, 97
Kerzner, Sol, 59
Konami Gaming, 15
Kyl, Jon, 118

L
Labor unions, 69–70
Lansky, Meyer, 4
Las Vegas, Nevada
    commercial casinos, 39–40
    corporate casino owners and operators, 13–15
    tourism, 70
Las Vegas Boulevard, 39
Las Vegas Convention and Visitors Authority, 70
Law enforcement, 121
Legislation and treaties
    Foreign Travel or Transportation in Aid of Racketeering Enterprising Act, 118
    Indian Gaming Regulatory Act, 5, 53–54, 57
    Internet gambling, 115–119
    Interstate Transportation of Wagering Paraphernalia Act, 118
    Interstate Wire Act, 117–118, 121
    Patriot Act, 121
    Proposition 1A (California), 5
    Racketeer Influenced and Corrupt Organizations Act, 37
    Statute of Anne, 2
    Unlawful Internet Gambling Enforcement Act, 5, 113, 118–119, 121
List of Excluded Persons, 16
Lobbying, 74–75
Local government, 19
Long, Earl, 44
Lotteries
    economic effects, 85–86, 88
    gambler demographics, 83–84
    games, 79–81, 79*t*
    group play, 84
    history, 2, 3, 4–5, 77–79
    multistate games, 82
    operations, 82–83
    proceeds, cumulative distribution of, 87*t*–88*t*
    psychological issues, 91–92
    retailers, 15, 16

sales, 79f
   sales and profit, by state, 86t
   scratch games, 81
   social effects, 89–91
   state games, 80t
   states with, 19, 78f
   Texas, 83f, 84t
   why people play, 84–85
Lotto. *See* Lotteries
Louisiana
   casino activity, 45t
   cockfighting, 109–110
   commercial casinos, 42, 44–45, 46f
   legalization of gambling, 3
   lottery, 78
   tribal casinos, effect of, 64

M

Magna Entertainment, 15
Major League Baseball, 111
Mare reproductive loss syndrome (MRLS),
   102
Marketing
   casinos, 33
   Internet gambling, 121
   Las Vegas, Nevada, 70
Martin, J. R., 106
Maryland horse racing, 101f
Mashantucket Pequot Tribe, 59
Masterson, Bat, 3
McNeil, Charles, 106
Medieval period, 1–2
Mega Millions, 82
MGM Mirage, 14
Michigan, 48–49, 49f
Military, U.S., 18
Military slot machines, 18
Miller, Donald, 89
Mississippi, 40–42, 43t, 44f
Missouri
   casino attendance, 48(f4.5)
   commercial casinos, 47–48
   Gaming Commission, 71t, 73
   gaming revenue, 48(f4.4)
Mobsters. *See* Organized crime
Mohegan Sun Casino, 59
Money laundering, 122
Montana, 108
Moral acceptability of gambling, 7, 9f, 9t,
   10(f1.3)
MRLS (mare reproductive loss syndrome),
   102
Multi-State Lottery Association (MUSL),
   82
Multistate lotteries, 82
Mutual funds, 15
MUTUALS.com, 15

N

National Council on Problem Gambling, 24
National Gambling Impact Study
   Commission (NGISC), 7, 65
National Indian Lottery, 92
National Labor Relations Board (NLRB),
   69–70
Native American tribal casinos
   California, 60–61
   commercial-tribal ventures, 57–58
   Connecticut, 59–60, 60f, 60t
   corporate management, 14
   effects, 63–65
   employment, 68–70
   federal recognition criteria, 54–55
   gambling classification, 53–54
   government regulation, 54
   growth of gaming operations, 58f
   history, 5, 53
   jobs creation, 70f
   off-reservation casinos, 58–59
   overview, 19
   revenue, 55–58, 55t, 57f
Native Americans
   history of gambling, 2
   lotteries, 92
NCAA athletics, 111, 111t
Nevada
   commercial casinos, 37–40
   corporate casino owners and operators,
      13–15
   gaming revenue, 38f, 39t
   history of gambling, 3–4
   illegal sports gambling, 109
   List of Excluded Persons, 16
   race book gambling, 96(f8.1)
   sports book gambling, 107f, 108f, 108t
   sports gambling, 106–107
   suicide rate, 72
Nevada Gaming Control Board, 4, 16
New Hampshire, 78
New Jersey, 40, 41t
New Orleans, Louisiana, 3, 42, 45
New York City, 19
New York City Off-Track Betting
   Corporation, 97
NGISC (National Gambling Impact Study
   Commission), 7, 65
NIMBY factor, 63
Nineteenth century, 2–3
NLRB (National Labor Relations Board),
   69–70
Numbers games, 16

O

Odds
   casino games, 29–30
   horse racing, 99–100
   sports books, 106

Off-reservation tribal casinos, 58–59
Off-track betting
   New York City, 19
   pari-mutuel gambling, 95
Oneida Tribe of Indians v. Wisconsin, 53
Oregon, 107–108
Organized crime
   gambling enterprises, 16
   Nevada casinos, 4, 37, 71
   sports gambling, 109

P

Paragon Casino and Resort, 64
Paraphernalia Act. *See* Interstate
   Transportation of Wagering
   Paraphernalia Act
Pari-mutuel gambling
   consumer spending on racetrack casinos,
      by state, 105f
   Florida pari-mutuel handle, by industry,
      103f
   future, 104–106
   money payouts, 99t
   overview, 94–95
   thoroughbred handle, 96(f8.2)
PartyPoker, 113, 114, 119
Pathological gamblers, 7, 22–25
   See also Problem gamblers
Patriot Act, 121
PayPal, 121
Pede Duane, 118
Penn National Gaming, 14
People v. World Interaction Gaming Corp.,
   117–118
Pet-Abuse.com, 109, 110
Pharmacology, 25
Point shaving, 110, 111
Poker
   casinos, 28
   consumer spending, 35f
   Internet sites, 114
   participation, 36f
   popularity, 32
   televised games, 32
Poker Alice, 3, 51
Politics, 74–75
Poverty, 89–90
Powerball, 5, 82, 84, 92
Problem gamblers
   addiction, 6–7
   casinos, 73
   characteristics, 21–22
   family problems related to gambling,
      22(t2.4)
   Internet gambling, 122–123
   Iowa Gambling Treatment Program
      admittees, 74(t6.5)
   lotteries, 91–92
   pathological gamblers, 22–24

rates, by state, 23*f*
self-assessment questionnaire, 22(*t*2.5)
treatment programs, 24–25, 24*t*, 73
See also Pathological gamblers
Professional sports, 111
Progressive jackpot slot machines, 29
Prohibition Era, 4
Proposition 1A (California), 5
Psychological issues
   casinos and consumer behavior, 33
   Internet gambling, 122–123
   lotteries, 84–85, 91–92
   problem gambling, 6–7, 21–24
   treatment programs, 24–25
Public opinion
   approval of legalized gambling, 10(*f*1.4)
   casinos, 28, 30–32, 31(*f*3.3), 63, 64*t*
   gambling encourages people to gamble
       more than they can afford, 11*f*
   Internet gambling, 7–8, 114–115
   lotteries, 92
   moral acceptability of gambling, 7, 9*f*,
       9*t*, 10(*f*1.3)
   sports gambling, 93–94, 94(*t*8.1)
Publicly held gambling corporations, 15

R

Race book gambling, 95, 96(*f*8.1)
Race books, 106–107
Race/ethnicity
   gamblers, 21*t*
   lotteries, 89–91
Racetrack casinos, 105–106, 105*f*
Racketeer Influenced and Corrupt
   Organizations Act, 37
Regulation. *See* Legislation and treaties
Retailers and lottery ticket sales, 15, 16, 83,
   85–86
Revenue
   casinos, 27, 65–67
   Colorado casinos, 51*f*
   commercial casinos, 65–66, 66*f*
   Illinois gaming taxes, 47(*t*4.8)
   Indiana gaming taxes, 47(*t*4.7)
   Iowa casinos, 50*f*
   Louisiana casinos, 45*t*, 46*f*
   Michigan casinos, 49*f*
   Mississippi casinos, 44*f*
   Missouri gaming revenue, 48(*f*4.4)
   Native American tribal casinos, 66–67
   Nevada casinos, 38, 38*f*, 39*t*
   New Jersey casinos, 41*t*
   South Dakota casinos, 52*f*
   tribal gaming, 55–58, 55*t*, 57*f*, 60*f*, 60*t*
Revitalization efforts, 70–71
Riverboat gambling
   history, 3
   Illinois, 46–47
   Indiana, 45–46

Iowa, 50
Louisiana, 44–45
Mississippi, 41–42
Missouri, 47–48
Romans, 1
Rose, Pete, 111
Rosenthal, Frank "Lefty," 107
Roulette, 29–30

S

Schwarzenegger, Arnold, 60
Scratch games, 81
Second-chance games, 81
Self-exclusion programs, 73
Self-help groups, 6–7
Seminole Tribe of Florida v. Butterworth,
   53
Senior citizens, 20–21
Siegel, Benjamin "Bugsy," 4, 37
Slot machines
   casinos, 28–29
   military, 18
   odds against gamblers, 30
   underage gambling, 74
Small businesses, 15–16
Snyder, Jimmy "the Greek," 107
Social effects
   casino gambling, 32
   illegal sports gambling, 110–111
   lotteries, 89–91
Social impact, 6–7
South Carolina
   lottery players, 84
South Dakota
   casino revenue, 52*f*
   commercial casinos, 51–52
South Oaks Gambling Screen test, 91–92,
   122
Spain, 82
Spending, consumer
   casinos, 28*f*, 38*t*
   poker, 35*f*
   racetrack casinos, 105*f*
Sports gambling
   animal fighting, 109–110
   California horse racing, 100
   consumer spending on racetrack casinos,
       by state, 105*f*
   demographics, 93–94
   Florida pari-mutuel handle, by industry,
       103*f*
   greyhound racing, 102–104, 104*t*
   horse racing, 95–100, 99*f*, 100*f*, 101*f*,
       102
   illegal, 109, 110–111
   Montana, 108
   Nevada, 96(*f*8.1), 106–107, 107*f*, 108*f*,
       108*t*
   Oregon, 107–108

pari-mutuel gambling, 94–95, 96(*f*8.2),
   104–106
participation, 94(*t*8.1)
public opinion, 93–94, 94(*t*8.2)
student-athlete gambling, 111*t*
thoroughbred racing, 95, 96(*f*8.2),
   97–98, 97*t*, 98*f*
Sports tampering, 110–111
States
   casino locations, by category, 29*f*–30*f*
   casino trips by residents, 33*f*, 34*f*
   casinos, 28
   charitable gambling fees and regulations,
       17–18
   charitable gambling receipts and
       proceeds, 18*f*
   commercial casinos tax revenue, 66*f*
   consumer spending on casino
       gaming, 38*t*
   consumer spending on racetrack casinos,
       by state, 105*f*
   gambling enterprises, 18–19
   Internet gambling laws, 119
   legal gambling operations, 5–6, 6*t*
   lotteries, 77–79, 78*f*, 80*t*
   lotteries, economic effect of, 85–86, 88
   lotteries, history of, 4–5
   lottery games, 79–81
   lottery operations, 82–83
   lottery proceeds, cumulative distribution
       of, 87*t*–88*t*
   lottery sales and profit, 86*t*
   multistate lottery games, 82
   Native American tribal casino
       regulation, 54
   new lotteries, 92
   problem gambling rates, 23*f*
   revenue from casinos, 65–67
   sports gambling, 108–109
   suicide rates, 72*t*
   thoroughbred horse races, 97*t*
Station Casinos, Inc., 14–15
Statistical information
   arrests, by type of crime, 17*t*
   arrests made by Missouri Gaming
       Division, 71*t*
   California horse racing handle, 100*f*
   casino markets, top 20, 40*t*
   casino trips, by state, 33*f*, 34*f*
   charitable gambling receipts and
       proceeds, 18*f*
   Colorado casino revenue, 51*f*
   commercial casino jobs, by state, 69*f*
   commercial casinos tax revenue, by
       state, 66*f*
   consumer spending on casino gaming,
       28*f*
   consumer spending on casino gaming, by
       selected states, 38*t*
   consumer spending on racetrack casinos,
       by state, 105*f*

education level of casino gamblers, 31(*f*3.4)

Florida pari-mutuel handle, by industry, 103*f*

gamblers, by demographic characteristics, 21*t*

gamblers' favorite games, 34*t*

gambling winnings that must be reported to the IRS, 18*t*

greyhound breeding statistics and number of dogs killed, 104*t*

horse racing takeout dollar distribution in California, 99*f*

Illinois gaming taxes, 47(*t*4.8)

income of casino gamblers, 32(*t*3.2)

income of Internet gamblers, 117*f*

Indiana gaming taxes, 47(*t*4.7)

Iowa casino revenue, 50*f*

Iowa Gambling Treatment Program admittees, 74(*t*6.5)

legal gambling operations, by state, 6*t*

life stage of casino gamblers, 32(*t*3.1)

lottery proceeds, cumulative distribution of, 87*t*–88*t*

lottery sales, 79*f*

lottery sales and profit, by state, 86*t*

Louisiana casino activity, 45*t*

Louisiana casino revenue, 46*f*

Michigan casino revenue, 49*f*

Mississippi casino revenue, 44*f*

Mississippi commercial casinos, 43*t*

Missouri casino attendance, 48(*f*4.5)

Missouri gaming revenue, 48(*f*4.4)

money payouts on pari-mutuel bets, 99*t*

Nevada gaming revenue, 38*f*, 39*t*

Nevada race book gambling, 96(*f*8.1)

Nevada sports book gambling, 107*f*

Nevada sports book gambling, by sport, 108*f*

Nevada sports book gambling on Super Bowls, 108*t*

New Jersey casino revenue, 41*t*

online *vs.* casino gamblers, by age, 116(*f*9.2)

online *vs.* casino gamblers, by educational attainment, 116(*f*9.3)

online *vs.* casino gamblers, by gender, 115*f*

poker, consumer spending on, 35*f*

poker participation, 36*f*

problem gamblers, 22(*t*2.4)

problem gambling rates, by state, 23*f*

public approval of legalized gambling, 10(*f*1.4)

public opinion on casinos, 31(*f*3.3), 64*t*

public opinion on historical gambling events, 8*f*

public opinion on moral acceptability of gambling, 9*f*, 9*t*, 10(*f*1.3)

public opinion on sports gambling, 94(*t*8.2)

public opinion that gambling encourages people to gamble more than they can afford, 11*f*

South Dakota casino revenue, 52*f*

sports gambling participation, 94(*t*8.1)

student-athlete gambling, 111*t*

suicide rates, by state, 72*t*

Texas lotteries, amount spent on, 84*t*

Texas lottery players, 83*f*

thoroughbred racing, 98*f*

thoroughbred racing handle, 96(*f*8.2)

tribal gaming jobs creation, 70*f*

tribal gaming operations, growth of, 58*f*

tribal gaming payments to Connecticut state general fund, 60*f*, 60*t*

tribal gaming revenue, 56*t*, 57*f*

tribal gaming revenue, by region, 55*t*

underage gambling, 74(*t*6.6)

Statute of Anne, 2

"The Strip," 39

Suicide, 72, 72*t*

Summa Corporation, 4

Super Bowl, 107, 108*t*

Supply and demand, 13

T

Taxes and fees
    charitable gambling, 17–18
    lottery winnings, 18*t*, 88–89

Televised poker games, 32

Texas, 83–84, 83*f*, 84*t*

Texas Hold 'Em, 32

thoroughbred racing, 95, 96(*f*8.2), 97–98, 97*t*, 98*f*

Thunder Valley Casino, 58

Tourism, 70–71, 102

Trans America Wire, 109

Travel Act. *See* Foreign Travel or Transportation in Aid of Racketeering Enterprising Act

Treaties. *See* Legislation and treaties

Treatment programs, 24–25, 24*t*, 73, 74(*t*6.5)

Tribal sovereignty, 70

Triple Crown, 97

Twelve-step program, 24*t*

U

Unclaimed lottery winnings, 86

Underage gambling
    casinos, 74, 74(*t*6.6)
    Internet gambling, 123

Unlawful Internet Gambling Enforcement Act, 5, 113, 118–119, 121

U.S. Commission on the Review of the National Policy toward Gambling, 4

U.S. Department of Justice, 121

U.S. Federal Trade Commission (FTC), 123

V

Vice Fund, 15

Victoria, Queen, 3

Video lottery games, 81–82

W

Washington, George, 77

Western United States, 3

Winnings, taxation of, 18, 18*t*, 88–89

Wire Act. *See* Interstate Wire Act

Wisconsin, Oneida Tribe of Indians v., 53

WMS Gaming, 15

World Interaction Gaming Corp., People v., 117–118

World Interactive Gaming Corporation, 117–118

World Sports Exchange, 118

World Trade Organization (WTO), 118

Y

Youth, 21, 123